Turbo Pascal® Express

250 Ready-To-Run
Assembly Language Routines
That Make Turbo Pascal®
Faster, More Powerful,
And Easier To Use

Robert Jourdain

A Brady Utility
Published by Prentice Hall Press
New York, New York 10023

A Brady Utility
Published by Prentice Hall Press
A Division of Simon & Schuster, Inc.
Gulf + Western Building
One Gulf + Western Plaza
New York, New York   10023

PRENTICE HALL PRESS is a trademark of Simon & Schuster, Inc.

Manufactured in the United States of America

1 2 3 4 5 6 7 8 9 10

Library of Congress Cataloging-in-Publication Data

Jourdain, Robert, 1950–
  Turbo Pascal express.

  "A Brady book."
  On t.p. the registered trademark symbol "®"
is superscript following "Pascal" in the title.
  Includes index.
  1. Assembler language (Computer program
language) 2. Subroutines (Computer programs)
3. Turbo Pascal (Computer program) I. Title.
QA76.73.A8J68   1987   005.13'6   86-30394

ISBN 0-13-535337-8

This book is dedicated to my parents

Acknowledgements

Many thanks to Kathleen Doler of Borland International and to Terry Anderson and the staff at Brady. Especial thanks to Carol Crowell, who designed the book and patiently shepherded it through a particularly complicated round of typesetting. I also owe much to Judy Frank, who unfailing lent a sympathetic ear when I'd moan and groan about going mad if I had to do *one more thing* 250 times.

Contents

Other Brady Books by Robert Jourdain

Programmer's Problem Solver for the IBM PC, XT & AT

Introduction

Somebody once said that there are two kinds of people in the world, those who divide humanity into two kinds of people and those who don't. Being among the former, I long ago split computer programmers into separate species, and I think that I've got it right. There are the *artistes* and there are the *Rambos*.

For artistes, programming is but a means to an end. Artistes think only of what the program will do and how it will look. When artistes code, every screen is a rococo masterpiece, every control code a mnemonic delight. Artistes invented feature-creep. They load their software with sub-sub-sub-menus, modes within modes, and help screens for the cybernetically handicapped. Many artistes lack solid computer training, and they tend to favor compiled BASIC. On their own, artistes tend to produce an absolutely marvelous approximation of software.

Rambos, on the other hand, take pride in how fast and how well they can get the job done. For Rambos, competence is synonymous with self-esteem. Rambos obsess over the tightest and fastest algorithms; they quote from Donald Knuth's *Art of Computer Programming* like Talmudic scholars. Rambos stake their personal identity on whether or not their code runs correctly the first time (Rambos *never* use GOTOs). At their most obnoxious, Rambos will boast how easy it is to throw together a text processor in an afternoon. Left to their own devices, Rambos produce the kind of program that makes the computer look and feel like a teletype machine.

Now, people of the type that think there are no types point out that anyone who perseveres long enough to become a successful programmer must be a combination of artiste and Rambo. If you're not enough of a Rambo, you'll never get it done. And if you're not enough of an artiste, the world doesn't want your efforts. Yet in today's highly competitive market, the two types need each other's skills more than ever.

So I've written this library of Rambo-artiste subroutines for Turbo Pascal programmers. Rambos will like the routines because they are written in assembly language, making them compact and extremely fast. Artistes will wax enthusiastic over the artful programming the routines make possible. And absolutely everybody should appreciate the tremendous time saving they bring. With a bit of imagination and little labor, these routines can transform a slow or blasé program into snappy, professional-looking software.

There are already subroutine libraries available for Turbo Pascal. Why another? The obvious reasons are that this library is faster, more compact, cheaper, and better documented than others. But it is the *kind* of routines I've written that I think will make the library especially worth your while. Many libraries simply give access to hardware features that Turbo Pascal doesn't. It is indeed useful to be able to change the shape of the cursor or to find a file's size, and this library includes these sorts of services. At the other extreme, Borland's own libraries for graphics, text, and data bases are highly specialized. You have to do things *their* way, and you have to incorporate large blocks of code to make use of a single feature.

This library takes the middle ground, performing tasks that appear again and again in commercial software, but that are never made part of a computer language. Consider the mundane matter of setting up a little chart on the screen with block characters. Perhaps you would want a full-screen box separated into eight columns with four dividers across, some of the lines single and some of them double. Good luck. You'll have loops all over the place, and you'll need to reset the cursor sixty times to print special characters at intersections. The result will be painfully slow and dangerously large. And what about when you want to make a change?

It's far easier to use three routines you'll find here: *DrawBox*, *VerticalLine*, and *HorizontalLine*. They draw boxes and lines within boxes in any combination of single- or double-line characters, and they automatically fill in the correct character whenever two lines meet. They'll draw the chart in under one-hundredth of a second, at any position, in any dimensions, and in any color. The code may be set up in only a few minutes, and changes take but seconds. And once you've devoted 725 bytes of code space to the three routines, you can apply them a thousand ways in the same program with little additional code.

If you have never written a Turbo Pascal program that is broken into pieces, you may feel a bit of trepidation at using a subroutine library. Fear not. Every routine is in its own file. The routine *WrapLine*, for example, resides in the file **WRAPLINE.PAS**. At the start of your Turbo program, you need merely add the line {**$I WRAPLINE.PAS**}. When Turbo Pascal compiles your program, it automatically incorporates the *WrapLine* function, just as if it were a function you had written yourself. That is all it takes to have output to the printer automatically word-wrapped (or use *JustLine* to right-justify the output, or *Wrapln* to wrap screen output, or *WrapInput* to wrap keyboard input, or *WrapString* to wrap a string array, and so on).

The library was written for Turbo Pascal version 3.0, operating on an IBM PC, XT, or AT. When Borland releases a new version of Turbo Pascal, it is expected to support modular programming. That is, it will let you develop a program in pieces so that all of the code does not have to be recompiled each time a change is made. But this doesn't mean that programs written using the library in its current form will become obsolete. On the contrary, I've taken special care to write the routines so that they should be able to cope with a larger memory model, provided that Borland continues to support all former compiler features, which is a reasonable expectation.

Before getting started, you should read Chapter 1 (experienced programmers can get by with the Hacker's Quick Reference that precedes Chapter 1). You'll find a discussion of a number of small points that you should be aware of to keep out of harm's way. Chapter 1 also explains how to use the program **ROUTINES**, which generates the routines from the compressed files that you'll find on the accompanying diskettes. **ROUTINES** manages the multitude of files, freeing you from dealing with endless directory listings of cryptic file names. Besides originating the routines in any of three forms, it can consult a list of routine names and create one file containing all the routines your program uses.

Next come eight chapters of documentation. The documentation tells about each routine, lists its parameters, and gives its declaration. There is really no need *ever* to look at the *Inline* files themselves unless you want to modify them or study them as examples of assembly language coding. The documentation includes one or more examples for each kind of routine. Since it contains notes about idiosyncrasies and error-checking, you won't have to experiment to find out how the routines behave under extreme circumstances.

The final chapter is a technical discussion for assembly-language programmers. It shows how to develop assembly-language routines for Turbo Pascal. When you take a look at the files, you'll no doubt conclude that only a madman would choose to code 250 routines in the machine code *Inline* format used by Turbo Pascal. You're right. I started this project by writing a program that automatically converts assembler **.lst** files into *Inline* form. You'll find this program on one of the diskettes, along with its Pascal source code, should you want to modify it. You'll also find a tiny, memory-resident debugging tool, TURBOBUG, which lets you watch your assembly routines as they run within a Turbo Pascal program. It's written entirely in assembler, and the source is included. Heavily commented source code is included for all routines.

This library is royalty-free. You may use any of the 250 routines in commercial software (subject to the limitations stated in the disclaimer on the copyright page). I have tested the daylights out of these routines. It's something you just have to do with assembly language subroutines because when they fail, they can easily bring down the machine. Still, if you use a routine in software that will be distributed to others, you should thoroughly test it in its full range of applications. If you have trouble, sit down and read the documentation notes carefully. If that won't do it, drop me a note in care of Brady Books, Prentice Hall Press, Reference Division, Gulf + Western Building, One Gulf + Western Plaza, New York, NY 10023.

Many happy RETurns,

Robert Jourdain

The Hacker's Quick Reference

—The routines are written in *Inline* form, that is, as text files. You may bring them into your programs by an include directive such as {**$I DRAWBOX.PAS**}, or by incorporating them into the source text.

—All routines are stand-alone; they do not access other routines. The documentation gives an approximation of how much code space a routine actually consumes (the figure is somewhat larger than the number of bytes of Inline code).

—The library is compressed into eight files found on the accompanying diskettes. Each file corresponds to a chapter of documentation. The routines are unpacked by a program on the diskettes called ROUTINES (ROUTINES.COM is on both diskettes). It is entirely menu- and prompt-driven and requires no instruction.

—Any of the routines may be generated in three forms: (a) as Inline code with notes (the notes are assembler mnemonics and comments); (b) as compressed Inline code *without* notes; and (c) as assembler source code.

—The ROUTINES program unpacks routines in three ways: It generates single routines; it generates all routines held in a single source file; or it reads an ordinary text file listing the names of all the functions and procedures you want generated and writes them into a single file. The file containing the list must have the extension **.LST**, and it generates the routines in a file having the same name, but with a **.LIB** ("library") extension. Place the names of the functions or procedures in the list file (not their file names), one to a line. For example:

DrawBox
BinaryToInteger
Wrapln
GetScan

—All string parameters, including values returned by functions, are declared as being of *stype* ("string type"). Routines that handle strings are self-adjusting to handle strings of any length. To make a routine process strings of more than one size, set *stype* to the type of the largest string and turn off type-checking by the compiler directive {$V-}. Or you may leave type-checking in force, using each routine for strings of a single type alone. In this case, open the Inline files and change the word *stype* to whatever other type you have defined.

—Some routines directly access variables not passed as parameters. If you want to use a variable name other than that given in the documentation, open the relevant Inline files and change the name in the Pascal statments that appear immediately following the declaration. (The unconventional way in which some parameters are handled is explained in Chapter 10.)

—Video routines in chapters 6 and 7 come in both BIOS and memory-mapping forms. The BIOS routines require a global integer variable named *VideoPage* that tells which video page the routine writes on. The memory-mapping routines look for the video buffer address in an integer variable named *VideoBuffer* (normally $B000 or $B800).

—In most screen-output routines, screen attributes are set by a parameter. To calculate the values for the attributes conveniently, set up a global integer variable named *Color*, making it the parameter. Then use the routines in Section 3 of Chapter 6 that change the bit settings in Color to create any screen attribute.

The routines contain enough error-checking to avoid crashes and confusion. When parameters are outside the permissible range, the routines generally return without doing anything at all. The *NOTES* in the documentation tell what error-checking is performed.

1

Using the Subroutine Library

The 250 assembly language routines in this collection are ready to run. They require no knowledge of assembly language whatsoever. You need only insert them into your Turbo Pascal program and call them like any Pascal procedure or function that you have written yourself. But there are some things you should know before you get to work, and you would do well to take the time to read this chapter carefully. You will learn here about the various ways to unpack the routines from the files they are compressed into. You will find out how to set up the routines for maximum flexibility. And you will acquire some important pointers about how to keep out of trouble. If you are an experienced programmer, you can get started at once by consulting the Hacker's Quick Reference that precedes this chapter.

For starters, you may wonder just what assembly language is and what its advantages are. You probably have heard that assembly language is very fast, and indeed you will be amazed at the speed of these routines. Where's the magic? Assembly language lets a programmer make optimum use of a computer's resources by directly controlling the machine's hardware. In Pascal you can write a statement like **Copy(Strg,X,Y)** and—voila!—the machine returns part of a string. Doing the same in assembly language takes many lines of code. An assembler program manipulates the dozen-odd *registers* that are the heart of the *CPU* (central

1

processing unit—the 8088 or 80286 chip). The program tracks variables to particular memory locations, shifts them character by character into registers, and then juggles the register contents—adding, dividing, shifting, rotating, negating, comparing.

Assembly language performs these operations through terse instructions ("mnemonics") like **MOV** and **CMP**. The instructions are converted into machine code by an *assembler*, which is to assembly language what a compiler is to a high-level language. *Machine code* is the form in which the instructions are used by the CPU. A single instruction is reduced to one or more bytes of code, in which the pattern of the eight bits making up each byte conveys what the instruction is and how it should work. You will see both the assembler mnemonics and their machine-code equivalents in the files that make up this subroutine library (but don't worry, you don't have to understand a thing about either to use the routines).

Now, a high-level language like Pascal also generates machine code; it has no choice, since machine code is the only language the CPU understands. So why is Pascal less efficient than assembly language? The answer lies in the difference in intelligence between a piece of software and a human brain. A compiler tends to do everything in the dumbest way since it has no way of recognizing when there are opportunities to do things more cleverly. For example, in a **for...to** loop, a compiler will probably move the counter variable onto the CPU, increment it, compare it, and then return it to memory until the next swing through the loop. An assembly-language programmer might see that a register is free to keep the variable on the chip throughout the loop. As a result, thousands of time-consuming memory accesses and extra code can be avoided. It is hard for a compiler to spot such opportunities because it sees only the matter at hand and cannot devise grand strategies. In the future, artificial intelligence techniques will help make compilers smarter.

Assembly language routines are very fast for another reason. High-level languages tend to have a very limited repertoire of capabilities. In Turbo Pascal, for example, you ordinarily use the **Copy** function to look at the contents of a string variable. If you want to write a function that eliminates all instances of a particular character from a string, you would repeatedly call **Copy**, first to test for the character and then to eliminate it. Every time a program calls a procedure or function, it incurs considerable overhead; all sorts of information in the CPU must be saved so that the computer can continue when the call is completed, and parameters may need to be copied to a holding area in memory (the *stack*). In some applications, the overhead associated with making calls can take up nearly half of total CPU time. An assembly-language routine, on the other hand, entails only a single call. Once it comes into action, there are no further calls since the routine does everything on its own.

There is a downside to all of this, however. A compiler has a built-in library—that mass of code that makes even a short program fairly hefty. When a Pascal program runs, it constantly reaches down to use the routines in this library. Assembly-language routines, however, can't get at the library. This is unfortunate, since there are times when it would be much easier to use this existing resource than to build it from scratch, especially when a service requires a lot of code.

There is another limitation. Programs written entirely in assembly language are made up of procedures that call other procedures, just as in Pascal. But isolated assembly-language subroutines inserted into a language like Turbo Pascal (in its current form, at least) have no practical means of using one another. Code must be duplicated.

For this reason, the routines in this collection are not always as compact as you might expect. Pure assembly-language programs can be a third the size of those generated by a high-level language, but that degree of compactness is simply not possible in a library like this one. Still, even with the disadvantages, the extra code these routines add to your Turbo COM files will be less than that incurred by writing the same service from scratch in Pascal.

The structure of a routine

There are two ways to integrate an assembly-language subroutine into a Turbo Pascal program. One way is to create the routine as a COM file and then include it through the **external** command. The file contains nothing but machine code, so the declaration for the procedure or function must be written separately in the program. Since this approach has a number of limitations and inconveniences it was not used for this subroutine library.

Instead, all of the routines here were developed in **Inline** form, which means that they exist as *text* files that Turbo Pascal reads and converts to machine code. There are several advantages. The entirety of the routine is included in the file, including the procedure or function's declaration. To illustrate, let's look at a routine called **BinaryToInteger**, which converts a string representation of a binary number such as **11010011011** to its integer equivalent. Here's the code:

```
Function BinaryToInteger(BinaryString: stype): integer;
Var
   X : integer;
Begin
   X := SizeOf(stype);
   Inline
      ($2B/$C0/          {      SUB   AX,AX          ;clear AX                    }
       $8B/$76/$FC/       {      MOV   SI,[BP-4]       ;sizeof stype                }
       $83/$C6/$04/       {      ADD   SI,4            ;offset from BP              }
       $BB/$01/$00/       {      MOV   BX,1            ;bit mask at bottom of BX }
       $2B/$C9/          {      SUB   CX,CX           ;clear CX                    }
       $BF/$04/$00/       {      MOV   DI,4            ;pt to string descriptor  }
       $8A/$0B/          {      MOV   CL,[BP][DI]     ;string length in CX         }
       $49/              {      DEC   CX              ;dec for text                }
       $83/$F9/$0F/       {      CMP   CX,15           ;non-0 & within 16 bits?  }
       $77/$10/          {      JA    L3              ;quit routine if not         }
       $41/              {      INC   CX              ;readjust                    }
       $03/$F9/          {      ADD   DI,CX           ;pt to first digit of str }
       $B2/$31/          {      MOV   DL,'1'          ;used to read string         }
       $38/$13/          { L1:  CMP   [BP][DI],DL     ;is the char a '1'?          }
       $75/$02/          {      JNE   L2              ;if not, jump ahead          }
       $0B/$C3/          {      OR    AX,BX           ;set corresponding bit       }
       $D1/$E3/          { L2:  SHL   BX,1            ;shift mask to next bit      }
       $4F/              {      DEC   DI              ;pt to next byte of strg  }
       $E2/$F5/          {      LOOP  L1              ;go do the next byte         }
       $89/$02);         { L3:  MOV   [BP][SI],AX     ;set result for return       }
End;
```

As you can see, the routine begins with the function's declaration. The declaration in no way differs from that of an ordinary Pascal subroutine. Generally, a subroutine's declaration is the only part that will concern you. A copy of the declaration appears in the documentation that makes up chapters 2 through 9 of this book, so there is no need to look into the Inline files on disk. More about that in a moment.

Like any Pascal procedure, *BinaryToInteger* starts and ends with **Begin** and **End;**. The assembly-language routine runs along the left margin of the example, beginning from **Inline**. This is machine code, written with each byte represented by a two-digit number. The numbers are hexadecimal (written in base 16) as shown by the leading dollar sign. Slashes separate the individual bytes. There may be from one to five such numbers on a line, and taken together they constitute one machine-code instruction.

To the left is the assembly-language source code from which the machine code was generated. First come the assembly language mnemonics. On the first line, for example, you'll see **SUB AX,AX**. This causes the CPU to clear one of its registers. This instruction is encoded as two bytes with the values **42** and **192**, which when encoded in Inline form become $2B/$C0/—the same as you will see at the start of the line. To the right of the mnemonics are notes of explanation.

Notice that both the mnemonics and the notes are nested within braces—they are merely Pascal program notes and are treated as such. It is the machine code that does the work. If you know nothing of assembly language and don't care to learn, you can ignore these notes. As you will see, it is a simple matter to generate the routine without the notes, so that it looks like this:

```
Function BinaryToInteger(BinaryString: stype): integer;
Var
   X : integer;
Begin
   X := SizeOf(stype);
   Inline
     ($2B/$C0/$8B/$76/$FC/$83/$C6/$04/$BB/$01/$00/$2B/$C9/$BF/$04/$00/$8A/$0B/
      $49/$83/$F9/$0F/$77/$10/$41/$03/$F9/$B2/$31/$38/$13/$75/$02/$0B/$C3/
      $D1/$E3/$4F/$E2/$F5/$89/$02);
End;
```

Turbo Pascal can compile the program ever so slightly faster when it is in this form, since it does not have to take the time to read through the notes. Another advantage is that the files take up considerably less disk space.

Sometimes you will find some Pascal code in the Inline files, as in the previous example. Most often it reads **X := Ofs(variable)** or **X := Seg(variable)** or **X := SizeOf(variable)**. This code is a roundabout way of getting Turbo Pascal to cough up information about the location of variables and the size of strings named in the declaration. It tends to make the routines a little larger, but it also makes the routines more flexible and contributes to their compatability with future versions of Turbo Pascal. See Chapter 2 if you want to understand how these bits of code work.

Bringing the routines into your program

There are two ways to bring a routine into your program. You can place an *include directive* in the program, and when it is compiled, Turbo Pascal will automatically look for the file containing the routine and read it. Or, since Inline code is in text form, you can simply copy the file into your source code.

The latter approach has several virtues. The routine's declaration is there to see without fumbling through the documentation. Compilation is faster since no time is taken for disk access. There's no fussing with potentially dozens of small files clogging your directory listings. You can also more conveniently rename the routines if you like. Of course, if your source file is pushing the 64K limit, it may be better not to include the assembly routines. It's usually a good idea to generate the routines without notes when they will be included in this way.

The Turbo editor allows you to read a file from disk and include it in the text being edited. The insertion is made at the current cursor position. When you type **Ctrl-KR**, a prompt at the top of the screen asks for the file name. To bring *Binary-ToInteger* into the source file you should first move the cursor to the left edge of the screen. Then enter the routine's file name, **BIN2INT.PAS** and strike Enter. The file instantly appears, and it is cast in low intensity as if it were selected for a block move. To undo its block status, simply type **Ctrl-KBKK**.

When the file is to be left on disk until compilation, you must add one simple line of code to the source file. This is the *include directive*. It looks like a Pascal note in that it is surrounded by braces. Type **$I** for "include" and then the file name. For *BinaryToInteger*, for example, the directive is {**$I BIN2INT.PAS**}. When there is no file-name extension, Turbo assumes a **.PAS** ending, so you could also write {**$I BIN2INT** }.

There are several points to note. First, there is no terminating semicolon. Second, the directive must be alone on the line; no other code or notes are allowed. Third, when you omit the extension, the file name must be followed by a space. Fourth, the **$I** must immediately follow the opening brace; otherwise, the directive is taken to be a note, and its content is disregarded. Fifth, the file name may be preceded by a drive specifier or subdirectory path, as in {**$I B:BIN2INT** } or {**$I \ROUTINES\BIN2INT** }. Finally, be sure to note that include files may not be nested. This is to say that you may not include the assembly routines from a file that is itself an include file for the main Pascal program.

You may be wondering *where* in your source text you should place the include directives or routine copies. The answer is simple. The routines are like any function or procedure that you write, and they go to the same place: after the declaration of the main program and before the main program itself begins. In case you are unclear about this, here are two short programs that use *BinaryToInteger*. The examples are identical except that the first uses an include directive, while the second copies the noteless form of *BinaryToInteger* directly into the source text. The programs merely enter a binary string from the keyboard and display the integer equivalent.

Case 1:

```
Program ConvertValue;
Type
  stype = string[16];
Var
  BinaryString : stype;
{$I BIN2INT.PAS}
Begin
  Clrscr;
  Writeln('Enter a binary string:');
```

```
   Readln(con,BinaryString);
   Write(BinaryToInteger(BinaryString));
End.
```

Case 2:

```
Program ConvertValue;
Type
   stype = string[16];
Var
   BinaryString : stype;
Function BinaryToInteger(BinaryString: stype): integer;
Var
   X : integer;
Begin
   X := SizeOf(stype);
   Inline
     ($2B/$C0/$8B/$76/$FC/$83/$C6/$04/$BB/$01/$00/$2B/$C9/$BF/$04/$00/$8A/$0B/
      $49/$83/$F9/$0F/$77/$10/$41/$03/$F9/$B2/$31/$38/$13/$75/$02/$0B/$C3/
      $D1/$E3/$4F/$E2/$F5/$89/$02);
End;

Begin
   Clrscr;
   Writeln('Enter a binary string:');
   Readln(con,BinaryString);
   Write(BinaryToInteger(BinaryString));
End.
```

The documentation

The routines are split into eight groups, with each group treated in its own chapter of documentation. The chapters are broken into two to four sections, and each section contains several entries that, in turn, contain all related routines. Each section begins with a few paragraphs describing the routines it contains. You may want to spend an hour leafing through these introductions for an overview of the library.

Each entry in the documentation starts with the declarations of the routines it describes. You then find the names of the files holding the routines and a value for the number of code bytes that each routine generates. *Code bytes* means the number of bytes the routine adds to your program's length. You may need to know these numbers if your program is pushing the 64K limit. Because it is difficult to anticipate the amount of code that will be created for the Pascal statements included in the routines, regard the values given for code bytes as close estimates.

Next, the documentation gives a statement of the purpose of the routines, followed by a description of all of the parameters in the declarations. One thing to watch for is mention of *global variables* by the routine. A global variable is one that is declared in the main program, such that it can be accessed from any procedure or function. In certain routines, it seemed wisest to have you set up a global variable for parameters that are constants. For example, for fast screen operations, some routines need to know the memory address of the video buffer (discussed below). This variable is set at the start of the program, and thereafter, all of the screen output routines consult this variable, saving you the trouble of writing it each time one of the routines is called.

Following the description of the parameters are notes about the peculiarities of the individual routines. These notes point out what the routines can and cannot do, and what kind of errors are checked. They also may suggest unusual applications of the routines.

Finally, there are examples. Routines that do only something very simple tend to have very short, simple examples. But the more versatile routines may be accompanied by something more imaginative. Often, a combination of routines produces startling results. Keep your eyes open for new possibilities.

The disk files

The two disks that accompany this book contain thirteen files in total. Each of eight files hold all routines in a chapter. The file **ROUTINES.COM** generates the individual routines from these eight aggregate files; a copy is found on both diskettes. The other four programs are of no interest to you unless you will be writing your own assembly-language programs for Turbo Pascal. The file **INLINE.COM** converts assembler files into the Inline format, and **INLINE.PAS** is the Turbo Pascal source code for this program. The file **TURBOBUG.COM** is a tool for debugging assembly-language routines while they run within a high-level language. Its source code is found in the file **TURBOBUG.ASM**.

The routines have been joined into eight files for a number of reasons. For starters, the directory space in two floppy disks cannot hold all the routines. Even with more slots in a directory, disk space would fall short. In fact, the routines have been compressed, as you can see by looking into one of the eight files. The compression is simple: strings of spaces have been replaced with code characters, using the *CompressText* and *DeCompressText* routines in Chapter 4. As we'll see in a moment, it is easy to generate from these large files any routine or group of routines that you need. And while generating them, you may choose whether the routines will be created with or without notes or as assembly-language source code.

The routines weren't compressed into large files simply to save space on the floppy disks. Stop and consider how much disk space would be taken up by 250 separate files. On a 10-megabyte PC XT hard disk, for example, a minimum of ten disk sectors of 512 bytes are allocated to a file, no matter how small. The library would require nearly two megabytes! If you own a hard disk, you will find it most convenient to place the eight files and **ROUTINES.COM** in a subdirectory. Altogether, they take up about 540K. From that subdirectory, the ROUTINES program will readily generate the routines your program requires in any other directory.

Unpacking the routines

The ROUTINES program is simple to use. Because it is entirely menu- and prompt-driven, there is really nothing to learn about the program except its capabilities. When you enter **ROU-TINES** from the DOS prompt, a starting menu gives three choices:

1. Generate single routines

2. Generate all routines in a chapter

3. Generate a group of routines in one file

In this and all subsequent menus, choices are made by striking the number key corresponding to the number of the menu entry.

To create single routines, strike the **1** key. Note that you can exit the program from any point by typing **Ctrl-Q**, and typing **Esc** returns you to the main menu.

The first menu choice generates a single routine in its own file; there is nothing more to say about it. The second choice causes all routines in a chapter to be generated as single files. If you have adequate hard disk space, you can unpack all 250 routines by making this choice eight times. Or you may generate the library on three diskettes. One arrangement is to place the system, bits, and string routines on the first diskette, the keyboard and screen routines on the second, and the graphics, files, and printer routines on the third.

The third choice helps manage multiple files. As you develop a program, you could find yourself using dozens of these routines. As a result, many little files would clog your subdirectories and many include directives would lengthen your source code. To avoid this confusion, ROUTINES can be made to look for a simple text file containing the names of all routines used by your program. It then generates a *single* file that holds all the routines, one after another. One include directive in your Pascal source is all that is needed to read in all the routines. Much compilation time is saved by reducing the number of disk accesses.

The file holding the routine names should have the extension **.LST**. It may be given any name, and ROUTINES prompts you for the name. You can create the file with the Turbo editor, the Sidekick notepad, any word processor, or the DOS *Copy* command, as you would a batch file. The file should contain only the names of the routines, one to a line. For example:

```
DrawBox
BinaryToInteger
WrapIn
GetScan
```

Note that these are the names of the routines as they appear in the declarations; they are not the associated file names (which are not used because they are harder to keep straight). There must be only one name on a line. ROUTINES ignores leading and trailing spaces, and blank lines. Case is also ignored, making

DrawBox, **DRAWBOX**, and **drawbox** all valid. Misspellings (or just plain nonsense) result in an error message.

The output file is given the same name of the list file, except that the file name extension is **.LIB** (for "library"). Thus the file **ZBASE.LST** holds the list of routines that are written to **ZBASE.LIB**. Once the routine file is created, your source requires only one include directive, in this case {**$I ZBASE.LIB**}.

Using the list option carries a constraint. All source files must be in the same subdirectory as ROUTINES. Generally speaking, this means that your system must have a hard disk or a 1.2-megabyte floppy drive. The list feature can be used with a 360K floppy disk when no request is made for routines from source files not present on the disk.

Choosing a format

Once you have made a selection from the main menu, a second menu asks which format to use. You choose between Pascal code with notes, Pascal code without notes, and assembly-language source code. Once you make a choice, all files are generated in this format. If you want different formats for different choices, you must return to the main menu after each file (or group of files) is created.

After choosing a format, you are asked for the location of the source files and for the name of the disk drive and subdirectory in which you want the program files generated. You will find it convenient to keep the ROUTINES program in the same subdirectory with all eight source files if you own a hard disk or 1.2-megabyte floppy drive.

What happens next depends on which of the three options you have chosen. When generating a whole chapter of files, the program asks for the chapter number, quickly writes the twenty to fifty files to disk, and then returns to the main menu. If you choose to write single files, you move on to a multipage menu that lists the names of all of the files. Its operation is intuitive. Use the left and right cursor keys to shift between listings for the eight chapters. All routines are listed, and each is numbered. When you find the routine you want, type its number and strike the Enter key. With that, the file is created and you are asked whether or not to do another.

Finally, if you choose to create a file of routines, you are prompted for the name and location of the list file, and as the file of routines is created, the name of each routine is displayed on the screen. An error message appears when the routine named in the list file cannot be found; the output file is completed without the missing routines. The program returns to the main menu once the LIB file is finished.

Altering the routines

Two kinds of changes can be made to a routine. You can alter the code itself if you know how to program in assembly language. Have ROUTINES generate the assembler source code for a routine, change it, and then use the INLINE program (discussed in Chapter 2) to return the code to Inline form. The second choice is to make simple changes in the routine's declaration; any Pascal programmer can do this.

If you don't like the name given to a function or procedure, simply open the routine's file and change the name in the declaration. Keep in mind that you won't be able to change the routine's listing in the ROUTINES program, and this may cause confusion. When you write a function in Pascal, the function's name appears at least once in the body of the function when the return value is set; to change the function's name, you need to scan the file for all instances. This is not required by these assembly-language routines.

Another possibility is that you might want to change the names of parameters to expressions you find clearer. Again, just open the routine file and make the change. But in this case, you need to scan the Inline code for the parameter name you alter. Parameter names preceded by *var* are sometimes incorporated into Inline code. During compilation, Turbo Pascal converts the name to the address of the variable. You may feel a little nervous about making changes in the Inline code itself, but no harm should result. If you fail to make a necessary change, the compiler will let you know about it.

Finally, some routines access global variables, and you may want to change their names. In this case, at the start of the routine, Pascal code returns the *Seg* and *Ofs* of the variable. Change the name at these locations.

String parameters

Turbo Pascal has a number of string-related functions, such as *Copy* and *Concat*. These functions have a different status than those you write yourself. As part of the compiler library, they are privy to the compiler's knowledge of the size of any string variable. As a result, these functions can accept a string of any size, whether its *type* is declared as **string[20]** or **string[200]**. On the other hand, when you write a function to process a string, it will accept only strings of the *type* named in the function's parameter declaration.

Turbo includes *Untyped parameters* to remedy these problems. These are string parameters that are passed to a subroutine without a type declaration. Unfortunately, the untyped parameter feature is inflexible, and it has not been extensively used in this library. This leaves three remaining options, two of which are bad, and one not quite so bad. You can make all string variables the size of the largest required, wasting vast amounts of data space. You can write several copies of the function, using different names and different string types. Or you can simply turn off the compiler's type-checking feature.

When you switch off type-checking, Turbo Pascal goes into moron mode. It does whatever your program code tells it to, and if the instruction leads to a hundred-byte string written to a memory location allocated for fifty bytes, so be it. The result of this mischief is that adjacent data is overwritten; when variables are subsequently read from the damaged data area, the program starts to process nonsense, and all sorts of bizarre events occur. What makes this situation disastrous is that the code inflicting the damage appears to be doing fine, and the finger is pointed at the code that uses the damaged data. You can spend days trying to debug code that is operating perfectly. Type-checking was invented for just this reason. Type-checking is turned off by writ-

Turbo Pascal Express

REPLACEMENT ORDER FORM

Please use this form when ordering a replacement for a defective diskette.

A. If Ordering within Thirty Days of Purchase

If a diskette is reported defective within thirty days of purchase, a replacement diskette will be provided free of charge. *This card must be totally filled out and accompanied by the defective diskette and a copy of the dated sales receipt.* In addition, please complete and return the Limited Warranty Registration Card.

B. If Ordering after Thirty Days of Purchase but within One Year

If a diskette is reported defective after thirty days but within one year of purchase and the Warranty Registration Card has been properly filed, a replacement diskette will be provided to you for a nominal fee of $5.00 (send check or money order only). *This card must be totally filled out and accompanied by the defective diskette, a copy of the dated sales receipt, and a $5.00 check or money order made payable to Simon & Schuster, Inc.*

NAME _____ PHONE NUMBER (___) _____

ADDRESS _____

CITY _____ STATE _____ ZIP _____

PURCHASE DATE _____

PURCHASE PRICE _____

COMPUTER BRAND & MODEL _____

Please send all requests to Technical Support Center, Simon & Schuster, Inc., Route 9W, Englewood Cliffs, NJ 07632; ATTN: Replacements

NOTE: Simon & Schuster reserves the right, at its option, to refund your purchase price in lieu of providing a replacement diskette.

0-13-535337-8

Turbo Pascal Express

LIMITED WARRANTY REGISTRATION CARD

In order to preserve your rights as provided for in the limited warranty, this card must be on file with Simon & Schuster within thirty days of purchase.

Please fill in the information requested:

NAME _____ PHONE NUMBER (___) _____

ADDRESS _____

CITY _____ STATE _____ ZIP _____

COMPUTER BRAND & MODEL _____ DOS VERSION _____ MEMORY _____ K

Where did you purchase this product?

DEALER NAME _____

ADDRESS _____

CITY _____ STATE _____ ZIP _____

PURCHASE DATE _____ PURCHASE PRICE _____

How did you learn about this product? (Check as many as applicable.)

STORE DISPLAY _____ SALESPERSON _____ MAGAZINE ARTICLE _____ ADVERTISEMENT _____

OTHER (Please explain) _____

How long have you owned or used this computer?

LESS THAN 30 DAYS _____ LESS THAN 6 MONTHS _____ 6 MONTHS TO A YEAR _____ OVER 1 YEAR _____

What is your primary use for the computer?

BUSINESS _____ PERSONAL _____ EDUCATION _____ OTHER (Please explain) _____

Where is your computer located?

HOME _____ OFFICE _____ SCHOOL _____ OTHER (Please explain) _____

0-13-535337-8

Simon & Schuster, Inc.

Brady Books

One Gulf+Western Plaza

New York, New York 10023

ATTN: **PRODUCT REGISTRATION**

ing {**$V-**} at the start of the program. It can be turned back on at any point by writing {**$V +** }.

In the declarations of all procedures and functions in this collection, string parameters are declared as being of *stype* ("string type"). To use the routines with strings of any size, simply set *stype* equal to the largest-type string that will be sent to any routine. Imagine a program that has an array of strings of up to 80 characters (*longtype*), and a second array for 40-character strings (*shorttype*). You might want to use the assembly-language routine *UpperCase* to convert strings from either array to uppercase. The type declaration would be:

```
Program WhatsIt;
{$V-}
Type
   longtype = string[80];
   shorttype = string[40];
   stype = string[80];
```

Type-checking has been turned off, and *stype* is set to receive strings of up to 80 characters. Like all routines in this library, since *UpperCase* already uses the expression *stype* in its declaration, there is no need to modify the routine file in any way. In fact, the easiest approach is to simply set *stype* to **255**—the longest string possible—and then use any of the routines to your heart's content. But be very, very careful that parameters and return values never exceed the ranges permitted by your data declarations.

What if you want to leave type-checking in force and use a routine for strings of only one type? Go ahead. The routines adjust automatically to any type size. Simply make *stype* equal to the desired string size. Or you may modify the routine, altering the expression "stype" to another word. In fact, you *must* make alterations in some routines when different type declarations are used. For example, you might want to leave the word *stype* in *UpperCase*, sizing it to 80 bytes, and change *stype* to *shorttype* in *LowerCase*, sizing it to 40 bytes.

Finally, you may turn type-checking off only when you call one of the routines in this collection that receive or return strings.

Place {**$V-**} immediately before the statement calling the routine and follow it with {**$V +** }. For example:

```
Strg1 := ConvertString(Strg2);
{$V-}
Test := Compare(Strg1,Strg3);
{$V+}
```

Compare is a function from Chapter 4 that reports whether strings are equal, regardless of case. **ConvertString**, on the other hand, is assumed to be a function written in Pascal. Here, type-checking ensures that **ConvertString** returns a proper-length value to **Strg1**. But **Compare** takes strings of any type.

When you go into a routine to change a string parameter's type declaration, you may need to change more than the word in the declaration proper. Below the declaration you may find a line of Pascal code that sometimes reads **X : = SizeOf(stype)**. Change this instance of **stype** as well. (The **SizeOf** statement is used by the routine in its automatic adjustment to any string size.)

If this discussion sounds a bit intimidating, don't let it be. Once you have made the leap into a world free of type-checking by setting {**$V-**}, the rest is simple. You may size **stype** to 255— the largest possible string—and forget about string sizes altogether. When these two simple actions have been taken, you can use any routine in the library without ever looking into a single file.

Video operations

Two chapters of routines concern the video display. There are a few things you should know to use these routines effectively. Many routines are offered in two forms: a memory-mapping version and a *BIOS* version (Basic Input-Output System— the part of the operating system built into the machine). The BIOS contains primitive routines that write single characters on the screen (the PC AT BIOS adds string-writing capabilities, but using them robs a program of its basic PC compatibility). BIOS versions of the routines use these operating-system services, and by doing so, they are guaranteed compatibility with future IBM machines.

The *memory-mapping* versions of the video routines go around the operating system. They write characters on the screen by sending data directly to video memory. Now, the only difference between the two forms is that the memory-mapping versions can sometimes operate at fifty times the speed of the BIOS versions. So why use the BIOS routines?

There are two reasons, and compatibility is not one of them. Nearly all IBM-compatible computers have video hardware that accommodates the memory-mapping conventions, and IBM has announced that it won't change the essentials in future machines. By using the BIOS versions, however, you can ensure that, first, the program will work with any of the new operating environments like IBM's TopView or Microsoft Windows, and second, that the program will work with future, multitasking versions of DOS. Still, the incredible speed of the memory-mapped versions is seductive. There really is no good reason *not* to use them when your software is bound for stand-alone operation.

All memory-mapping routines need to know the address of video memory. This address, which differs between monochrome and color systems, is expressed as a hexadecimal number, either **$B000** for the monochrome adaptor, or **$B800** for the color graphics adaptor. Either value can be used with the EGA (Enhanced Graphics Adaptor), depending on which screen mode you select. Note that these addresses refer only to text modes. This library contains no dot-addressed graphics routines.

The memory-mapping routines look for the video memory address in a global integer variable named *VideoBuffer*. A variable is *global* when it is declared in the body of a Pascal program; it is called "global" because any procedure or function can get to it. When you use one or more of the memory-mapping routines, declare the variable *VideoBuffer* (**VideoBuffer: integer**) and assign a value to it before a memory-mapping routine is used (**VideoBuffer := $B000;** or **VideoBuffer := $B800;**). (Numbers beginning with "$" are *hexadecimal*; you don't need to understand them—just assign the values for *VideoBuffer* as shown.) A program can use an equipment determination routine from Chapter 2 to determine the kind of video adaptor in use.

Video adaptors may have several *pages* of video memory, meaning that they can hold several full-screen text images. Display can be switched from one page to another. Video pages are numbered from 0 upward. In 80-column modes, the monochrome adaptor has only one page (page 0), the color graphics adaptor has four (0-3), and the EGA can have up to eight in either monochrome or color modes (0-7). Successive pages begin at higher memory locations. Page 0 begins at **$B000** or **$B800**, page 1 starts **$100** higher, and so on. When you want one of the memory-mapping routines to write on a higher-numbered page, you must add multiples of **$100** to the **VideoBuffer** value. Hence, on the color graphics adaptor, page 0 is at **$B800**, page 1 is at **$B900**, page 2 is at **$BA00**, etc.

The BIOS versions of the video routines do not require the **VideoBuffer** variable. Instead, they use a global variable called **VideoPage** that tells which video page to write on. Usually, this value is 0. Setting **VideoPage** to 2 causes the BIOS routines to write on page 2. If you fail to set up **VideoPage** or **VideoBuffer**, the routines that need them won't compile, and Turbo points to the error.

One last word about paging. Turbo Pascal always writes to page 0 and displays page 0. It is the *current page*. Chapter 6 has routines that can bring other pages into view. Any page may be written on before or while it is displayed. Note that when you clear the current page, the effect is to clear the screen. The **ClrScr** command always clears the current page; the **ClearPage** procedure in Chapter 7 clears pages out of view.

The other concern when using the video routines is setting up screen *attributes*. An *attribute* is some characteristic of a character's display: its foreground or background color and intensity, whether it is blinking, or perhaps whether it is underlined. Most of the video routines have a parameter called **Color** that sets the attribute in which the characters written by the routine are displayed. Now, video memory devotes two bytes to each character position on the screen. The first holds the character's code, and the second holds its *attribute byte*. The **Color** parameter is the value given to the second byte. The parameter is set up as an integer to keep procedure declarations simple. But it should contain only values that fit into a byte—that is, numbers from 0 to 255.

Attribute bytes determine colors using particular bit patterns. Bits are counted from 0 to 7, in which bit 0 corresponds to the value 1, bit 1 corresponds to 2, bit 2 to 4, bit 3 to 8, and so on up to 128. Bits 0 through 2 set the foreground color, where bit 0 turns on blue, bit 1 turns on green, and bit 2 turns on red. The various combinations create any of eight colors, including white when all bits are on, and black when all are off. Bit three sets the foreground color to high intensity, altering the shade of the eight basic colors so that there are sixteen in all.

The same logic applies to the high four bits, except here they set a character's background color. Bit 4 sets blue, 5 sets green, and 6 sets red. In this case however, the fourth, highest bit does not usually affect the color's intensity; rather, it turns blinking on and off.

On a monochrome display, since only black and white exist, a "normal image" results when the three main foreground bits are turned on and the three main background bits are turned off. A reverse image is the opposite. Underlining is an anomaly, where bit 0 is turned on and bits 1 and 2 are off. The figure below diagrams the bit settings for color and monochrome adaptors.

Once you have decided on a bit pattern, you must add up the values of each bit to make one value, which is what is sent as

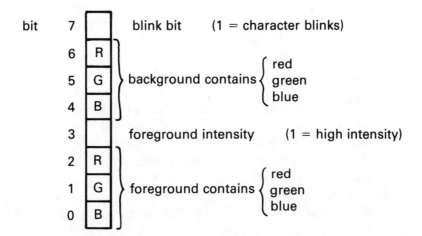

the *Color* parameter. Figuring out the bit patterns for every color is a lot of work (note that Chapter 3 has routines to help). It is much easier to use the special routines in Chapter 6 that automatically set up attribute bytes using codes for the various colors and characteristics (the Turbo Pascal facilities for setting character color don't apply). These routines look for a global variable named *Color* and make the appropriate changes in its bit pattern. By using this variable when you call a video routine, all the work is done for you.

For example, a routine called *BlinkOn* turns blinking on, and another called *BlinkOff* does the opposite. Say that you are using the procedure *Wrt*, which memory-maps a string starting from the current cursor position. *Wrt* takes two parameters: first the string, and then the attribute. You might write:

```
Wrt('Only the word ',Color);
```

Here, *Color* might contain the value **112**, which creates reverse-image on a monochrome display. To make the next word blink, write:

```
BlinkOn;
Wrt('blink',Color);
```

BlinkOn changes a bit setting in the variable *Color*, leaving the rest of the attribute untouched. To finish the sentence in nonblinking characters:

```
BlinkOff;
Wrt(' actually blinks',Color);
```

Error-checking

Finally, a word about error-checking. Most of the routines have a fair amount of error-checking built in. They check that the parameters your programs send them are in range. These checks prevent the routines from doing damage to the program's data or from crashing outright. But in most cases, they cannot detect the sort of errors that result from asking the routine to do something valid but not very sensible. For example, some routines can clear a rectangular area of the screen. You supply the coordinates of the top left corner of the area and its width and depth. If the coordinates are at the bottom right corner of the display, there won't be enough room to clear, and odd patches on the screen are affected.

Such errors could be detected but only at the cost of making the routines larger and slower. As a result, error-checking has been taken only far enough to halt disaster. The rest is up to you. When the parameters you send are out of range, usually a routine simply returns without doing anything. So when a routine appears to do nothing at all, it means that a parameter is in error. Some of the more complicated routines return error codes, as described in their documentation.

A final word

You're ready to go! If you feel a bit overwhelmed by the discussions of type-checking, video buffers, and attribute bytes— don't worry. Just follow these simple rules at first:

For strings: Place the line {**$V-**} at the start of the program, with nothing else on the line. Then make a type declaration for *stype*, where **stype = string[255]**.

For video: Declare integer variables named *VideoBuffer* and *VideoPage*. Make **VideoBuffer := $B000** if you are using a monochrome monitor, or **VideoBuffer := $B800** if a color monitor. Set *VideoPage* to **0**. When a procedure calls for a value for *Color*, use **7** for normal white-on-black.

Although a few of these routines are rather large, most take up only some tens of bytes of code space. Three or four dozen routines may consume only a few kilobytes of the precious sixty-four. Familiarize yourself with the library, so that when opportunities arise, you will spot them. Experiment freely. At the least you'll save time; at most you'll find new avenues to creativity.

2
The System

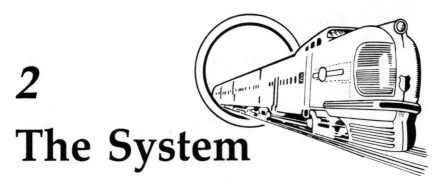

Section 1: Equipment determination

This section holds routines that tell your programs what equipment is present in the machine. *MachineType* tells which type of IBM microcomputer (PC, PC AT, and so on) your program is running on. *DOSVersion* reports which DOS version is loaded. *NumberSerial* and *NumberParallel* tell how many serial and parallel ports the machine has. And *GamePort* finds out if a game port is present.

Several routines center on the video system. *MDAPresent*, *CGAPresent*, *EGAPresent*, and *HerculesPresent* seek out the various video cards. *CurrentAdaptor* reports which video adaptor is currently used by the operating system when more than one is present in the machine. *EGAMonitor* tells whether an EGA is connected to a high resolution monitor, and *EGAMemory* tells how much memory is loaded on the EGA card.

Finally, several routines search out information about disk drives. *NumberFloppy* and *NumberFixed* report how many floppy- and fixed-disk drives are present. *DiskType* tells what kind of disk drive is present at a particular drive number. And *DiskSize* reports a disk's capacity (the *FreeSpace* routine in Chapter 8 tells how much disk space is available).

Function *MachineType: integer;*

FILE NAME: IBMTYPE.PAS   (33 code bytes)

PURPOSE: *MachineType* returns a code number that tells the kind of IBM machine that the program is running on. The codes are:

1. IBM PC
2. IBM PC XT or Portable PC
3. IBM PCjr
4. IBM PC AT
5. IBM Convertible
6. Undetermined

NOTES:

1. The value **6** ("Undetermined") may be returned by IBM compatibles of any kind.

2. Early models of the PC XT may return the code for a standard PC.

3. The code is a conversion of the value found in memory at **F000:FFFE**.

EXAMPLE: To find out if the machine is an AT:

```
if MachineType = 4 then Write('This is an IBM AT');
```

Function DOSVersion: integer;

FILE NAME:	DOSVERS.PAS (43 code bytes)
PURPOSE:	**DOSVersion** returns the number of the DOS version under which the Turbo Pascal program is running. A version number consists of two parts. For version **2.1**, the **2** is the *major version number*, and the **1** is the *minor version number*. The latter should actually be regarded as the two-digit number **10**. Rather than return separate values for the two parts of the version number, this routine returns a three-digit decimal number, where the hundred's place holds the major version number, and the other two digits hold the minor version number. Thus, version 2.1 is reported as **210**.
NOTES:	1. This routine helps keep software user-friendly. Rather than have your program crash when it is used with a version of DOS that is too early, check that a correct version is loaded and inform the user if it isn't.
EXAMPLE:	To check that the version is at least 2.0:

```
if DOSVersion < 200 then Write('Must use DOS 2.0 or later');
```

Function NumberSerial: integer;
Function NumberParallel: integer;

FILE NAMES:	NUMSRIAL.PAS	(26 code bytes)
	NUMPARLL.PAS	(26 code bytes)

PURPOSE: *NumberSerial* returns the number of serial ports in the machine while *NumberParallel* does the same for parallel ports.

NOTES: 1. The values returned by the functions merely reflect the presence of the port hardware; they do not indicate whether devices are connected to the ports.

EXAMPLE: To report the number of serial ports:

```
Write('Number serial ports: ', NumberSerial);
```

Function GamePort: boolean;

FILE NAME:	GAMEPORT.PAS (28 code bytes)
PURPOSE:	*GamePort* returns TRUE when the machine has a game port. It doesn't indicate whether any device is actually connected to the port.
NOTES:	1. This routine tests the port (201h) directly.
EXAMPLE:	To report the presence of a game port:

```
Write('There is ');
if GamePort then
  Write('a')
  else Write('no');
Write(' game port present');
```

The result:

```
There is a game port present
```

. . . or . . .

```
There is no game port present
```

Function MDAPresent:boolean;
Function CGAPresent:boolean;
Function EGAPresent:boolean;
Function HerculesPresent:boolean;

FILE NAMES:

MDAPRES.PAS	(51 code bytes)
CGAPRES.PAS	(51 code bytes)
EGAPRES.PAS	(34 code bytes)
HERCPRES.PAS	(51 code bytes)

PURPOSE:

Each of these routines checks to see if a particular video adaptor is present in the machine. **MDAPresent** looks for the IBM Monochrome Adaptor, **CGAPresent** for the IBM Color Graphics Adaptor, and **EGAPresent** for the IBM Enhanced Graphics Adaptor. In addition, **HerculesPresent** searches for the ubiquitous Hercules monochrome graphics card. When only one adaptor is present, it necessarily is the *current adaptor*. When there are two adaptors, use the **CurrentAdaptor** function in this section to find out which is in control.

NOTES:

1. **MDAPresent** and **CGAPresent** check for an adaptor by writing to the cursor-address register on the video-controller chip. The original value is restored. **EGAPresent** checks the BIOS data area at **40:0087** for an EGA-status byte.

2. **MDAPresent** returns TRUE when a Hercules card is present. **HerculesPresent** tests a video control register for vertical retrace. It works only when the machine is set for monochrome mode.

3. When an EGA is set to a CGA mode, **CGAPresent** returns TRUE. Similarly, **MDAPresent** returns TRUE when the EGA is in monochrome mode.

EXAMPLE: This example displays a message telling
                        which adaptors are present:

```
Write('MDA');
if not MDAPresent then Write(' not');
Writeln(' present');
Write('CGA');
if not CGAPresent then Write(' not');
Writeln(' present');
Write('EGA');
if not EGAPresent then Write(' not');
Writeln(' present');
```

Function CurrentAdaptor: integer;

FILE NAME: CRNTADAP.PAS   (53 code bytes)

PURPOSE: *CurrentAdaptor* determines which of the IBM adaptors is the *current adaptor*, that is, the one to which BIOS and DOS calls are directed. It returns one of three codes:

1   Monochrome Display Adaptor
2   Color Graphics Adaptor
3   Enhanced Graphics Adaptor

NOTES: 1. For simultaneous output to a second adaptor, write directly to the video buffer. For example, if the color graphics adaptor is current but a monochrome adaptor is also present and connected to a second monitor, any of the memory-mapping routines in Chapters 6 and 7 write to the second monitor when they are given $B000 as the value for **Buffer**.

2. The memory-mapping routines in Chapters 6 and 7 use a global variable named *VideoBuffer* to find out the base address of the adaptor in use. Ordinarily the value given *VideoBuffer* is **$B000** for the monochrome adaptor modes, and **$B800** for color text modes. Use *CurrentAdaptor* to set *VideoBuffer*.

EXAMPLE: To be sure that a graphics program is supported:

```
if CurrentAdaptor = 1 then WrongAdaptorError;
```

Function EGAMonitor: integer;

FILE NAME: EGAMONTR.PAS   (70 code bytes)

PURPOSE: *EGAMonitor* returns a code that indicates
                    the kind of monitor connected to the EGA:

        0   no EGA present
        1   monochrome monitor
        2   low-resolution color monitor
        3   high-resolution color monitor

EXAMPLE: To test that an advanced color graphics
                    mode is allowed:

```
if EGAMonitor <> 3 then WrongMonitorError;
```

Function EGAMemory: integer;

FILE NAME:	EGAMEM.PAS	(41 code bytes)

PURPOSE: *EGAMemory* reports how much memory is mounted on an EGA. It returns one of five codes:

0	no EGA present
1	64K
2	128K
3	192K
4	256K

EXAMPLE: To test that the EGA has at least 128K:

```
If EGAMemory < 2 then EGAEquipError;
```

Function NumberFloppy: integer;
Function NumberFixed: integer;

FILE NAMES: NUMFLOPY.PAS   (34 code bytes)
               NUMFIXED.PAS   (57 code bytes)

PURPOSE: **NumberFloppy** returns the number of floppy-disk drives in the machine, and **NumberFixed** does the same for hard disk drives. Both routines return **0** when no drive of that type is found.

NOTES: 1. **NumberFloppy** uses the equipment status byte returned by BIOS INT 11H. The value may reflect drive specifiers set aside for RAM disks (virtual disks).

2. Use the **DiskType** function (the next in this section) to find out which drive numbers correspond to which disk types. The capacity of a disk drive may be found with the **DiskSize** function (also in this section).

3. **NumberFixed** works by testing the disk type at drive numbers above those allocated to floppies.

EXAMPLES: To report the number of floppy drives:

```
Writeln('There are ', NumberFloppy, ' floppy drives');
```

And the number of fixed disks:

```
Writeln('Number fixed disks: ', NumberFixed);
```

Function DiskType(DriveNumber: integer): integer;

FILE NAME: DISKTYPE.PAS   (54 code bytes)

PURPOSE: **DiskType** checks the disk at a specified drive number and returns one of the following code numbers:

0	no drive at that specifier
1	single-sided, 9-sector
2	double-sided, 9-sector
3	single-sided, 8-sector
4	double-sided, 8-sector
5	high density, 15-sector
6	fixed

PARAMETERS: **DriveNumber** is the drive number, where 0 = default, 1 = A:, 2 = B:, etc.

NOTES: 1. The routine works through function 1CH of INT 21H, which returns a pointer to the FAT identification byte. This means that the interrupt must access the diskette in the disk drive. If there is none, DOS is thrown into a critical error condition (the **"Abort, Retry, Ignore"** message). That's why you shouldn't use this routine to find floppy-disk drives.

EXAMPLE: To find out whether drive B is a floppy or fixed disk:

```
Write('Drive B is a ');
if DiskType(2) = 6
  then Write('fixed')
  else Write('floppy');
Write(' disk');
```

Function DiskSize(DriveNumber: integer): integer;

FILE NAME:	DISKSIZE.PAS	(60 code bytes)

PURPOSE: *DiskSize* returns the capacity of the disk found at a specified drive. The capacity is given in kilobytes. The function returns **0** when there is no disk drive at the specified drive number.

PARAMETERS: *DriveNumber* is the drive number, where 0 = default, 1 = A:, 2 = B:, and so on.

NOTES: 1. *FreeSpace*, a routine found in Chapter 8, reports the available disk space.

            2. If *DiskSize* is used to access a floppy-disk drive when no floppy disk is present, the DOS error condition occurs. The only recovery is for the user to insert a diskette into the drive and to request "retry." If "abort" is chosen, the Turbo Pascal program is terminated, and control returns to DOS.

EXAMPLE: To find the size of a fixed disk at C:

```
Write('Drive C: holds ', DiskSize, ' kilobytes');
```

Section 2: Memory

Three kinds of random-access memory are available to IBM microcomputers. First, there is the 1-megabyte space within which DOS makes use of the lowest 640K. This is what we conventionally think of as "memory". The function *RamSize* tells how much of this kind of memory is installed in the machine.

The second kind of memory—*extended memory*—can be installed only in a PC AT. An AT can address up to sixteen megabytes when it is driven by the proper operating system, and the second through sixteenth megabytes constitute extended memory. At present, Turbo Pascal programs cannot make use of extended memory. Still, to help with equipment checks, this section contains the function *ExtendedSize*.

The third kind of memory, *expanded memory*, was devised to increase the amount of memory available to programs confined to a 1-megabyte address space. It operates by a technique called *bank switching*, which is discussed below. Up to eight megabytes of expanded memory can be installed in a PC, XT, or AT. This technology, developed by several industry leaders, rather than by IBM, is called the "Lotus-Intel-Microsoft Expanded Memory Specification," or LIM EMS. A second standard, AQA EMS, is a superset of the LIM EMS; software that works with LIM works with AQA too.

Here is how the LIM standard works: Within the conventional 1 megabyte of memory space, DOS uses only the lowest 640K. Higher addresses go unused because they are cut off from the low 640K by the memory buffers employed by video adaptors. The LIM standard takes any available 64K stretch of high memory addresses and uses them as a window into the two to eight megabytes of memory it provides. At any moment, 64K of the LIM memory is "visible" to the 8088 or 80286 CPU at these memory positions. It is a program's job to switch into "view" whatever data is currently required by the program and perhaps to transfer the data from high memory down to a position in the 640K used by the program. The 64K window is treated as four 16K partitions, with each one individually selectable. At any moment, you can call to view 16K swatches of memory from any four locations in expanded memory. The four window partitions are referred to here as windows 0 through 3. Taken together, they are called the "page frame."

Working in assembly language, you can keep program code in expanded memory and run it from there. The concern here, however, is with giving you the means to use very large data sets with your Turbo Pascal programs. The eight expanded memory routines in this section give you all the control you need to allocate pages and switch between them. Your Pascal programs may access the data directly in high memory (using the **Mem** or **MemW** commands), or they can transfer the data between high memory and ordinary variables in low memory.

The workings of the EMS standard are straightforward. By reading this section and studying the examples, you will quickly learn to use it. In the first step, **SeekExpanded** tells whether expanded memory is present in the machine and **NumberPages** shows how many 16K pages are installed. **FrameAddress** returns the position of the 64K block in high memory used by the EMS. And **AvailablePages** tells how many 16K pages are available for use by your program.

AllocatePages allocates as many pages of expanded memory as your program needs. When pages are allocated, an identification number (a "handle") is returned; this number identifies the whole group of pages. Individual pages within the group are referred to by numbers counted from 0 upward. A particular 16K page is named by its handle and its page number. If your program allocates twelve pages, it thereafter calls on pages 0 through 11 under the particular handle returned. Pages from subsequent allocations are also numbered from 0 upward.

The **SelectPage** procedure uses a handle and page number to bring a particular page into view in one of the four positions in high memory. Once that is done, the **MoveData** and **ExchangeData** procedures can exchange data between the page and low memory. Finally, **DeallocatePages** releases pages when your program is finished to make them available to subsequent programs. A complete example of all routines used together is presented with **DeallocatePages**.

Function *RamSize: integer;*

FILE NAME:	RAMSIZE.PAS	(19 code bytes)

PURPOSE: *RamSize* reports the amount of RAM (to 640K) loaded in the machine.

NOTES: 1. *RamSize* uses the BIOS equipment determination interrupt (INT 12H).

EXAMPLE: To report the amount of RAM:

```
Write(There are ',RamSize,' kilobytes of RAM');
```

Function ExtendedSize: integer;

FILE NAME: EXTDSIZE.PAS   (32 code bytes)

PURPOSE: *ExtendedSize* is used with a PC AT to find out how much extended memory is present in the machine. The routine returns **0** when there is no extended memory; otherwise, it returns the number of kilobytes of extended memory installed.

NOTES: 1. The routine uses function 88H of INT 15H. It returns a value other than 0 only in a PC AT equipped with 640K of RAM.

EXAMPLE: To report the amount of extended memory:

```
Write(There are ',ExtendedSize,' KB of extended memory');
```

Function SeekExpanded: boolean;
Function NumberPages: integer;

FILE NAMES:	EXPANDED.PAS	(29 code bytes)
	NUMPAGES.PAS	(29 code bytes)

PURPOSE: *SeekExpanded* returns TRUE when EMS memory is installed and functioning properly. It returns FALSE when EMS hardware is present but the EMS device driver has not been loaded.

NumberPages returns the number of 16K pages of expanded memory present in the machine. The function returns −1 when no EMS hardware is found, or when the EMS hardware or software has malfunctioned. Thus, it also can serve as an equipment-determination routine.

NOTES: 1. Since *NumberPages* returns −1 when no EMS board is present, it never returns 0.

EXAMPLES: To report whether an EMS board is present:

```
if SeekExpanded = 1 then write("EMS board present");
```

To report the amount of expanded memory, you must overcome Turbo Pascal's inability to handle long integers. Since a page is roughly sixteen and one-third kilobytes, these lines do the job:

```
Write('There are roughly ');
Write(NumberPages*16 + Round(NumberPages/3));
Writeln(' kilobytes of expanded memory.');
```

Function FrameAddress: integer;

FILE NAME:	FRAMADDR.PAS (27 code bytes)
PURPOSE:	In machines equipped with expanded memory, **FrameAddress** returns the memory segment at which the 64K expanded memory window begins. The routine returns −1 when no EMS board is present, or when the EMS hardware or software malfunctions.
NOTES:	1. The address that is returned points to the lowest position in the EMS page frame.
EXAMPLE:	This short example displays the lowest byte in the window. First, the integer variable *I* is given the window address. Then the byte variable **A** receives the byte value held in memory at **I:0000**, in which **I** is the start of the segment, and **0000** is the first byte of the 64K bytes (0000 to FFFF) held in the segment.

```
I := FrameAddress;
A := Mem[I:0000];
Write(chr(A));
```

More concisely:

```
Write(chr(Mem[FrameAddress:0]));
```

Function AvailablePages: integer;

FILE NAME:	AVLPAGES.PAS (22 code bytes)
PURPOSE:	*AvailablePages* returns the number of 16K expanded memory pages available.
NOTES:	1. The number returned does not necessarily reflect the capacity of the EMS hardware. Memory-resident programs may have allocated EMS pages for their own use. Use *NumberPages* (also in this section) to find out how many pages of expanded memory are actually installed.
EXAMPLE:	Say that your laboratory measurements entail a data set of 700,000 integer values, requiring roughly 1.4 megabytes of memory. Also assume that you will keep all the data in expanded memory. A 16K page of memory is actually 16384 bytes (2 to the 14th power). So you need 1400000/16384 = 85.45 pages—that is, 86 pages. To test for their availability:

```
If AvailablePages < 86 then InsufficientMemory;
```

Function AllocatePages(Number: integer): integer;

FILE NAME:	ALLOPAGE.PAS (31 code bytes)
PURPOSE:	**AllocatePages** allocates a specific number of 16K pages of expanded memory for use by your program. The function returns an integer-length *handle*—an arbitrary identification number by which your program can refer to the group of pages allocated. The routine returns −1 when the allocation cannot be made owing to unavailability or some other error.
PARAMETERS:	**Number** is the number of pages to allocate.
NOTES:	1. Your program should store the handle for subsequent use. The handle is required when a request is made to switch a particular page into view.

2. Any number of allocation requests may be made. It is a good idea to allocate all the pages you will need for any one data set so that all data will fall under one handle and one sequence of page numbers. For example, if you need to store a 64K array, allocate four pages, enabling you to refer to pages 0 through 3 under handle A. If, instead, the program allocates three pages and then goes back for one more, your data structures must deal with three quarters of the data being held in pages 0 through 2 under handle A and the rest residing in page 0 under handle B.

3. Allocating a page isn't the same as bringing it into the 64K window in high memory. The **SelectPage** procedure does this.

4. Use the **AvailablePages** function first to avoid errors. Note that a request for **0** pages is treated as an error.

EXAMPLE:

This example assumes a data set of 30000 50-byte records. This amounts to 1.5 megabytes; because 327 50-byte records fit into a 16K page, 92 pages are required. To make the allocation:

```
Handle1 := AllocatePage(92);
```

Now test that the allocation was successful:

```
if Handle1 = -1 then AllocationError;
```

Function SelectPage(Handle,PageNumber,Window: integer): integer;

FILE NAME: SELECTPG.PAS   (34 code bytes)

PURPOSE: *SelectPage* switches a specified expanded-memory page into one of the four 16K windows in high memory. The function returns **0** when the allocation has been made successfully, and otherwise it returns one of the following error codes:

131   there is no such handle

138   the page number is out of the range of those allocated

139   the page frame was not within 0–3

OTHER   other non-zero codes indicate equipment problems

PARAMETERS: *Handle* is the handle returned when the page was allocated.

PageNumber is the number of a page allocated under *Handle*.

Window is a number from **0** to **3** that corresponds to one of the 16K partitions of the 64K page frame in high memory used by the EMS. The lowest-address window is **0**.

NOTES: 1. Each window is $400 paragraphs large. If the base address of the 64K window in high memory is **$E000**, then page frame 0 is at **$E000**, frame 1 is at **$E400**, frame 2 is at **$E800**, and frame 3 is at **$EC00**.

2. The page numbers are merely arbitrary identifiers; they bear no intrinsic sequential order. Think of them as blank sheets of paper spread out on a table, not as blocks of memory at particular positions

as you would think of ordinary RAM. When you use *SelectPage* to bring a particular page into the 64K frame, you may position it in any of the four windows.

EXAMPLE: Assume that ten pages were allocated and that the handle was assigned to the integer variable *ArrayHandle*. To bring page 3 to window 2:

```
SelectPage(ArrayHandle,3,2);
```

Procedure MoveData(Seg1,Ofs1,Seg2,Ofs2,NumberBytes: integer);
Procedure ExchangeData(Seg1,Ofs1,Seg2,Ofs2,NumberBytes: integer);

FILE NAMES:	MOVEDATA.PAS	(48 code bytes)
	XCHGDATA.PAS	(68 code bytes)

PURPOSE: These two procedures move data between expanded memory and program memory. They may be used to move data directly to and from Turbo Pascal variables. In both cases, you must specify the *absolute addresses* of the two memory locations (that is, the lowest address in each). **MoveData** moves a specified number of bytes of data from **Seg1:Ofs1** to **Seg2:Ofs2**. **ExchangeData** exchanges data between the two locations.

PARAMETERS: **Seg1** and **Ofs1** are the segment and offset *from* which data is transferred by **MoveData**. In **ExchangeData**, they point to one of the two areas between which data is swapped. In both cases, **Seg1** and **Ofs1** mark the beginning (lowest address) of the data.

Seg2 and **Ofs2** are the segment and offset *to* which data is transferred by **MoveData**. In **ExchangeData** they mark the second of the two areas between which data is exchanged.

NumberBytes is the number of bytes to be transfered. This value may be up to 65535 bytes (that is, 64K). Since integers in Turbo Pascal are limited to **32767**, the corresponding negative number must be used for higher values (see note 4 below).

NOTES: 1. These procedures may be used for purposes other than data transfer to and from expanded memory. For example, they could swap data between expanded memory pages or between Turbo Pascal arrays.

2. *MoveData* copies the data starting from the lowest byte of the source to the lowest byte of the target, then the next highest byte, and so on. This means that the source and target areas must not overlap when the source is at a lower location in memory than the target.

3. Within a 16-bit integer, 65536 bit patterns are possible. Rather than devote all patterns to a sequence of positive numbers from 0 to 65535, the top half of the sequence is regarded as representing negative numbers, where $65535 = -1$, $65534 = -2$, and so on. As a result, Turbo Pascal's integers range from -32768 to 32767. But when *MoveData* and *ExchangeData* receive the value -1 for *NumberBytes*, they regard it as 65535 and proceed to move or exchange 65535 bytes of data. Thus, values from 32768 to 65535 are supplied to the routines by sending the equivalent negative integer. To calculate this integer, subtract 65536. For example, to move 40000 bytes: $40000 - 65536 = -25536$.

4. You must be certain that the offset plus *NumberBytes* is not greater than 65535. For example, if *Seg2:Ofs2* is **E000:0005**, trying to move a full 65535 block means that the processor needs to reach 65540 bytes above the segment value **E000**. Since it cannot do this, it instead "wraps around" its addressing pointer so that the last five bytes of the series are taken starting from **E000:0000**.

EXAMPLES: First, assume that expanded memory is to contain 100-byte records, and that record positions 13–14 (counting from 0) are to hold an integer value. Say that your program needs to insert this value into record 22 of the series (also counting from 0), and that the value is currently held in the Pascal variable **Age**. Furthermore, assume that the series of records begins at the start of page 0, that page 0 has been brought to view in window 0, and that the four EMS windows begin at segment **E000**. To move the data into place, first calculate its offset in the series of records:

```
Position := 22 * 100 + 13;
```

Now, the memory position of the variable **Age** can be found with Turbo's **Seg** and **Ofs** functions. Since the integer is two bytes long, **NumberBytes** equals 2. To move the integer to expanded memory:

```
MoveData(Seg(Age),Ofs(Age),$E000,Position,2);
```

This is a lot of trouble to store a single variable (**MemW** would do as well), but if **Age** referred to an array of 5000 integers starting at E000:0000, the whole array could be moved as easily:

```
MoveData(Seg(Age),Ofs(Age),$E000,0,10000);
```

To move the array from expanded memory to the Pascal variable:

```
MoveData($E000,0,Seg(Age),Ofs(Age),10000);
```

As you can see, the strategy is to keep many data records, of which Turbo Pascal sees only a few. From Turbo's perspective, it is always manipulating the same data object; but, in fact, the contents of that object may be constantly changed. Managing the data exchange can become quite complex, however. If, for example, you wish to create a very large string array, it is easy enough to allocate page after page of, say, eighty-one-byte records in expanded memory, keeping a table in Turbo's memory that tracks the range of elements held by each page number. But performing array operations—moves, copies, searches—can become very complicated, and performance may be slowed considerably by constant data transfers. Sometimes, greater speed can be attained by *swapping* data, at once saving the just-modified data while reading in the next.

In this example, **ExchangeData** swaps a 4000-byte array between Turbo's data segment and window 2. Assume that the expanded memory page contains four such arrays, and that the program wants the highest. The segment address would be that of the page-frame address (say, **$E000**), plus two times **$400** to point to the start of window 2, giving **$E800**. The offset would be three times 4000 bytes: 12000 bytes. (It is often convenient to state the segment in hexadecimal and the offset in decimal—there is no reason not to.) To make the swap:

```
ExchangeData(Seg(Array1),Ofs(Array1),$E800,12000,4000);
```

Function DeallocatePages(Handle: integer): integer;

FILE NAME: DEALPAGE.PAS   (29 code bytes)

PURPOSE: *DeallocatePages* deallocates all pages previously allocated to a program under a particular handle. Pages allocated separately (that is, under a different handle) are unaffected. The function returns 0 if the deallocation has been made successfully, and −1 if not. With deallocation, pages will be available to subsequent programs.

PARAMETERS: *Handle* is the handle issued for the group of pages when they were allocated by *AllocatePages*.

NOTES: 1. Partial deallocation of a group of pages isn't possible. You must deallocate all pages and then call the *AllocatePages* function once again.

2. The error value **−1** is returned when a non-existent handle has been given to the function, or when no expanded-memory board is installed or operating properly. By the time your program comes to deallocate pages, it ought already to have used the equipment determination routines to learn of any hardware problems, so the error message is really intended to indicate a bad handle.

EXAMPLE: *DeallocatePages* is the last of the expanded-memory commands, and it is here assembled with all other commands to show how they work together. In this example a program reads a large number (perhaps megabytes) of 30-byte records from a disk and stores them all in expanded memory. For clarity, only 500 records are stored per page, taking up 15K of the 16K available. The records are

read one by one from disk into a single record variable (**PersonRecord**) and then transferred to expanded memory. Only window 0
is used, so all records are within a 15,000
byte offset of the 64K frame address. Once
500 records are written on one page, the next
page is brought into the window. Here is the
structure of the record:

```
Type
  nametype : string[18];
  passtype : string[8];
  statistics = record
              Name : nametype;
              AccessNumber : integer;
              Password : passtype;
              end;
```

Note that the two string types contribute
nineteen and nine bytes to the record, respectively, adding an extra byte for the
descriptors that tell the length of the strings
they hold. Only one such record is required
in Turbo's data segment:

```
Var
  PersonRecord : statistics;
```

Assume that the data is stored in a file
named **PASSWORD.DAT** and that the file is
assigned to **PersonFile**:

```
Var
  PersonFile : file of Statistics;
```

Make the file assignment:

```
Assign(PersonFile,'PASSWORD.DAT');
```

If you want to make a dummy file for experimentation, try this code, which places the record number in *AccessNumber*:

```
Rewrite(PersonFile);
for I := 0 to 1999 do  {60K file}
  begin
    with PersonRecord do
      begin
        Name := 'NNNNNNNNNNNNNNNNNN';
        AccessNumber := I;
        Password := 'PPPPPPPP';
      end;
  end;
Close(PersonFile);
```

Now you are ready to load the file. First, check that expanded memory is present in the machine:

```
if SeekExpanded <> 1 then EMSError;
```

Most programs allocate all available pages to themselves:

```
Available := AvailablePages;
Handle := AllocatePages(Available);
```

Next, find out the page-frame address:

```
Frame := FrameAddress;
```

To load the file, open it, read the records one by one, and then transfer them to EMS memory using *MoveData*. The loop that reads the records must constantly watch for a page to fill and then switch to another. (Page 0 is brought into Window 0 before the loop is entered.) Here, a variable called *Ptr* keeps track of offsets within window 0, *RecordCount* counts the number of records entered onto a page, *PageCount* tallies the number of EMS pages used, and *RecordTotal* counts the total number of records read from the file. Two more values, *Sgmt* and *Ofst*, hold the address of the *PersonRecord* record used for data transfer.

```
Reset(PersonFile);
Sgmt := Seg(PersonRecord);
Ofst := Ofs(PersonRecord);
Ptr := 0;
Pagecount := 0;
RecordCount := 0;
RecordTotal := 0;

ErrorChk := SelectPage(Handle,0,0);   {initial page}
if ErrorChk <> 0 then OutOfPagesError;

while not EOF(PersonFile) do
  begin
    Read(PersonFile,PersonRecord);   {get record}
    MoveData(Sgmt,Ofst,Frame,Ptr,30);   {transfer to EM}
    RecordCount := RecordCount+1;
    Ptr := Ptr+30;
    if RecordCount = 500 then   {new page}
      begin
        PageCount := PageCount+1;
        ErrorChk := SelectPage(Handle,PageCount,0);
        if ErrorChk <> 0 then OutOfPagesError;
        RecordTotal := RecordTotal+500;
        RecordCount := 0;
        Ptr := 0;
      end;
  end;
RecordTotal := RecordTotal + RecordCount;
Close(PersonFile);
```

The data is loaded. It is easy to fetch a particular record by calculating the EMS page number and bringing it into window 0. For record #603:

```
RecordNum := 603;
PageNeeded := RecordNum div 500;
ErrChk := SelectPage(Handle,PageNeeded,0);
```

Next, calculate the record's offset and move it into *PersonRecord*:

```
RecordOffset := RecordNum mod 500;
MoveData(Frame,RecordOffset*30,Sgmt,Ofst,30);
```

To view the record:

```
with PersonRecord do
  begin
    Writeln('Name: ',Name);
    Writeln('AccessNumber ',AccessNumber);
    Writeln('Password: ',Password);
  end;
```

Later, after writing the altered data back to disk, don't forget to deallocate the pages:

```
ErrorChk := DeallocatePages(Handle);
```

Section 3: The time and date

This section has routines that access the DOS time and date settings, set by the DOS TIME and DATE commands, or perhaps by an internal real-time clock. *GetTime* reports the hour, minutes, and seconds, and *SetTime* sets these values. Similarly, *GetDate* reports, and *SetDate* sets, the day, month, and year.

Two other routines concern the day of the week. *DayOfWeek* reports the day corresponding to the current date. DOS contains an algorithm to make this calculation, and it is possible to exploit it to find out the day of any date, provided that it falls within 1980–2099. *FindDay* performs this service.

Procedure GetTime;
Procedure SetTime;

FILE NAMES: GETTIME.PAS   (56 code bytes)
               SETTIME.PAS   (54 code bytes)

PURPOSE: *GetTime* returns the time of day kept by DOS, which is entered by the TIME command or set by an internal real-time clock. The values for the hour, minutes, and seconds are placed in three integer variables held in a record named *Time*. The variables are *Time.Hour*, *Time.Minutes*, and *Time.Seconds*, and they should be declared in that order. *SetTime* *sets* the DOS time reading using the contents of these three variables.

PARAMETERS: *Time.Hour* is an integer variable accessed by the routine. The hours are counted from 0 to 23, where 0 = midnight.

Time.Minutes and *Time.Seconds* are integer variables accessed by the routine. Both are counted from 0 to 59.

EXAMPLES: This example shows the setup for the *Time* record:

```
Type
  timetype = record
             Hour : integer;
             Minutes : integer;
             Seconds : integer;
             end;

Var
  Time : timetype;
```

To set the time to 2:31:56 PM:

```
Time.Hour := 14;
Time.Minutes := 31;
Time.Seconds := 56;
SetTime;
```

To report the time:

```
GetTime;
Write('The time is ',Time.Hour,':');
Write(Time.Minutes,':',Time.Seconds);
```

Procedure GetDate;
Procedure SetDate;

FILE NAMES: GETDATE.PAS   (60 code bytes)

                          SETDATE.PAS   (54 code bytes)

PURPOSE: *GetDate* returns the date kept by DOS, which is entered by the DATE command or set by an internal real-time clock. The values for the day, month, and year are placed in three integer variables held in a record named *Date*. The variables are *Date.Year*, *Date.Month*, and *Date.Day*, and they should be declared in that order. *SetDate* *sets* the DOS date with the contents of these three variables.

PARAMETERS: *Date.Year* is an integer variable accessed by the routine. It must be a number from 1980 to 2099.

         Date.Month is an integer variable accessed by the routine. The months are counted from 1 to 12.

         Date.Day is an integer variable accessed by the routine. It is a number from 1 to 31.

EXAMPLES: To set up the record:

```
Type
  datetype = record
             Year : integer;
             Month : integer;
             Day : integer;
             end;

Var
  Date : datetype;
```

To set the date to 6/21/1987:

```
Date.Year := 1987;
Date.Month := 6;
Date.Day := 21;
SetDate;
```

To report the date:

```
GetDate;
Write('The date is ',Date.Month,'/');
Write(Date.Day,'/',Date.Year);
```

Function DayOfWeek: integer;

FILE NAME: DAYWEEK.PAS   (23 code bytes)

PURPOSE: *DayOfWeek* tells which day of the week cor-
               responds to the current date. It returns a
               value from 0 to 6, where 0 is Sunday, 1 is
               Monday, and so on.

NOTES: 1. If the DOS date reading hasn't been set,
                  the random value found is the one used
                  for calculating the day of the week.

EXAMPLE: To display the day:

```
Day[0] := 'Sunday';
Day[1] := 'Monday';
Day[2] := 'Tuesday';
Day[3] := 'Wednesday';
Day[4] := 'Thursday';
Day[5] := 'Friday';
Day[6] := 'Saturday';
Write('It is ',Day[DayOfWeek]);
```

Function FindDay(Month,Day,Year: integer): integer;

FILE NAME: FINDDAY.PAS   (48 code bytes)

PURPOSE: *FindDay* takes any date from 1980 to 2099 and tells which day of the week it falls on. It returns a value from 0 to 6, which 0 is Sunday, 1 is Monday, and so on.

PARAMETERS: *Month* is the month, from 1 to 12.

                      Day is the day, from 1 to 31.

                      Year is the year, from 1980 to 2099.

NOTES: 1. The year is limited to the given range because the routine makes use of the DOS function that calculates the day of the week of the current date, which is limited to that range.

EXAMPLE: To find out the day of the week of 6/21/87:

```
Day[0] := 'Sunday';
Day[1] := 'Monday';
Day[2] := 'Tuesday';
Day[3] := 'Wednesday';
Day[4] := 'Thursday';
Day[5] := 'Friday';
Day[6] := 'Saturday';
Write('6/21/87 is on a ',Day[FindDay(6,21,1987)]);
```

3

Bit Operations

Section 1: Change a value's representation

This chapter is broken into two sections. The first contains routines that convert bit patterns between their decimal, binary, and hexadecimal representations. The second section provides routines that change individual bits within bit patterns.

Turbo Pascal accepts numbers in decimal or hexadecimal form, and it writes out numbers only in decimal form. This is an unfortunate limitation, since some kinds of information are far more intelligible when expressed as binary or hex numbers. The routines in this section more than remedy the problem. *ByteToBinary* and *IntegerToBinary* convert byte and integer values into character strings of 0s and 1s. The number **129**, for example, is returned as **10000001**. *ByteToHex* and *IntegerToHex* change the number to hexadecimal form, so that **129** would be returned as **81**. *BinaryToByte* and *BinaryToInteger* take binary strings and convert them into a byte or integer. **10000001** would be returned as **129**.

There are also four routines that read *bit fields*—a sequence of bits within a byte or integer; a field may contain from 1 to 16 bits. The bits are numbered 0 to 7 or 0 to 15. *ByteField* and *IntegerField* return a bit field as an integer. You might ask for the value of bits 3 through 5 in a byte or integer and the result would be an integer from 0 to 7—the range of values that can be held by three bits. **ByteFieldString** and **IntegerFieldString**, on the other hand, return binary representations of a bit field. Their reading of bits 3 through 5 would be a three-character string such as **101**. Section 2 contains counterparts to these routines that let you change bit fields without altering the rest of the byte or integer.

Function ByteToBinary(Value: byte): stype;
Function IntegerToBinary(Value: integer): stype;

FILE NAMES:	BYTE2BIN.PAS	(70 code bytes)
	INT2BIN.PAS	(70 code bytes)

PURPOSE: **ByteToBinary** and **IntegerToBinary** convert a numeric value to a binary character string, removing leading zeros. For example, they return **10000001** when **Value** is **129** and **11** when it is **3**.

PARAMETERS: **Value** is the byte or integer that is converted to a binary string.

stype must be at least **string[8]** for **ByteToBinary** and **string[16]** for **IntToBinary**.

NOTES: 1. Although **IntegerToBinary** is set up to receive an integer value, it will accept byte values, even without changing the word **integer** in the function declaration. Conversely, **ByteToBinary** will accept integer values, but it will return the bit pattern of only the lowest eight bits.

2. The routines return a single '0' character when the input value is zero.

EXAMPLES: To see the bit pattern of **255**:

```
Writeln(ByteToBinary(255));
```

This is what is displayed:

```
11111111
```

Or, with an integer:

```
Writeln(IntegerToBinary(-1));
```

The result:

```
1111111111111111
```

Function ByteToHex(Value: byte): stype;
Function IntegerToHex(Value: integer): stype;

FILE NAMES: BYTE2HEX.PAS   (52 code bytes)
               INT2HEX.PAS   (61 code bytes)

PURPOSE: *ByteToHex* and *IntegerToHex*, respectively, convert a byte or integer value to a two- or four-byte hexadecimal string. Leading zeros are included in the string.

PARAMETERS: *Value* is the byte or integer that is converted to a hexadecimal string.

NOTES: 1. *IntegerToHex* will work for byte values— even without changing the word **integer** to **byte** in the function declaration. The result, however, will be four bytes long, with the first two digits always zero.

EXAMPLES: To find the hexadecimal equivalent of **255**:

               ```
               Writeln(ByteToHex(255));
               ```

               The result is:

               ```
               FF
               ```

               IntegerToHex, on the other hand, always returns four digits:

               ```
               Writeln(IntegerToHex(255));
               ```

               The result:

               ```
               00FF
               ```

Function BinaryToByte(BinaryString: stype): byte;
Function BinaryToInteger(BinaryString: stype): integer;

FILE NAMES:	BIN2BYTE.PAS	(68 code bytes)
	BIN2INT.PAS	(68 code bytes)

PURPOSE: *BinaryToByte* and *BinaryToInteger*, respectively, convert a binary string of up to eight or sixteen digits into a byte or integer value.

PARAMETERS: *BinaryString* is a string containing only the characters "0" and "1". It may be from one to sixteen characters long.

NOTES:

1. The routines return zero when the input string is null or when it is longer than eight or sixteen characters.

2. The routines test for the "1" character and assume a "0" when "1" isn't found. As a result, any characters in the string other than "1" are interpreted as "0."

EXAMPLES: To find out the value of the string **11111111**:

```
Writeln(BinaryToByte('11111111'));
```

The result:

255

Integers, of course, treat the high bit as a minus sign:

```
Writeln(BinaryToInteger('1111111111111111'));
```

The result:

−1

Function ByteField(Value: byte; StartBit,NumberBits: integer): integer;
Function IntegerField(Value: integer; StartBit,NumberBits: integer): integer;

FILE NAMES: BYTFIELD.PAS   (55 code bytes)
               INTFIELD.PAS   (55 code bytes)

PURPOSE: *ByteField* and *IntegerField* return an integer
               that gives the value held in a bit field. For
               example, a value from 0 to 7 would be re-
               turned for a three-bit field. Both the starting
               point and the size of the bit field must be
               specified.

PARAMETERS: *Value* is the byte or integer from which the
               bits are read.

               StartBit is the number of the lowest bit in the
               field. Bits are counted from 0 to 7 in bytes
               and from 0 to 15 in integers, where 0 is the
               least significant bit.

               NumberBits is the number of bits in the
               field.

NOTES: 1. The routines check that there is room for
                  the field between the starting bit and the
                  end of the byte or integer; when the field
                  does not fit, 0 is returned.

               2. When *StartBit* or *NumberBits* are out of
                  range, the routines return 0.

EXAMPLES: In this example, *ByteField* finds out the
               background color of the top-left character on
               the video display. The video buffer begins at
               memory segment **$B800** for the color graph-
               ics adaptor, and the attribute byte for the
               first character is at offset **0001**. The back-
               ground color, numbered from 0 to 7, is held
               in bits 4–6.

```
Writeln(ByteField(Mem[$B800:$0001],4,3));
```

Or use **MemW** to retrieve the integer at that location at offset **0000**. Bits 8–15 are the attribute byte, and the background color is held by bits 12–14:

```
Writeln((IntegerField(MemW[$B800:0000],12,3));
```

Function ByteFieldString(Value: byte; StartBit,NumberBits: integer): stype;
Function IntegerFieldString(Value,StartBit,NumberBits: integer): stype;

FILE NAMES:	BYTFSTRG.PAS	(74 code bytes)
	INTFSTRG.PAS	(74 code bytes)

PURPOSE: *ByteFieldString* and *IntegerFieldString* return a character string of 1s and 0s that shows the bit settings of a field in a byte or integer.

PARAMETERS: *Value* is the byte or integer from which the bits are read.

StartBit is the number of the lowest bit in the field. Bits are counted from 0 to 7 in bytes and from 0 to 15 in integers, where 0 is the least significant bit.

NumberBits is the number of bits in the field.

NOTES: 1. The routines check that there is room for the field between the starting bit and the end of the byte or integer; a null string is returned when the field doesn't fit.

2. When *StartBit* or *NumberBits* are out of range, the routines return a null string.

EXAMPLES: A code telling what video adaptor is active is held in memory at **0040:0010**. Bits 4 and 5 are **11** for the monochrome adaptor, **10** for the color adaptor in 80 columns, and **01** for the color adaptor in 40 columns. To find the bit pattern:

```
Writeln(ByteFieldString(Mem[$40:$0010],4,2));
```

If the monochrome card is active, this string is returned:

11

The next higher byte in memory holds a second byte of information about equipment. The two high bits of this byte tell how many parallel ports are present in the machine. In this second example, both equipment-status bytes are read together as an integer value, placing the parallel port information in bits 14 and 15:

```
Writeln(IntegerFieldString(MemW[$40:$0010],14,2);
```

When two parallel ports are present, the result is:

```
10
```

Section 2: Change bit settings

Section 1 provides routines to *read* bit patterns. The routines in this section let you *set* them. First come four routines that rotate the bits within bytes or integers. Rotation operations are cousins to shift operations, which Turbo Pascal provides with its **shl** and **shr** operators. Rightward rotation by one bit shunts all bits downward by one position and the bottom bit moves to the top. Leftward rotation does the opposite. Clever application of these routines can simplify bit manipulations.

SetByteBits and *SetIntegerBits* take a bit pattern in character form (for example, **11101**) and write it into a byte or integer at any position you specify. *SetBits8* and *SetBits16* do the same, but the new value for the bit field is expressed as an integer. You can use these routines to effortlessly bit-pack data. *SetMemByte* and *SetMemWord* also replace bit fields, using a bit string to specify the new value, but they operate directly on specified memory locations. *SetMem8* and *SetMem16* are similar routines that use integers rather than bit strings. These four procedures are useful for modifying attributes in the video buffer, or status information in the BIOS data area. Next come *BitCopy8* and *BitCopy16*, which copy a bit field of specified length from one byte or integer to any position within another byte or integer.

Finally, two pairs of routines compress and uncompress byte or integer data: *Compress8*, *Compress16*; and *Expand8*, *Expand16*. Often data consist of numbers much smaller than can be held in the bytes or integers they occupy. For example, a sequence of one million laboratory measurements might always have values between 0 and 500. An integer is required to hold a number up to 500, but only the lowest 9 bits of the 16 available are used. The compression routines can snip out these 9-bit fragments and lay them end-to-end, greatly reducing the data's disk-storage requirements.

Function RotateByteLeft(Value: byte; NumberBits: integer): byte;
Function RotateByteRight(Value: byte; NumberBits: integer): byte;
Function RotateIntegerLeft(Value, NumberBits: integer): integer;
Function RotateIntegerRight(Value, NumberBits: integer): integer;

FILE NAMES:

ROLBYTE.PAS	(25 code bytes)
RORBYTE.PAS	(25 code bytes)
ROLINT.PAS	(25 code bytes)
RORINT.PAS	(25 code bytes)

PURPOSE:

These four routines return a value in which the bits have been rotated left or right. For example, when a byte is rotated to the right by one bit, bit 0 becomes bit 7, bit 7 becomes bit 6, bit 6 becomes bit 5, and so on. Conversely, when a byte is rotated to the left by one bit, bit 7 shifts to bit 0.

PARAMETERS:

Value is the byte or integer value in which the rotation is made.

NumberBits is the number of bits that the byte or integer is rotated to the left or right.

NOTES:

1. These routines use the ROR and ROL instructions—not RCL and RCR—and so they do not rotate the bits through the CPU carry flag.

EXAMPLE:

In this example, the byte variable **Attribute** is prepared for insertion into the video buffer in four-color graphics mode. Each pair of bits in the byte corresponds to a pixel, and all are to be made the same color: binary **10**. This value is placed in a byte variable, **Mask**, which acts as a mask for setting the bits in **Attribute**. **Attribute** is cleared, the bottom two bits are ORed, then the byte is rotated by two bits at a time until all of the bit pairs are set. **Mask** is returned to its original pattern by the end of the loop.

```
Mask := 2;
Attribute := 0;
for I := 1 to 4 do
  begin
    Attribute := Attribute or Mask;
    Attribute := RotateByteRight(Attribute,2);
  end;
```

The resulting bit pattern:

```
10101010
```

Procedure SetByteBits(var Value: byte; Bits: stype; Position: integer);
Procedure SetIntegerBits(var Value: integer; Bits: stype; Position: integer);

FILE NAMES:	BYTEBITS.PAS	(81 code bytes)
	INTBITS.PAS	(81 code bytes)

PURPOSE: *SetByteBits* and *SetIntegerBits* change a bit field in a byte or integer variable. The pattern for the bit field is supplied as a binary character string. Other bits in the byte or integer are untouched.

PARAMETERS: *Value* is the byte or integer variable in which bits are changed.

Bits is a string variable in which the pattern of 1s and 0s describes the bit pattern to be placed in the bit field. Since this parameter defines the length of the bit field, the string may need to be padded with leading zeros to give it as many characters as the field has bits.

Position, which defines the starting point of the field, is the number of the bit in the byte or integer corresponding to the lowest bit of the field. *Position* is counted from 0 to 7 in bytes and from 0 to 15 in integers.

NOTES: 1. The routines check that there is room for the field between the starting bit and the end of the byte or integer; no change is made when the field doesn't fit.

2. When *Bits* is a null string or *Position* is out of range, the routines return without changing the byte or integer.

EXAMPLE: This example uses *SetByteBits* to assemble a screen attribute byte for a monochrome display. It assumes that a number of Boolean variables have been initialized to set the various characteristics.

```
Attribute := 0;
if Normal then SetByteBits(Attribute,'111',0);
if Underline then SetByteBits(Attribute,'001',0);
if Reverse then SetByteBits(Attribute,'111',4);
if Intense then SetByteBits(Attribute,'1',3);
if Blink then SetByteBits(Attribute,'1',7);
```

Procedure SetBits8(var Value: byte; Replacement,Position,Bits: integer);
Procedure SetBits16(var Value: integer; Replacement,Position,Bits: integer);

FILE NAMES:

SETBIT8.PAS   (61 code bytes)
SETBIT16.PAS   (62 code bytes)

PURPOSE:

SetBits8 and *SetBits16* change a bit field in a byte or integer variable. The new value for the bit field is given in integer form. Other bits in the byte or integer are untouched.

PARAMETERS:

Value is the byte or integer variable in which bits are changed.

Replacement is the value inserted into the bit field.

Position, which defines the starting point of the field, is the number of the bit in the byte or integer corresponding to the lowest bit of the field. *Position* is counted from 0 to 7 in bytes and from 0 to 15 in integers.

Bits is the number of bits in the field, from 1 to 16.

NOTES:

1. The routines check that there is room for the field between the starting bit and the end of the byte or integer; no change is made when the field doesn't fit or when *Position* is out of range.

2. When *Replacement* is too large for the specified bit field, as many bits as can fit are taken from the low end of the value.

EXAMPLE:

This example is similar to that given for *SetByteBits* (also in this section). It assembles a screen attribute byte for a monochrome display, giving the values for the bit fields as decimal numbers (such as **7** for "normal" attribute, rather than the bit pattern **111**).

```
Attribute := 0;
if Normal then SetBits8(Attribute,7,0,3);
if Underline then SetBits8(Attribute,1,0,3);
if Reverse then SetBits8(Attribute,7,4,3);
if Intense then SetBits8(Attribute,1,3,1);
if Blink then SetBits8(Attribute,1,7,1);
```

Procedure SetMemByte(Bits: stype; Position,Segment,Offset: integer);
Procedure SetMemWord(Bits: stype; Position,Segment,Offset: integer);

FILE NAMES: MEMBYTE.PAS   (84 code bytes)
                    MEMWORD.PAS   (84 code bytes)

PURPOSE: *SetMemByte* and *SetMemWord* change one or more bits at any position in a specified byte or word in memory. The bit pattern is supplied as a binary character string. Other bits in the memory byte or word are unaffected.

PARAMETERS: *Bits* is a character string in which the pattern of 1s and 0s describes the bit pattern for the bit field that will be changed. Since this parameter defines the length of the bit field, the string may need to be padded with leading zeros.

Position, which defines the starting point of the field, is the number of the bit that is the lowest in the field. *Position* is counted from 0 to 7 in memory bytes, and from 0 to 15 in memory words.

Segment is the segment and *Offset* the offset of the memory byte or word.

NOTES: 1. The routines check that there is room for the field between the starting bit and the end of the byte or word; no change is made when the field doesn't fit.

2. The routines return without changing the byte or integer when *Bits* is a null string or *Position* is out of range.

EXAMPLES: One use for this routine is to change attribute bytes directly in the video buffer. Two bytes are devoted to every screen position: the first holds the character, and the second holds its attribute. The attribute sets the color of a character and other features such as whether or not it blinks. Characters are at even-numbered positions in video RAM, and attribute bytes are at odd-numbered positions—that is, each attribute immediately follows the character it controls.

This example causes the top line of the screen to blink. Since it assumes the presence of a monochrome card, it uses the segment and offset **$B000:0000** to point to the top-left corner of the screen. Blinking occurs when bit 7 of an attribute byte is set to 1.

```
Writeln('Here is some text that soon will be blinking');
Delay(1000);
for I := 0 to 79 do
  begin
    SetMemByte('1',7,$B000,I*2+1);
  end;
```

Repeating this action with the string ′0′ would stop the blinking. The same results could be obtained with **SetMemWord**:

```
for I := 0 to 79 do
  begin
    SetMemWord('1',15,$B000,I*2);
  end;
```

Procedure SetMem8(Replacement,Position,Bits,Segment,Offset: integer);
Procedure SetMem16(Replacement,Position,Bits,Segment,Offset: integer);

FILE NAMES:

SETMEM8.PAS (61 code bytes)
SETMEM16.PAS (62 code bytes)

PURPOSE:

SetMem8 and *SetMem16* change the value held in a bit field at any position in a specified byte or word in memory. The new value for the bit field is given as an integer. Other bits in the memory byte or word are unaffected.

PARAMETERS:

Replacement is the value inserted into the bit field.

Position, which defines the starting point of the field, is the number of the bit in the byte or integer corresponding to the lowest bit of the field. *Position* is counted from 0 to 7 in bytes and from 0 to 15 in integers.

Bits is the number of bits in the field, from 1 to 16.

Segment is the segment and *Offset* the offset of the memory byte or word.

NOTES:

1. The routines check that there is room for the field between the starting bit and the end of the byte or word; no change is made when the field doesn't fit or when *Position* is out of range.

2. When *Replacement* is too large for the specified bit field, as many bits as can fit are taken from the low end of the value.

EXAMPLE:

This example makes characters on a monochrome screen invisible by changing bits 0-2 of their attribute bytes to **0**. The address of the video buffer (**$B000:0000**) points to the top left corner of the screen. After a delay the characters are redisplayed by changing bits 0-2 back to **7**. First, clear the screen and write some text:

```
ClrScr;
LowVideo;
for I := 1 to 25 do
  begin
    GotoXY(20,I);
    Write('Here is some text');
  end;
```

Now change the attributes:

```
for I := 0 to 1999 do
  begin
    SetMem8($B000,I*2+1,0,0,3);
  end;
```

After a delay, repeat the loop using **7** as the replacement value:

```
Delay(5000);
for I := 0 to 1999 do
  begin
    SetMem8($B000,I*2+1,7,0,3);
  end;
```

Procedure BitCopy8(var Target: byte; Source,TStart,SStart,Number: integer);
Procedure BitCopy16(var Target: integer; Source,TStart,SStart,Number: integer);

FILE NAMES: BITCPY8.PAS   (69 code bytes)
                 BITCPY16.PAS   (69 code bytes)

PURPOSE: These two procedures copy a bit field from a
                 specified position in a *source* variable to a
                 (possibly different) position in a *target* vari-
                 able. No other bits are affected in the target
                 variable. **BitCopy8** operates on byte targets,
                 and **BitCopy16** operates on integer targets.

PARAMETERS: **Target** is the byte or integer to which the bit
                 field is transferred.

                 Source is a byte or integer from which the bit
                 field is copied. **Source** is declared as being of
                 type *integer*. The procedures, however, ac-
                 cept and use an argument of *byte* type with-
                 out generating an error message. As a result,
                 when **Source** is a byte value, there is no need
                 to change the declaration to **Source: byte**.

                 TStart is the bit number in the **Target** at
                 which the low end of the field is written. The
                 bits are numbered from 0 to 7 in bytes and
                 from 0 to 15 in integers.

                 SStart is the bit number in the **Source** from
                 which the field begins. The bits are num-
                 bered from 0 to 7 in bytes and from 0 to 15 in
                 integers.

                 Number is the number of bits in the field.

NOTES: 1. The routines have no error checking to
                 ensure that the bit field will fit between
                 TStart and the end of the variable.

                 2. The routines are identical except for their
                 declarations, and in fact, either can han-

dle integer target variables. The two versions are provided for programming clarity and convenience.

EXAMPLES: This example copies bits 3 through 5 from **Source** to bits 7 through 9 in **Target**. **Target** is an integer, and **Source** may be either an integer or a byte.

```
BitCopy16(Target,Source,7,3,3);
```

The next example packs data into a byte array. Four-bit data fields are taken from the lowest four bits of an array of integer values. The variable *Pt* toggles between pointing to bits 0 and 4 of the target bytes.

```
Num := 0;    {points to packing array}
Pt := 4;     {points to start bit in packing array}
for I := 1 to DataNumber do
  begin
    if Pt = 4 then
      begin
        Pt := 0;
        Num := Num + 1;
      end else Pt := 4;
BitCopy8(PackedData[Num],Data[I],Pt,0,4);
  end;
```

Function Compress8(var SA:atype1;var TA:atype2;Bits,Pos,Num:integer):integer;
Function Compress16(var SA:atype1;var TA:atype2;Bits,Pos,Num:integer):integer;

FILE NAMES: COMPRS8.PAS   (121 code bytes)

COMPRS16.PAS   (121 code bytes)

PURPOSE: These routines compress an array of bytes or integers into a *packed* byte array. This is done by saving only the significant bits in the byte or integer (for example, in a series of integers where none holds a value over 500, only the lowest nine bits are required out of the sixteen available). The bit fields taken from the *source* array are laid out end-to-end in the *target* array. You may specify the size and position of the bit fields transferred to the target array. The functions return the number of bytes filled with data. The data is uncompressed by the **Expand8** and **Expand16** procedures found in this section.

PARAMETERS: **SA** stands for "source array," the name of the byte or integer array from which the source data is taken. The routine always reads the data starting from the first element of the array.

atype1 stands for "array type 1," an **array of byte** or an **array of integer**.

TA stands for "target array"—the name of the byte array into which the data is packed.

atype2 stands for "array type 2." It ordinarily would be an **array of byte**.

Bits is the number of bits taken from each element of the source array.

Pos is the position within the data element from which the bits are copied. Bit positions are numbered from 0 to 15.

Num is the number of elements in the source array to be compressed.

NOTES:

1. These routines are most useful for compressing positive integer data. Negative integers can't be compressed without special processing, since the high bit of the byte or integer is always set. To compress integers in the range −500 to +500, you need to move the "minus sign" indicated by the high bit down to bit 9 (counting from 0), and *then* you can compress the data, taking the lowest ten bytes.

2. The routines return −1 when an input parameter is out of range or the bit field does not fit between the starting bit and the end of the byte or integer.

EXAMPLE:

This example compresses an array of 1000 positive integers in which no value exceeds 1000. Since bits 0 through 10 count up to 1023, the top five bits of the integers may be discarded. Thus the target array need be only 10,000 bits long, equaling 1250 bytes:

```
Type
  atype1 = array[1..1000] of integer;
  atype2 = array[1..1250] of byte;
Var
  Data : atype1;
  PackedData : atype2;
```

Assume that the source array has been filled with data. Then to compress it, write:

```
NumberBytes := Compress16(Data,PackedData,10,0,1000);
```

and now **NumberBytes** tells how many bytes in **PackedData** were filled (including the last, possibly *partly* filled byte).

Procedure Expand8(var SA:atype2; var TA:atype1; Bits,Pos,Num:integer);
Procedure Expand16(var SA:atype2; var TA:atype1; Bits,Pos,Num:integer);

FILE NAMES:	EXPAND8.PAS	(106 code bytes)
	EXPAND16.PAS	(106 code bytes)

PURPOSE: These routines reverse the data compression made by **Compress8** and **Compress16**. Bit fields are *unpacked* from a byte array and distributed to byte or integer arrays. The fields may be laid down at any position in the target bytes or integers.

PARAMETERS: **SA** stands for "source array," the name of the byte array holding the compressed data.

atype2 stands for "array type 2," an **array of byte**.

TA stands for "target array"—the name of the byte or integer array receiving the decompressed data.

atype1, which stands for "array type 1," is an **array of byte** or an **array of integer**.

Bits is the number of bits in each compressed data element.

Pos is the position within the target byte or integer at which the data is inserted. Bit positions are counted from 0 to 15.

Num is the number of data elements contained in the source array.

NOTES: 1. Take care not to confuse the source and target arrays during decompression, since what was formerly the source is now the target and vice versa.

2. Since no other bits are affected in the target bytes or integers except those receiving the compressed data, more than one data series can be combined. But *you must*

clear the target array before decompressing the data.

3. The routines return −1 when an input parameter is out of range or the bit field does not fit between the starting bit and the end of the byte or integer.

EXAMPLE: This example decompresses the 1000-integer array compressed in the example given for the **Compress8** and **Compress16** routines. The arrays are given the same *type* declarations:

```
Type
  atype1 = array[1..1000] of integer;
  atype2 = array[1..1250] of byte;
Var
  Data : atype1;
  PackedData : atype2;
```

Since the arrays have been left with the same names, now **Packed** acts as the source. Be sure to first clear the target array (the Turbo Pascal **FillChar** procedure is convenient):

```
FillChar(Data,2000,0);
```

Then decompress the data:

```
Expand16(Packed,Data,16,0,1000);
```

4
String Operations

Section 1: Add characters

This chapter is divided into four sections. The first holds routines that add characters to strings, and the second holds routines that delete characters. The routines in the third section change characters in strings, substituting one for another. Finally, Section 4 has routines that count substrings within strings or that search for substrings within strings.

There are six routines in this section. The first four *pad* strings. That is, they add a particular character to a string again and again until it attains a given length. **PadLeft** and **PadRight** place the pad characters at the beginning and end of the string. **PadCenter** adds the characters at a specified position inside the string. **PadEnds** evenly divides the pad characters on the left and right of the string, surrounding it. Pad operations are useful for formatting data for display or printing. The first two routines may also be used to prepare data for output to files by making every element the same length.

The remaining two routines create strings made up of a single character or substring. **CharString** makes a string of any length from a single character, such as "-------". **StringString** returns a string made up of repetitions of a substring, such as "-*--*--*-". These strings may be used for line graphics on the display or printer and for many other purposes as well.

Procedure PadLeft(var Strg: stype; Ch: char; Length: integer);
Procedure PadRight(var Strg: stype; Ch: char; Length: integer);

FILE NAMES: PADLEFT.PAS   (84 code bytes)
                    PADRIGHT.PAS   (74 code bytes)

PURPOSE: *PadLeft* pads the beginning and *PadRight* pads the end of astring, extending it to the specified length.

PARAMETERS: *Strg* is the string variable that is padded.

                    Ch is the character used for padding.

                    Length is the length to which the string is padded.

NOTES: 1. The routines return without changing the string when *Length* cannot fit into *Strg*. This is also the case when the current length of *Strg* is greater than or equal to *Length*.

                  2. When *Strg* is null the routines return a string of the pad character that is as long as specified by *Length*.

EXAMPLES: This example adds a line of dashes to the right side of a string, preparing it as a section divider on a page:

```
Title := 'Section IX ';
PadRight(Title,'-',50);
```

Now **Title** looks like:

```
Section IX ---------------------------------------
```

Alternatively:

```
Title := 'Section IX';
PadLeft(Title,'-',50);
```

The result:

```
--------------------------------------- Section IX
```

Procedure PadCenter(var Strg: stype; Ch: char; Position,Length: integer);

FILE NAME: PADCENTR.PAS   (114 code bytes)

PURPOSE: *PadCenter* extends a string to a specified length by padding it at any position with a given character.

PARAMETERS: *Strg* is the string variable that is padded.

               Ch is the character used for padding.

               Position is the position in the string at which padding begins. The string positions are counted from 1 to 255. When position 3 of **ABCDE** is padded to seven characters with "-", the result is **AB--CDE**. Position 1 gives **--ABCDE** and position 6 gives **ABCDE--**.

               Length is the length to which the string is extended.

NOTES: 1. When *Position* is **0** it is treated as if it were 1. Any position greater than the length of the string causes the padding to occur at the end of the string.

               2. The routine checks that *Strg* can hold *Length*, and when it cannot, it returns without changing the string.

EXAMPLE: This example right-justifies the page numbers in a table of contents. Assume that the numbers are the last two digits in the string. Then:

```
Line[1] := '1. Gorilla behavior     37';
Line[2] := '2. Human response            76';
etc.
```

```
For I := 1 to NumberLines do
  begin
    PadCenter(Line[I],' ',Length(Line[I])-2,40);
  end;
```

The result is:

```
1. Gorilla behavior                    37
2. Human response                      76
etc.
```

Procedure PadEnds(var Strg: stype; Ch: char; Length: integer);

FILE NAME:	PADENDS.PAS (123 code bytes)
PURPOSE:	**PadEnds** extends a string to a specified length by padding it at both ends with any character you choose. This procedure is useful for centering strings when they are displayed or printed.
PARAMETERS:	**Strg** is the string variable that is padded.
	Ch is the character used for padding.
	Length is the length to which the string is extended.
NOTES:	1. When there is an odd number of fill characters, the extra character is placed at the left end (the beginning) of the string.
	2. The routine tests that **Length** can fit into **Strg**, and if it cannot, it returns without changing the string. This is also the case when **Length** is less than or equal to the initial length of **Strg**, or when **Strg** is null.
EXAMPLES:	To write a string centered on the display:

```
Strg := 'Chapter XI';
PadEnds(Strg,' ',80);
Gotoxy(1,1);
Write(Strg);
```

To add border characters to the centered string:

```
Strg := ' Chapter XI ';
PadEnds(Strg,'-',80);
Gotoxy(1,1);
Write(Strg);
```

Function CharString(Ch: char; Length: integer): stype;

FILE NAME:	CHARSTRG.PAS (65 code bytes)
PURPOSE:	*CharString* returns a string of specified length made up entirely of a given character.
PARAMETERS:	*Character* is the character used to build the string.
	Length is the length of the string returned; it may be from 1 to 255.
NOTES:	1. When *Length* is 0 or greater than 255, the routine returns an empty string.
	2. The routine checks that a string of size *Length* will fit into *Strg*, and when it doesn't, a maximum size string is returned.
EXAMPLE:	This example inserts a line of periods between a chapter name and a page number:

```
Chapter := 'Chapter 3 ';
Page := '74';
NumChars := 50-Length(Chapter)-Length(Page);
Write(Chapter+CharString('.',NumChars)+Page);
```

The result:

```
Chapter 3 ......................................74
```

Function StringString(Strg: stype; Length: integer): stype;

FILE NAME:	STRGSTRG.PAS (94 code bytes)
PURPOSE:	**StringString** returns a string of specified length made up of repetitions of a substring.
PARAMETERS:	**Strg** is the substring from which the string is made. When the substring is **--END**, for example, the string returned will be **--END--END--END** . . . .
	Length is the length of the string returned.
NOTES:	1. When **Length** is not an even multiple of the length of **Strg**, the returned string ends with only part of the substring. For example, **StringString("ABC",5)** returns **ABCAB**.
	2. The routine checks that a string of size **Length** will fit into **Strg**, and when it does not, a maximum size string is returned.
	3. When **Length** is 0 or greater than 255, the routine returns an empty string.
	4. **Strg** may be a single character, and hence this routine can serve the same function as **CharString** (also in this section). It is, however, about twice the size.
EXAMPLE:	This example surrounds a title with **-*-**:

```
Title := 'Recent Advances In Canine Psychoanalysis';
Title := StringString('-*- ',8) + Title;
Title := Title + StringString(' -*-',8);
```

The result:

```
-*- -*- Recent Advances In Canine Psychoanalysis -*- -*-
```

Section 2: Delete characters

This section contains eleven routines that delete characters from string variables. The first four—*DeleteLeft*, **DeleteLeftPlus**, **DeleteRight**, and **DeleteRightPlus**—remove characters from the ends of a string until they encounter a border character. The "plus" versions of the routines remove the border character as well. Then come two related routines, *DeleteMiddle* and *DeleteMiddlePlus*, which remove characters from a starting point anywhere in a string up to specified boundary characters on either side.

The next routine, **DeleteAll**, also works from any starting position in a string. It looks for a particular character and, if it finds it, it removes the character and then goes on to delete any matching characters to the left or right. Because the routine works from within a string as well as at the ends, it is very versatile. For convenience, there are two similar routines, *DeleteSpcLeft* and *DeleteSpcRight*, that remove leading and trailing spaces from strings.

The section concludes with two routines that scan strings and remove all instances of characters. *DeleteChar* removes every instance of a single specified character. *DeleteRange* removes every instance of every character from a range of ASCII codes. These routines are particularly useful in processing communications data.

Procedure DeleteLeft(var Strg: stype; Border: char);
Procedure DeleteLeftPlus(var Strg: stype; Border: char);
Procedure DeleteRight(var Strg: stype; Border: char);
Procedure DeleteRightPlus(var Strg: stype; Border: char);

FILE NAMES:

DELLEFT.PAS   (50 code bytes)
DELLEFT&.PAS   (58 code bytes)
DELRGHT.PAS   (44 code bytes)
DELRGHT&.PAS   (46 code bytes)

PURPOSE:

DeleteLeft deletes all characters from the beginning of a string variable up to, but not including, the first incidence of a boundary character. *DeleteLeftPlus* does the same, but it deletes the boundary character as well. *DeleteRight* and *DeleteRightPlus* are counterparts that make the deletions from the end of the string.

PARAMETERS:

Strg is the string from which characters are deleted.

Border is the character at which deletion stops.

NOTES:

1. **DeleteLeftPlus** and **DeleteRightPlus** delete only the first instance of the border character. In the string **AAAZZZBBB**, for example, if **Z** is the border character, then **DeleteLeftPlus** would return **ZZBBB**.

2. No characters are deleted by *DeleteLeft* and *DeleteRight* when *Border* is the same as the first or last character in the string, respectively. *DeleteLeftPlus* and *DeleteRightPlus*, however, will delete this first instance of the character.

3. The entire string is deleted when the border character is not found.

EXAMPLE:

In the following example, end-of-line notes are eliminated from a Pascal source file.

Here, every character from the right up to and including "{" is eliminated.

```
SampleLine := 'for I := 1 to 10 do {look up the index}';
DeleteRightPlus(SampleLine,'{');
```

Now, SampleLine is:

```
for I := 1 to 10 do
```

Procedure DeleteMiddle(var Strg: stype; Position: integer; Left,Right: char);
Procedure DeleteMiddlePlus(var Strg: stype; Position: integer; Left,Right: char);

FILE NAMES: DELMDDL.PAS   (104 code bytes)
                DELMDDL&.PAS   (100 code bytes)

PURPOSE: These two routines start at any position in a string and delete all characters to either side until they encounter specified boundary characters. Different characters may be named for the left and right boundaries. *DeleteMiddle* deletes all characters up to, but not including, the boundary characters; *DeleteMiddlePlus* deletes the boundary characters as well. When one or both of the boundary characters aren't encountered, the deletion continues to the ends of the string.

PARAMETERS: *Strg* is the string in which the deletion is made.

                Position is the position within *Strg* from which the deletion begins.

                Left and *Right* are the borders characters to the left and right of *Position*.

NOTES: 1. When the left or right border character is found at *Position*, the routine seeks the second border character and deletes all between. If the second border character is adjacent, no deletion is made by *DeleteMiddle*.

EXAMPLES: This example changes the text contained within braces in a line from a Pascal program file. The *SearchRight* function (found in Section 4 of this chapter) locates the leftmost brace.

```
Strg := 'if I < 5 then TryAgain; {error message}';
Position := SearchRight(Strg,'{',1);
if Position <> 0 then
  begin
  DeleteMiddle(Strg,Position+1,'{','}';
    Insert('display warning',Strg,Position+1);
  end;
```

The result:

```
if I < 5 then TryAgain; {display warning}
```

To eliminate the whole note, use DeleteMiddlePlus:

```
DeleteMiddlePlus(Strg,Position+1,'{','}';)
```

Procedure DeleteAll(var Strg: stype; Ch: char; Position: integer);

FILE NAME: DELALL.PAS   (99 code bytes)

PURPOSE: Beginning from a specified position within a
                 string, **DeleteAll** looks for a specified charac-
                 ter and, if it finds it, it deletes the character
                 and all adjacent instances of the character to
                 the left and right.

PARAMETERS: **Strg** is the string variable in which the dele-
                 tion is made.

                 Ch is the character that is deleted.

                 Position is the position in the string from
                 which deletion begins. The position is
                 counted from 1 to 255.

NOTES: 1. The routine returns without altering the
                    string when **Position** is **0** or when it ex-
                    ceeds the length of the string.

EXAMPLES: This example eliminates all trailing space
                 characters from a string.

```
DeleteAll(Strg,' ',Length(Strg);
```

                 As a more complicated example, consider
                 the case where there are a number of strings
                 consisting of a phone number followed by a
                 name, with a variable number of space char-
                 acters between. To separate all of the names
                 from the phone numbers by exactly five
                 spaces, first delete all spaces between, then
                 reinsert five spaces.

```
for I := 1 to ListLength do
  begin
    DeleteAll(List[I],' ',9);   {8-char number}
    Insert('     ',List[I],9);
  end;
```

Procedure DeleteSpcLeft(var Strg: stype);
Procedure DeleteSpcRight(var Strg: stype);

FILE NAMES:	DELSPCRT.PAS	(46 code bytes)
	DELSPCLF.PAS	(49 code bytes)

PURPOSE: *DeleteSpcLeft* and *DeleteSpcRight* remove all space characters from the left or right end of a string.

PARAMETERS: *Strg* is the string from which the spaces are deleted.

NOTES: 1. The *DeleteAll* routine (also in this section) can do the work of both these routines. They are included for convenience, and also for extra speed and compactness when the flexibility of *DeleteAll* is not required.

EXAMPLE: To remove all trailing spaces from a string:

```
DeleteSpcRight(Strg);
```

Procedure DeleteChar(var Strg: stype; Ch: char);

FILE NAME:	DELCHAR.PAS (69 code bytes)
PURPOSE:	*DeleteChar* removes all instances of a specified character from a string variable.
PARAMETERS:	*Strg* is the string variable from which the character is eliminated.
	Ch is the character that is eliminated.
NOTES:	1. No change is made when the character is not found in the string.
EXAMPLE:	One use for this routine is to process incoming communications data. This example eliminates all NUL characters (ASCII 0) from a string:

```
DeleteChar(ComString,chr(0));
```

Procedure DeleteRange(var Strg: stype; Ch1,Ch2: char);

FILE NAME:	DELRANGE.PAS (85 code bytes)
PURPOSE:	*DeleteRange* removes from a string variable all characters that fall within a specified range. The range is given by two ASCII characters, and those characters and all intermediate characters in the ASCII set are eliminated.
PARAMETERS:	*Strg* is the string variable from which the characters are eliminated.
	Ch1 and *Ch2* are the two characters that define the range. It does not matter which has the higher ASCII code.
NOTES:	1. The range extends from the low number ASCII code to the high number code, no matter the order in which they are listed. The range will not *wrap around* from the high end of the ASCII set to the low end.
	2. When *Char1* and *Char2* are the same, only that character is eliminated.
EXAMPLE:	This example eliminates all characters in a string that come from the *extended ASCII set*—numbers 128 through 255.

```
DeleteRange(SampleString, chr(128), chr(255));
```

Section 3: Change characters

This section contains routines that change characters in strings, generally without changing the string's length. The first four routines are exceptions: they convert strings of numerals to *integer* or *real* form. Written as functions rather than as procedures (unlike the Turbo Pascal *Str* instruction), they are included because other routines in the library require them. The next routine also wanders from this section's theme—it is *SwapStrings*, which quickly exchanges two string variables.

Next are two routines that replace awkward combinations of the Turbo Pascal *Insert* and *Delete* procedures. *OverWrite* writes a substring over any position within a string. *Replace* replaces a specified number of characters within a string with a substring of any length. Then there are routines that seek out particular characters and change them. *ChangeCharacter* replaces all instances of a specified character; *ChangeRange* does the same for any instance of a range of ASCII codes. *UpperCase* and *LowerCase* convert the case of all alphabetic characters. And *Translate* replaces every character in a string with a corresponding character taken from a translation table. Finally, *ExpandTabs* replaces tab characters with the number of space characters required to extend to the next tab position.

This section ends with a pair of routines compressing strings that contain long sequences of the same character. The program files that constitute this collection, for example, use sequences of spaces to format the code and notes. *CompressText* removed these spaces so that the routines take up less disk space. *DecompressText* operates within the ROUTINES program to restore the code to its original form. These routines are very fast.

Function IntStr(Value: integer): stype;
Function IntStrg(Value: integer): stype;
Function RealStr(Value: real): stype;
Function RealStrg(Value: real): stype;

FILE NAMES: INTSTR.PAS   (61 code bytes)
              INTSTRG.PAS   (78 code bytes)
              REALSTR.PAS   (150 code bytes)
              REALSTRG.PAS   (125 code bytes)

PURPOSE: These four functions convert numeric values to string form. Turbo Pascal does not provide a *function* to perform these conversions. The screen output routines in this collection require such a function since they handle only string arguments. **IntStr** converts either byte or integer values to numeric strings while **RealStr** does the same for real values. **IntStrg** and **RealStrg**, respectively, do the same, but they return the string with exactly one space character added at each end so that it is formatted for insertion into a text string.

PARAMETERS: **Value** is the number that is converted to string form.

NOTES: 1. There is a little cheating going on here: these routines contain no assembly language at all. They are written entirely in Turbo Pascal to avoid wasteful duplication of code.

EXAMPLE: The **Display** procedure found in Section 4 of Chapter 6 can display about 1000 80-character strings per second on a monochrome display. **Display** handles only string arguments, however, and so this example uses *IntStrg* to have it write an integer too.

```
Num := 34;
Display('Enrollment includes'+IntStrg(Num)+'baboons',3,3,7);
```

The result:

```
Enrollment includes 34 baboons
```

Procedure SwapStrings(var Strg1,Strg2: stype);

FILE NAME: SWAPSTRG.PAS   (65 code bytes)

PURPOSE: *SwapStrings* exchanges two string variables.

PARAMETERS: *Strg1* and *Strg2* are the two string variables.

NOTES:
1. Be sure that the two string variables can accommodate each other. You must be concerned with the actual length of the strings that the two variables hold, not their type declarations. For example, *Strg1* may be declared as **string[80]**, and *Strg2* may be declared as **string[100]**; you must see to it that the string held in *Strg2* doesn't exceed 80 bytes.

2. It is trivial to swap strings with standard Pascal code. The virtue of this routine is that no intermediate holding variable is required, and that it works extremely quickly.

EXAMPLE: This example simply swaps two strings:

```
Like := 'Baboons';
Dislike := 'Gorillas';
SwapStrings(Like,Dislike);
Writeln('I like playing with '+Like);
Writeln('I dislike playing with '+Dislike);
```

The result:

```
I like playing with Gorillas
I dislike playing with Baboons
```

Procedure OverWrite(var Strg: stype; Substrg: stype; Position: integer);

FILE NAME: OVERWRT.PAS   (61 code bytes)

PURPOSE: *OverWrite* overwrites part of a string with a given substring, starting from a specified position within the string.

PARAMETERS: *Strg* is the string variable that is overwritten.

                Substrg is the substring that replaces characters in **Strg**.

                Position is the character in *Strg* at which overwriting begins. The positions are numbered from 1 to 255.

NOTES: 1. The substring may be a single character, or it may have as many characters as the string itself, but it must fit within the original string length. The substring "**ABCDE**", for example, can overwrite the string "**12345**," but only when *Position* is 1. Other positions cause the routine to return without modifying the string.

                2. The routine also makes no change when either the string or the substring is null or when *Position* is a number greater than the length of **Strg**.

EXAMPLES: In the following string, the time of day is written in the tenth through seventeenth character positions:

```
Appointment[934] := '12/03/87    12:35 PM    Hortense Yang';
```

To change the time to **12:45**:

```
OverWrite(Appointment[934],'12:45 PM',10);
```

Procedure Replace(var Strg: stype; SubStrg: stype; Position,Chars: integer);

FILE NAME:

REPLACE.PAS   (175 code bytes)

PURPOSE:

Replace deletes a specified number of characters from any position within a string and inserts a substring of any length at the same position. It performs the same service as the combination of the Turbo Pascal *Delete* and *Insert* commands, but it works about four times faster.

PARAMETERS:

Strg is the string variable in which the replacement is made.

SubStrg is the SubStrg that is written into *Strg* at *Position*.

Position is the position in the string from which characters are deleted and *SubStrg* is inserted. It is a number from 1 to 255, depending on the length of *Strg*.

Chars is the number of characters deleted at *Position* before *SubStrg* is inserted. *Chars* doesn't need to equal the length of *SubStrg*. When *Chars* is **0**, no characters are removed, and *SubStrg* is simply inserted at *Position*.

NOTES:

1. The routine returns without making any changes when *Strg* or *SubStrg* are null, when *Position* is a number greater than the length of *Strg*, or when the number of characters from *Position* to the end of the string is less than the value given by *Chars*.

2. *Replace* doesn't check that the new string it creates will not be longer than *stype* allows. Be careful.

EXAMPLE: This example replaces the first two charac-
                            ters in a string with a three-character
                            substring.

```
Text := '1. Preliminary Remarks';
Replace(Text,'[1]',1,2);
```

The result:

```
[1] Preliminary Remarks
```

Procedure ChangeCharacter(var Strg: stype; Search,Replace: char);

FILE NAME: CHGCHAR.PAS   (42 code bytes)

PURPOSE: **ChangeCharacter** changes every instance of a character in a string variable to a different character.

PARAMETERS: *Strg* is the string variable in which the characters are changed.

Search is the character that is replaced.

Replace is the character that replaces the *Search* character.

EXAMPLE: This example replaces parentheses with square brackets:

```
Line := 'Assembler (believe it or not) causes balding'.
ChangeCharacter(Line,'(','[');
ChangeCharacter(Line,')',']');
```

The result:

```
Assembler [believe it or not] causes balding.
```

Procedure ChangeRange(var Strg: stype; Replacement,Char1,Char2: char);

FILE NAME:

CHGRANGE.PAS   (54 code bytes)

PURPOSE:

ChangeRange seeks out every instance of a range of ASCII codes in a string variable and changes it to a specified character.

PARAMETERS:

Strg is the string variable in which the characters are changed.

Replacement is the character that replaces characters found in the range defined by **Char1** and **Char2**.

Char1 and *Char2* are the two characters that define the range of ASCII codes. They are included in the range.

NOTES:

1. It does not matter whether **Char1** or **Char2** is given the higher number code. For this reason, the range may not *wrap around* from the high end to the low end of the ASCII set.

EXAMPLE:

This example replaces all characters in the extended ASCII set (numbers 128 through 255) with spaces—perhaps to avoid problems printing the string.

```
ChangeRange(Text,' ',chr(128),chr(255));
```

Procedure UpperCase(var Strg: stype);
Procedure LowerCase(var Strg: stype);

FILE NAMES:	UPPERCAS.PAS	(44 code bytes)
	LOWERCAS.PAS	(44 code bytes)

PURPOSE: *UpperCase* and *LowerCase* change all alphabetic characters in a string variable to uppercase or lowercase.

PARAMETERS: *Strg* is the string variable in which the changes are made.

NOTES: 1. Turbo Pascal provides the *UpCase* function for changing single characters from lower- to uppercase. There is no corresponding function for upper-to-lower conversion.

EXAMPLE: This example applies both procedures to the same string:

```
Sample1 := 'But, my dear, roses ARE red!';
Sample2 := Sample1;
UpperCase(Sample1);
LowerCase(Sample2);
Writeln(Sample1);
Writeln(Sample2);
```

The results:

```
BUT, MY DEAR, ROSES ARE RED!
but, my dear, roses are red!
```

Procedure Translate(var Strg: stype; var Table: tabletype);

FILE NAME: TRANSLAT.PAS   (41 code bytes)

PURPOSE: *Translate* translates all characters in a string from one ASCII code to another in accordance with a translation table of up to 256 bytes. The table is set up as an array of *byte* or *char*; the first byte corresponds to ASCII 0, the second byte to ASCII 1, and so on.

PARAMETERS: *Strg* is the string variable that is translated.

      Table is an array of byte or char that is declared as being of **tabletype**, which is an array of byte or char.

NOTES: 1. If memory is especially cramped, you may choose to use a table shorter than 256 bytes as long as you are sure that the translated string won't contain characters from the deleted part. Only the high end of the table may be omitted since the routine always treats the start of the table as ASCII 0. Should a character appear in the string for which there is no counterpart in the table, the routine will simply use whatever random value it finds at the corresponding place in memory.

EXAMPLE: First, declare the table:

```
Type
  tabletype = array[0..255] of char;
Var
  Table : tabletype;
```

Next, initialize the table to normal character values:

```
for I := 0 to 255 do
  begin
    Table[I] := chr(I);
  end;
```

Now insert the bytes that you want changed. Here all instances of " { " and "[" (ASCII 91 and 123) are changed to "(", and " } " and "]" (ASCII 93 and 125) are changed to ")":

```
Table[91] := '(';
Table[123] := '(';
Table[93] := ')';
Table[125] := ')';
```

Finally, make the translation. Assume this value for the string:

```
Text := 'Here [at last] is the {simple} example.';
```

Translate:

```
Translate(Text,Table);
```

The result:

```
Here (at last) is the (simple) example.
```

Function ExpandTabs(Strg: stype; MaxLength: integer): stype;

FILE NAME: EXPNDTAB.PAS   (120 code bytes)

PURPOSE: *ExpandTabs* replaces all tab characters in a string with spaces. The string is expanded in the same way that it would be if it were displayed. Tab stops are assumed to be eight characters apart, with the first character of the string coinciding with the left margin of the screen or printer.

PARAMETERS: *Strg* is the string in which the tabs are expanded.

                  MaxLength is the maximum length to which *Strg* may be expanded. At least one space is inserted at each tab position. The tabs closest to the beginning of the string are expanded first, and when there is insufficient room, a tab character may be only partly expanded.

NOTES: 1. The routine returns without changing the string when *MaxLength* cannot fit into *Strg*.

EXAMPLE: This example expands the tabs in the string **DateTime**, limiting the result to an 80-column line.

```
DateTime := 'May 8, 1987'+chr(9)+chr(9)+'12:07';
DateTime := ExpandTabs(DateTime,80);
```

The result:

```
May 8, 1987             12:07
```

Function CompressText(Strg: stype; DelCh,FlagCh: char): stype;
Function DecompressText(Strg: stype; DelCh,FlagCh: char): stype;

FILE NAMES: CMPRSTXT.PAS   (125 code bytes)
               DEPRSTXT.PAS   (98 code bytes)

PURPOSE: These two routines compress character strings by stripping out all instances in which a specified character appears three or more times in succession. Each group of characters is replaced by two characters in which the first flags the position and the second tells how many instances of the target character are at that point. You must specify both the character being removed and the flag character replacing it.

PARAMETERS: *Strg* is the string that is compressed or decompressed.

               DelCh is the character stripped out of the string by *CompressText* and later reinserted by *DecompressText*.

               FlagCh is the character placed in the string by *CompressText* to flag that a sequence of *DelCh* has been deleted. It is followed by a byte that tells how many characters have been removed, from 3 to 127. The flag character should be a character that does not appear in the data that is compressed.

NOTES: 1. The foremost use for these routines is to strip spaces from special text files, like program files. (In fact, they compress and decompress this subroutine library to make it fit two floppy disks.) You may apply *CompressText* more than once to the same string, deleting a different character each time and inserting a different flag character.

2. You must ensure that the largest string returned by *DecompressText* won't exceed the string type assigned to the function.

3. *CompressText* adds 128 to the byte that follows *FlagCh* and shows how many characters have been deleted. This measure guards against insertion of control codes into the string that would confuse file operations.

EXAMPLE: This example removes the spaces from a Pascal program file and then restores them. A typical line in the file may contain many spaces (use the *ExpandTabs* routine—also found in this section—to convert tab characters to spaces before compression). This line, for example, has a stretch of 29 spaces:

```
while X>0 do                    {begin sort}
```

This code compresses the file, using "#" as the flag character:

```
for I := 1 to NumberLines do
  begin
    Line[I] := CompressText(Line[I],' ','#');
  end;
```

Now the above sample line would take the form:

```
while X>0 do#¥{begin sort}
```

The yen sign in the compressed line is ASCII character 157; it represents the 29 spaces (plus 128) that have been deleted from the string. To restore the program file to its original form:

```
for I := 1 to NumberLines do
begin
  Line[I] :=
DecompressText(Line[I],' ','#');
  end;
```

Section 4: Search strings

The routines in this section search strings for various kinds of information. Taken as a whole, they are rather a hodgepodge, but many are very useful, and their exceptional speed can make a lot of difference in programs operating on string arrays. First comes **Compare**, which reports whether two strings are equal regardless of the case of the alphabetic characters they contain. Then comes **CopyRight**, which returns a specified number of characters from the end of a string. It replaces the usual **Copy(Strg,Length(Strg)-X,X)** construction. Two more routines, **LeftEnd** and **RightEnd**, return part of a string taken from the left or right up to a specified border character. Another routine that returns parts of strings is **WrapString**, which prepares text for word-wrapping. It returns as much of a string as will fit, word-wrapped, between two specified margins.

The next three routines count characters within strings. **CharCount** simply counts the number of occurrences of a given ASCII code. **RangeCount** counts all instances of a range of ASCII codes. And **WordCount** counts the number of words contained in a string.

Finally, some routines seek substrings within a string and report the substring's position. **SeekChar** returns the position of a single character. While other search routines can do the same, **SeekChar** is considerably faster. **SeekRange** returns the position of the first instance of any character in a range of ASCII codes. **SearchRight** and **SearchLeft**, on the other hand, seek particular characters or substrings, also returning the position of the first match. **SearchLeft** starts the search from the beginning of the string, while **SearchRight** works backward from the end of the string. Unlike the Turbo Pascal **Pos** function, these two routines allow you to set a starting point for the search so that they can easily handle multiple instances of the substring. The last routine, **SeekString**, works like **SearchLeft**, but it matches characters regardless of case.

Function Compare(var Strg1: stype; Strg2: stype): boolean;

FILE NAME: COMPARE.PAS   (110 code bytes)

PURPOSE: *Compare* compares two strings, ignoring the case of the characters **a–z** and **A–Z**. It returns TRUE when the strings are equal.

PARAMETERS: *Strg1* and *Strg2* are the two strings that are compared.

NOTES: 1. Only Strg2 may be an immediate value. This design optimizes both flexibility and speed.

EXAMPLE: This example compares two instances of the same word, in which one is capitalized and one is not.

```
Target := 'Orangutan';
Source := 'orangutan';
Write(Compare(Target,Source));
```

The result:

```
TRUE
```

Function CopyRight(Strg: stype; NumberChars: integer): stype;

FILE NAME: COPYRGHT.PAS   (83 code bytes)

PURPOSE: *CopyRight* returns a specified number of characters from the *end* of a string. This routine saves your program the trouble of calculating the starting position for the Turbo Pascal **Copy** instruction when it fetches characters from the end of a string (with the expression **Copy(Strg,Length(Strg)-X,X)**). *CopyRight* operates at about the same speed, and so its value lies in its convenience and clarity.

PARAMETERS: *Strg* is the string from which the characters are taken.

                NumberChars is the number of characters to be copied from the end of the string.

NOTES: 1. When *Number* is larger than the length of the string, the routine returns the whole string (or null if the string is null).

EXAMPLE: To fetch the last three characters of a string:

```
Text := '1234567890';
Write(CopyRight(Text,3));
```

The result:

```
890
```

Function LeftEnd(var Strg: stype; Border: char): stype;
Function RightEnd(var Strg: stype; Border: char): stype;

FILE NAMES:	LEFTEND.PAS	(65 code bytes)
	RIGHTEND.PAS	(69 code bytes)

PURPOSE: *LeftEnd* and *RightEnd* return the portion of a string extending from its beginning or end up to a specified border character. The border character is not returned. The entire string is returned when the border character does not appear.

PARAMETERS: *Strg* is the string from which the substring is returned.

     Border is the border character.

NOTES: 1. A null string is returned when *Strg* is null or when the first character encountered is the border character.

EXAMPLES: To fetch the end-of-line note in an assembly language text file:

```
ProgLine := 'SUB CX,CX      ;Clear CX for loop';
Writeln(RightEnd(ProgLine,';'));
```

The string returned:

```
Clear CX for loop
```

To retrieve the code instead:

```
Writeln(LeftEnd(ProgLine,';'));
```

The result:

```
SUB CX,CX
```

Function WrapString(var Strg: stype; Length: integer): stype;

FILE NAME: WRAPSTRG.PAS   (137 code bytes)

PURPOSE: *WrapString* divides a series of strings into word-wrapped lines. It returns as many as *Length* characters from the beginning of a string, always returning whole words. Since these characters are deleted from the source string, the original string is divided between the return string and *Strg*.

PARAMETERS: *Strg* is the string from which the characters are removed.

        Length is the maximum number of characters returned—that is, the line length for the word-wrapped text.

NOTES: 1. *WrapString* follows a particular logic that ensures that normal text will be broken into strings that don't begin with space characters, allowing the strings to be properly left-justified when they are displayed or printed. This is done without removing any characters from the string. Instead, the last column is always reserved for spaces: either the space that follows a word within a sentence or else the second space of the two that separate sentences. The last column is filled with a character other than the space only when no spaces have been encountered up to that point, such that the "word" must be broken in two.

        2. You will find three ready-made word-wrap routines in this collection. *WrapLn* (Chapter 6) outputs a sequence of strings to the display. *WrapPrint* does the same for the printer, and it takes into account embedded control codes (Chapter 9). Fi-

nally, **WrapInput** word-wraps keyboard input, with a maximum of 255 characters (Chapter 5). Particularly for screen operations, **WrapString** gives more flexibility. Whereas **WrapLn** automatically manages cursor operations and varying string lengths, it will not let you arrange text files for scrolling up and down. **Wrap-String** makes this possible with only a little more coding (note that scrolling routines are found in Chapter 7).

3. **WrapString** does not expand tab characters. Use the **ExpandTabs** procedure found in Section 3 of this chapter to convert tabs to spaces before using this routine.

EXAMPLE: This example shows how to prepare an array of variable-length strings for output to the display or printer. The strings are first loaded into an array named **Text**; then they are reassembled into word-wrapped lines of roughly equal length in a second array called **Wrap**. Here are the first five strings in **Text**:

```
Text[1] := 'After a lot of heavy editing, a text array ';
Text[2] := 'can become ';
Text[3] := 'divided into fragments of many lengths, ';
Text[4] := '';
Text[5] := 'including null strings';
```

A call is made to the **WrapArray** function, which wraps the strings and transfers them to the **Wrap** array. The first parameter for this function gives the number of lines in **Text** to be converted, and the second gives the maximum length for the word-wrapped lines. The function returns the number of lines in **Wrap** that have been filled.

```
WrapLength := WrapArray(5,33);
```

To see the result:

```
for I := 1 to WrapLength do
  begin
    Writeln(Wrap[I]);
  end;
```

This is what would be displayed:

```
After a lot of heavy editing, a
text array can become divided
into fragments of many lengths,
including null strings.
```

Finally, here is the *WrapArray* function. It uses a string variable named *TempLine* to hold the characters that are fed to the *WrapString* assembly-language routine. The variables *TextPtr* and *WrapCount*, respectively, point to the (global) *Text* and *Wrap* arrays. The function contains two *while* loops nested in a larger *while* loop. The first keeps adding strings to *TempLine* from the *Text* array until *TempLine* is at least as long as the specified line length. The second *while* loop uses *WrapString* to extract as many word-wrapped lines as it can from *TempLine* before sending it around to the first loop for refilling. A final bit of code sets the remaining text fragment into the *Wrap* array.

```
Function WrapArray(NumberLines,LineWidth: integer): integer;
Var
  TempLine : stype;
  TextPtr,WrapCount : integer;
begin
  TempLine := '';
  TextPtr := 1;
  WrapCount := 1;
  while TextPtr <= NumberLines do
    begin
```

```
        while (Length(TempLine) < LineWidth)  and (TextPtr <=
NumberLines) do
          begin
            TempLine := TempLine + Text[TextPtr];
            TextPtr := TextPtr+1;
          end;
        while Length(TempLine) >= LineWidth do
          begin
            Wrap[WrapCount] := WrapString(TempLine,LineWidth);
            WrapCount := WrapCount+1;
          end;
      end;
  if TempLine <> '' then
    begin
      Wrap[WrapCount] := TempLine;
      WrapArray := WrapCount;
    end;
end;
```

Function CharCount(var Strg: stype; Character: char): integer;

FILE NAME:	CHARCONT.PAS (37 code bytes)
PURPOSE:	*CharCount* reports how many times a particular character occurs in a string.
PARAMETERS:	*Strg* is the string in which the characters are counted.
	Character is the character searched for.
NOTES:	1. You can use this routine to check for inadmissible characters by testing whether the count for a character is 0.
EXAMPLE:	To count the letter "i" in "Mississippi":

```
Word := 'Mississippi';
Write(CharCount(Word,'i'));
```

The result:

4

Function RangeCount(var Strg: stype; Char1,Char2: char): integer;

FILE NAME: RNGECONT.PAS   (55 code bytes)

PURPOSE: *CountRange* reports the number of oc-
                    curences in a string of characters falling
                    within a range of ASCII codes.

PARAMETERS: *Strg* is the string in which the count is made.

                    Char1 and *Char2* are the two characters de-
                    fining the range. The two characters are
                    themselves included in the range, which is
                    always defined from the series of ASCII
                    codes counted from 0 to 255, and whether
                    Char1 or *Char2* is the higher number is un-
                    important. This means that you can not de-
                    fine a range that begins, say, at ASCII 129,
                    and then wraps around to ASCII 31. Rather,
                    you must make two separate range checks.

NOTES: 1. *Char1* and *Char2* may be the same charac-
                       ter, in which case the routine counts that
                       character alone (like *CharCount*).

EXAMPLE: This example tests whether a string contains
                    any control codes (ASCII 0–31) other than
                    the carriage return (ASCII 13) or line feed
                    (ASCII 10).

```
I := RangeCount(Strg,chr(0),chr(9));
I := I + RangeCount(Strg,chr(11),chr(12));
I := I + RangeCount(Strg,chr(14),chr(31));
if I <> 0 then InadmissableChar;
```

Function WordCount(var Strg: stype): integer;

FILE NAME:	WORDCONT.PAS (49 code bytes)
PURPOSE:	*NumberWords* returns the number of words in a string. A word is defined as any series of characters other than the space character.
PARAMETERS:	*Strg* is the string in which the words are counted.
NOTES:	1. There are odd instances in which this routine may not give the exact number of words. For example, a double dash floating between spaces (" -- ") is counted as a word.
EXAMPLE:	This example counts the number of words in a text file. It assumes that individual words are not divided between the end of one line and the beginning of the next.

```
Total := 0;
for I := 1 to NumberLines do
  begin
    Total := Total + WordCount(Text[I]);
  end;
```

Function SeekChar(var Strg: stype; Ch: char; StartPt: integer): integer;

FILE NAME: SEEKCHAR.PAS   (63 code bytes)

PURPOSE: *SeekChar* searches a string from left to right and returns the position of the first instance of a specified character. The search may begin at any point in the string. The function returns **0** when the character is not found.

PARAMETERS: *Strg* is the string that is searched.

                Ch is the character searched for.

                StartPt is the starting position from which the search is made. The position is counted from 1 upward, in which 1 corresponds to the first byte of the string.

NOTES: 1. Other routines in this section can perform the same service as *SeekChar*, but not as quickly.

                2. When *StartPt* is larger than the length of *Strg*, the routine returns **0**.

EXAMPLES: To locate the first left brace (" { ") in a string:

```
FirstPos := SeekChar(Strg,'{',1);
```

                To search for a second:

```
if FirstPos <> 0 then
  SecondPos := SeekChar(Strg,'{',FirstPos+1);
```

Function SeekRange(var Strg: stype; Ch1,Ch2: char; StartPt: integer): integer;

FILE NAME: SEEKRNGE.PAS   (80 code bytes)

PURPOSE: *SeekRange* returns the position of the first instance of a character in a specified range of ASCII codes.

PARAMETERS: *Strg* is the string that is searched.

Ch1 and *Ch2*, the ASCII characters setting the range, are included in it. It does not matter which character has the higher ASCII code—the routine finds the lowest and uses it as the bottom of the range. This means that the range may not wrap around from the high end to the low end of the ASCII set. When *Ch1* and *Ch2* are identical, that character alone is counted.

StartPt is the starting position from which the search is made. The position is counted from 1 upward, in which 1 corresponds to the first byte of the string.

NOTES: 1. *SeekRange* may be used to find out if any of a particular class of codes is present in a string. For example, it can tell you whether there are any control codes (ASCII 0–31), or any codes from the ASCII extended character set (128–255). The *RangeCount* function in this section counts the number of codes in a given range.

EXAMPLE: This example seeks the first control code in a string:

```
ControlCode := SeekRange(Txt,chr(0),chr(31),1);
```

Function SearchLeft(var Strg:stype; Substrg:stype; StartPt: integer): integer;
Function SearchRight(var Strg:stype; Substrg:stype; StartPt: integer): integer;

FILE NAMES: SEARCHLF.PAS   (129 code bytes)
                     SEARCHRT.PAS   (109 code bytes)

PURPOSE: *SearchLeft* and *SearchRight* search for a specified substring in a string, returning its position if it is found or **0** if it is not. *SearchLeft* begins the search from the beginning of the string while *SearchRight* starts from the end. Since the routines are given a position in the string from which the search begins, multiple instances of the substring may be located.

PARAMETERS: *Strg* is the string in which the search is made.

Substrg is the substring that is searched for.

StartPt is the starting position from which the search is made. For *SearchLeft*, the position is counted from 1 upward, in which 1 corresponds to the first byte of the string. For *SearchRight*, the count also begins from 1, but in this case 1 corresponds to the last byte of the string.

NOTES: 1. For *SearchLeft*, both *StartPt* and the value returned are counted from the *beginning* of the string. *SearchRight*, however, counts *StartPt* from the *end* of the string but returns a value counted from the beginning. Although confusing at first, this approach is the most useful for programming when multiple searches and changes are made in a string. Consider the following examples.

EXAMPLES: The use of *SearchLeft* is straightforward. To find the first instance of the word "the" in a string:

```
FirstPosition := SearchLeft(Txt,'the',1);
```

To find the next instance:

```
SecondPosition := SearchLeft(Txt,'the',FirstPosition+1);
```

SearchRight is harder to use because the counting system is different. The value it returns is a position counted from the beginning of the string, but the starting position is counted from the end. For example, to find the last instance of the substring **"the"** in the string **"Give the cat the rat"**:

```
Txt := 'Give the cat the rat';
Position := SearchRight(Txt,'the',1);
```

Here, the parameter **1** corresponds to the **"t"** in **"rat."** The routine returns the value **14**, which is the fourteenth character, counting from the **"G"** in **"Give."** To resume the search, looking for the second instance of **"the,"** starting from the right, the start position would be **8**, that is, the eighth position from the right of the string. It could be calculated this way:

```
Txt := 'Give the cat the rat';
Pos1 := SearchRight(Txt,'the',1);
Pos2 := SearchRight(Txt,'the',Length(Txt)-Pos1+2);
```

Function SeekString(var Strg: stype; Substrg: stype; StartPt: integer): integer;

FILE NAME:	SEEKSTRG.PAS (220 code bytes)
PURPOSE:	*SeekString* searches for a substring within a string, moving from left to right, and starting from a specified position in the string. It ignores the case of alphabetic letters; the substring "apes," for example, matches with "apes," "Apes," and "APES." The function returns the starting position of the substring if it is found or **0** if it is not.
PARAMETERS:	*Strg* is the string in which the search is made.
	Substrg is the substring that is searched for.
	StartPt is the starting position from which the search is made. The position is counted from 1 upward, in which 1 corresponds to the first byte of the string.
NOTES:	1. *SeekString* operates at only one-seventh the speed of the *SearchLeft* or *SearchRight* functions (also found in this section).
EXAMPLE:	To find the number of occurrences of the word "rose" in the string "A rose is a Rose is a ROSE":

```
Strg := 'A rose is a Rose is a ROSE';
SubStrg := 'rose';
NumberTimes := 0;
StartPoint := 1;
While Position <> 0 do
  begin
    Position := SeekString(Strg,SubStrg,StartPoint);
    if Position <> 0 then
```

```
        begin
          NumberTimes := NumberTimes + 1;
          Startpoint := Position + 1;
        end;
  end;
```

5
Keyboard Input

Section 1: Intercept single keystrokes

"Keyboard input" is actually "keyboard-buffer input." The command **Read(kbd,Ch)** moves a code from the keyboard buffer into the *char* variable *Ch*. ASCII 27 flags that an extended code has arrived and that you should follow up with a second *Read* command to learn the extended code number. Except for telling whether the keyboard buffer is empty or not, Turbo Pascal offers no further help in finding out what the user has typed.

There are many other kinds of information about keyboard input, most of which are provided by the routines making up this section. Two routines clear the keyboard buffer. *ClearBuffer* simply clears the buffer, while *ClearChar* clears the buffer and then waits for a character. Note that the buffer is cleared by Turbo Pascal's **Write** and **Writeln** commands (presumably a bug). Turbo Pascal has the *KeyPressed* function to tell whether the buffer contains a character. The **NextKey** function does the same thing but reports what the next character is without removing it from the buffer. All these routines work through standard operating system calls (these days it is very risky to access the keyboard buffer directly since any of a multitude of operating environments and resident programs can change the structure of the buffer or its position in memory).

The Turbo *Read* procedure creates confusion by returning ASCII 27 when an extended code arrives. This 1-byte code rightfully belongs to the Esc key (and to Ctrl-[). The operating system functions instead return ASCII 0 as the first byte of an extended code, and since no keystroke can produce this code no confusion can arise. The **ReadChar** function works exactly as the Turbo **Read(Kbd,c)** command except that it signals extended codes with ASCII 0. There also is a function called **NoWait** which checks the buffer for a keystroke and returns it if one is found, but which does not wait for a keystroke if none is present.

Another point of confusion in interpreting key codes is whether ASCII codes 8, 9, 13, and 27 result from the Backspace, Tab, Enter, and Escape keys, respectively, or from the combinations of Ctrl-H, -I, -M, and -[. *ReadKey* is an otherwise ordinary key input function that checks for these distinctions and returns different codes for the four Ctrl-key cases. The distinctions can also be made with *GetScan*, which returns the scan code of the next keystroke in line in the buffer.

Often a keyboard input routine contains one input command followed by a long list of statements like **if Ch in ['a'..'z']**, which sort out whether the input is wanted by the program or not. These statements make for a great deal of coding, and often separate key input sequences must be created for different parts of a program. *FilterIn* waits for a keystroke and then compares it to tables that tell which codes are acceptable; keystrokes not in the tables are rejected. A related function, *FilterOut*, rejects all keystrokes that are found in the tables. When a different sort of input is required, you need merely change the lookup tables.

Finally, a special routine makes the keyboard do something it is not intended to do. *KeyPause* converts one or more keys into ON-OFF push buttons. For example, you can set up a key so that when it is pressed, a status line or help screen is displayed as long as the key is held down. When the key is released, the information instantly disappears. This routine works through the operating system, making it safe to use in any application.

Procedure ClearBuffer;

FILE NAME: CLRBUFFR.PAS   (22 code bytes)

PURPOSE: *ClearBuffer* clears the keyboard buffer.

NOTES:

1. A number of utility programs and operating environments change the size and position of the keyboard buffer. This procedure respects that fact and doesn't access the buffer pointers directly. Instead, it simply keeps reading from the buffer until no more characters are returned.

2. You may wish to use **ClearChar** (also in this section) to automatically clear the buffer and then wait for a keystroke.

EXAMPLE: In this example, the keyboard buffer is cleared before requesting a "Yes" or "No" reply:

```
Write('Exit without saving file?  Yes/No');
ClearBuffer;
Read(kbd,Ch);
If Ch in ['Y','y'] then...
```

Function ClearChar: char;

FILE NAME:	CLEARCHR.PAS (23 code bytes)
PURPOSE:	*ClearChar* clears the keyboard buffer and then waits for and returns the next incoming keystroke.
NOTES:	1. The routine returns ASCII 0 when it finds an extended code. In this case, fetch the second byte of the code with *Read(kbd,Character)* or *ReadChar* (also in this section). Do *not* use *ClearChar* to get the second byte, since it would instead erase the code and then wait for another keystroke.
	2. *ClearChar* uses function 7 of INT 21H. It intercepts Ctrl-Break, causing an in-memory program to return to the Turbo prompt and a .COM program to return to DOS.
EXAMPLE:	This function is generally required only in special cases where inadvertent keystrokes could be interpreted as commands. Compare this code to the example for *ClearBuffer* (also in this section):

```
Write('Quit without saving data?  y/n');
Answer := ClearChar;
if Answer in ['Y','y'] then...
```

Function ReadChar: char;

FILE NAME: READCHAR.PAS   (21 code bytes)

PURPOSE: *ReadChar* waits for and returns a keystroke exactly as the Turbo Pascal statement **Read(Kbd,character)**, except that it returns ASCII 0 (null) instead of ASCII 27 (escape) when an extended code is received.

NOTES: 1. Because the *Read* procedure returns the escape character when it finds an extended code, it is impossible to know when the code issues from the Escape key itself (as a 1-byte ASCII code). *ReadChar* overcomes this confusion by returning the standard null character for extended codes. Calling the function a second time returns the extended code itself.

2. This function intercepts Ctrl-Break, causing an in-memory program to return to the Turbo prompt, and a .COM program to return to DOS.

EXAMPLE: In the code below, **ReadChar** inputs a keystroke and tests for an extended code. The example checks for the "cursor right" extended code, 0;77, and for the one-byte backspace code, ASCII 8.

```
Ch := ReadChar;
if Ch = chr(0) then
  begin
    Ch := ReadChar;
    if Ch := chr(77) then... (cursor right)
    .
    .
```

```
        end;
    if Ch = chr(8) then... (backspace)
    .
    .
```

Function ReadKey: char;

FILE NAME: READKEY.PAS   (81 code bytes)

PURPOSE: *ReadKey* waits for and returns a keystroke, much as the *ReadChar* function that is also documented in this section. *ReadKey* returns special codes for **Ctrl-H**, **Ctrl-I**, **Ctrl-M**, and **Ctrl-[**. Normally, these key combinations return ASCII codes 8, 9, 13, and 27— the same codes as the backspace, tab, carriage return, and escape keys. *ReadKey* adds 200 to the four codes when they arise from the Ctrl key, giving **208**, **209**, **213**, and **227**.

NOTES: 1. The code numbers from 208–227 cause no confusion because there are no normal keystrokes that result in one-byte codes in this range. Of course, it would be more consistent to give over ASCII codes 1–26 to the Ctrl key sequence from ^A to ^Z, allotting the special codes to the Backspace, Tab, Enter, and Escape keys. However, since the usual codes for these keys are second nature to experienced programmers, they haven't been tinkered with.

EXAMPLE: This example waits for a keystroke and then distinguishes between the backspace key (ASCII 8) and the "Help" command (Ctrl-H, returned as ASCII 208):

```
Ch := ReadKey;
if Ch = chr(8) then Backspace;
if Ch = chr(208) then HelpScreen;
   .
   .
   .
```

Function NoWait: char;

FILE NAME:	NOWAIT.PAS (27 code bytes)
PURPOSE:	*NoWait* returns a keyboard code if one is in the buffer, or ASCII 255 ($FF) if not. Extended codes return **Chr(0)**. *NoWait* may be used to read the second byte of the code.
NOTES:	1. You may use any keyboard input function to read the second byte of an extended code, such as the Pascal *Read(kbd,Ch)* statement or the *ReadChar* function given in this chapter. Do not use *ClearChar*, which clears the buffer first.
EXAMPLE:	In this example, **NoWait** is placed within a loop that sends lines of text to the printer; it provides a convenient way of interrupting an ongoing operation:

```
Procedure PrintText(NumberLines: integer);
Var
  Ch : char;
begin
  for I := 1 to NumberLines do
    begin
      write(lst,TextArray[I]);
      Ch := NoWait;
      If Ch <> chr(255) then Goto LeaveLoop;
    end;
  If Ch in ['P','p'] then...
  If Ch in ['Q','q'] then...
end;
```

Function NextKey: char;

FILE NAME: NEXTKEY.PAS   (60 code bytes)

PURPOSE: *NextKey* returns the code of the next key-
                    stroke *without* removing it from the keyboard
                    buffer. When there is no code, it returns **255**
                    (**$FF**). The function indicates whether the
                    code is an ASCII code or an extended code
                    by setting a global Boolean variable,
                    ExtendedCode.

PARAMETERS: *ExtendedCode* is a global Boolean variable
                    that is set whenever the *NextKey* function is
                    called. When it is TRUE, the next code in the
                    buffer is an extended code, and the value re-
                    turned by *NextKey* is the second byte of the
                    code. When *ExtendedCode* is FALSE, the
                    next keystroke is a one-byte ASCII code, and
                    that code is returned by the function.

NOTES: 1. *NextKey* uses function 1 of INT 16H—it
                       doesn't access the keyboard buffer
                       directly.

                    2. The **Write** and **Writeln** commands clear
                       the keyboard buffer in Turbo Pascal. Be
                       careful that they don't defeat your use of
                       this function.

EXAMPLE: This example checks for the next keystroke
                    in the buffer and distinguishes between **F10**
                    (0;68) and **D** (ASCII 68):

```
Ch := NextKey;
if Ch = chr(255) then ...no code
if ExtendedCode then
  begin
    if Ch = chr(68) then ...F10
     .

     .
  end else
```

```
begin
  if Ch = chr(68) then ...'D'
    .
    .
end;
```

Function GetScan: integer;

FILE NAME: GETSCAN.PAS   (69 code bytes)

PURPOSE: *GetScan* returns the scan code of the next keystroke code in the keyboard buffer. The code is not removed from the buffer. ASCII 255 ($FF) is returned when the buffer is empty.

NOTES:

1. A scan code is one of 83 numbers (84 on the IBM AT) arbitrarily assigned to each key on the keyboard. IBM Technical Reference Manuals and many popular books (including the author's *Programmer's Problem Solver*) contain a table of scan codes.

2. The *GetScan* function finds out the scan code of a keystroke *before* it is read from the keyboard buffer, since in many instances it cannot be found out afterward.

3. The **Write** and **Writeln** commands clear the keyboard buffer in Turbo Pascal. Take care that they don't interfere with the use of this function.

EXAMPLE: ASCII codes 8, 9, 13, and 27 each arise from two different keystrokes: the backspace or Ctrl-H, the tab or Ctrl-I, the carriage-return or Ctrl-M, and Esc or Ctrl-[. One use for scan codes is to distinguish between these alternatives. This example checks whether the next keystroke is a backspace or Ctrl-H (used here to call up a help screen). It works in combination with *NextKey* (also found in this section) which reports the next character in the keyboard buffer without removing it.

First the example checks whether the next key code is ASCII 8. If so, it fetches the scan code and then "reads" the code from the buffer to clear it out of the way. Once that is done, the routine consults the scan code to see whether the backspace key (scan code 14) was depressed. If not, the keystroke must have been Ctrl-H.

```
Ch := NextKey;
if Ch = chr(8) then
  begin
    ScanCode := GetScan;
    Read(kbd,Ch);
    If ScanCode = 14 then BackSpace else HelpScreen;
  end;
```

Function FilterIn(AsciiString,ExtendedString: stype): char;
Function FilterOut(AsciiString,ExtendedString: stype): char;

FILE NAMES: FILTERIN.PAS   (204 code bytes)
                       FLTEROUT.PAS   (210 code bytes)

PURPOSE: These two functions enter a character from the keyboard and check to see if it is to be accepted by testing whether the character is present in one or two strings of characters, one for ASCII codes and one for extended codes. *FilterOut* rejects a character if it finds it listed in one of the filter strings; *FilterIn* rejects a character when it *doesn't* find it in the strings. When the character is rejected, the speaker beeps, and the routine discards it and goes on to wait for another keystroke. The character isn't echoed on the display.

PARAMETERS: *AsciiString* and *ExtendedString* are strings containing the characters to be accepted or rejected. The characters in *ExtendedString* are the *second* bytes of extended codes—the initial byte of ASCII 0 is omitted. When *FilterOut* is given the *AsciiString* '[]', square brackets are rejected. Similarly, the backtab is discarded when *ExtendedString* is chr(15). A *range* of characters may be defined in either string by writing the first, lower-numbered code twice, following it with the character at the high end of the range. The sequence 'aaz', for example, would cause *FilterOut* to reject all lowercase letters and *FilterIn* to accept no ASCII codes other than lowercase letters. A string may contain any number of ranges defined in this way, and any number of individual characters. Placing the code chr(255) in either string signals that all codes are to be accepted (or rejected); a null string signals that none are.

NOTES:

1. Like **ReadKey**, these functions return different codes in the four cases where an ASCII code may arise from different keystrokes. The numbers 8, 9, 13, and 27 are returned for the Backspace, Tab, Carriage Return, and Escape keys. Their counterparts—Ctrl-H, -I, -M, and -[—return 208, 209, 213, and 227. Any of these codes may be included in **AsciiString**.

EXAMPLES:

This example permits entry only of characters allowed in DOS file names. The first nine characters in the ASCII character string—**aaz**, **AAZ**, and **009**—set the ranges for a–z, A–Z, and 0–9. The remaining characters mark individual codes, with the apostrophe written as **chr(39)** to avoid confusing the compiler. The carrage-return character (ASCII 13) is added to the string to allow termination of input. The second parameter for **FilterIn** is a null string, rejecting all extended codes.

```
DOSFilter := 'aazAAZ009$&#@!%`()-{}_/\'+chr(39)+chr(13);
Ch := FilterIn(DOSFilter,'');
```

The next example rejects lowercase characters and otherwise accepts all ASCII and extended codes:

```
Ch := FilterOut('aaz','');
```

The null string indicates that there are no extended codes that should be filtered out. To *reject* all extended codes instead:

```
Ch := FilterOut('aaz',chr(255));
```

Procedure KeyPause(Code: char; ASCII: boolean);

FILE NAME:	KEYPAUSE.PAS	(68 code bytes)

PURPOSE: *KeyPause* transforms a key into an ON-OFF contact switch. For example, you can use it to make one or more function keys display a help screen. When the key is pressed down, the help screen appears. When the key is released, the help screen is erased. *KeyPause* is called after the particular keystroke is intercepted in an ordinary keyboard-input loop. But before *KeyPause* is called, the program would display the help screen. *KeyPause* watches the keyboard buffer, which is continuously filled with the same code until the key is released. Then **KeyPause** simply returns, having done nothing more than clear the buffer. The program would then go on to erase the help message and restore the contents of the prior screen.

PARAMETERS: *Code* is the code number of the key that is held down. It is either an ASCII code or the second byte of an extended code.

ASCII is TRUE when the *Code* represents a one-byte ASCII code; it is FALSE when *Code* is the second byte of an extended code.

NOTES: 1. *KeyPause* waits until the keyboard's "typematic" (automatic repeat feature has had enough time to pump another code into the buffer. Only then does it attempt to read the next keystroke from the buffer (otherwise the buffer would quickly be emptied, making it appear as if the key had been released). The routine adjusts for the time difference between the initial typematic delay and the subsequent repetition rate.

2. There is a slight delay from the time the key is released to the time that *KeyPause* returns. The keyboard typematic rate makes this unavoidable. Truly instantaneous response can only be achieved with the Shift and Toggle keys, as shown in Section 3 of this chapter.

EXAMPLE:

This example uses two procedures from Chapter 7. *GrabBox* saves an area of the screen and clears it; *RestoreBox* returns the original contents. You'll also find *Display*, which writes a character string. These routines are used here with *KeyPause* to make F10 display a reverse-image message box that appears when the key is pressed down and that disappears when the key is released.

First, intercept the keystroke with *Read-Char*. The code for F10 is **0;68**.

```
Repeat
  begin
    Ch := ReadChar;
    if Ch = chr(0) then   {extended code?}
      begin
        Ch := ReadChar;
        if Ch = chr(68) then ShowScreen(Ch);   {F10 code}
      end;
  end;
Until(Ch = 'q');   {strike 'q' to quit the loop}
```

Here is the procedure that draws and erases the message box. It is passed the extended code number for use by *KeyPause*. *GrabBox* clears the area it saves in reverse image (on a monochrome display) and the *Display* procedure writes the message in this same attribute. *KeyPause* is given the value FALSE for *ASCII* since it is used here with an extended code.

```
Procedure ShowScreen(Ch: char);
Type
  Boxtype = array[1..250] of byte;
Var
  BoxCopy : Boxtype;
begin
  GrabBox(BoxCopy,5,5,25,5,112); {draw the box}
  Display('Here is the message',8,7,112);
  KeyPause(Ch,FALSE);  {wait while F10 is down}
  RestoreBox(BoxCopy,5,5,25,5);  {erase the box and return}
end;
```

Section 2: Intercept multiple keystrokes

Turbo Pascal supplies the standard *Readln* function to enter strings from the keyboard. Unlike **Read(kbd,ch)**, *Readln* echoes input on the display, but with little flexibility. You cannot monitor the contents of the string and cannot control its length. This section contains a number of routines that receive strings in various formats and display them. All use BIOS functions to write on the screen and to beep the speaker when input errors occur. The simplest routine, *InputLine*, enters a string much like *Readln*, but also sets the echo color and maximum string length; it also can convert incoming alphabetic characters to upper- or lowercase.

Next is *InputRight*, which enters a string leftward from a starting point, so that the whole string shifts to the left with each additional keystroke, or to the right when backspaced. Thus, the string is always right-justified against its starting point. Even more elaborate is *WrapInput*, which automatically word-wraps keyboard input between any two columns on the screen. It is fully equipped for backspacing and for unusual input. Since both of these routines allow you to set a maximum length for the string, it can be confined to a particular area of the screen.

This section concludes with two routines that input numeric strings and return them as integer or real values. These routines display the input against a fixed right margin or decimal point, aligning columns of numbers. Rather like *InputRight*, *InputInteger* echoes a string from right to left, with the 1's place fixed at a given screen position. This function can be set up to return either integer or real values. *InputReal* inputs a real value around a fixed decimal point. It echoes numbers to the left of the decimal point until the period key is pressed, and then it echoes subsequent keystrokes at the right of the decimal point. Both routines support backspacing, and in both you can limit the number of digits the routine will accept.

Function InputLine(Col,Row,Color,MaxLen: integer; CharCase: char): stype;

FILE NAME: INPLINE.PAS   (240 code bytes)

PURPOSE: *InputLine* receives characters from the keyboard and assigns them to a string variable. The string is echoed in a given attribute starting from the specified cursor coordinates. Input ends when the carriage return is struck. Backspacing is supported, and the Escape key clears whatever has been written and starts over. You may set a maximum length for the string. Beyond this length, keystrokes other than the backspace or escape are discarded and the speaker beeps. The function can be made to convert all lowercase letters to uppercase or vice versa.

PARAMETERS: *Col* and *Row* set the initial cursor position from which the input is echoed. Columns are counted from 1 to 80 and rows are counted from 1 to 25.

Color is the attribute in which characters are displayed. It is a number from 0 to 255, where 7 is "normal" white-on-black. *Color* may be a global variable that is set by routines in Chapter 6.

MaxLen is the maximum number of characters allowed in the string, from 1–255.

CharCase flags whether all alphabetic characters should be converted to upper- or lowercase, or whether no conversion should be made. Use "U" or "u" to cause all characters to be converted to uppercase, and "L" or "l" for lowercase. Any other character results in no conversion taking place. The case conversion is made to both the characters

echoed on the display and the characters returned in the string.

NOTES:

1. Turbo Pascal accepts string input and echoes it using **Readln(StrgVar)**. This routine
   works in the same way, but it lets you fully
   control attributes, case conversion, and the
   string length. Turbo allows input of a string
   longer than *stype* and returns only as many
   characters as the string can hold. This routine beeps when the maximum length is
   reached and ignores additional characters,
   allowing you to limit user input to a particular region of the screen. The routine also
   beeps when the backspace reaches the initial cursor position.

2. All extended codes are ignored. Control
   codes (Ctrl-A through Ctrl-Z) are ignored
   except for Ctrl-H and Ctrl-M, which are
   interpreted as a backspace and carriage
   return. The tab key is ignored.

3. The backspace erases characters using the
   same attribute in which they are written.
   If underlining is used, backspacing will
   leave underlined spaces.

4. It is your responsibility to see to it that
   MaxLen does not exceed **stype**. The routine checks that *Row* and *Col* are in
   range, and that *MaxLen* is nonzero; it returns without taking input when these
   parameters are in error.

EXAMPLE:

In this example the user is asked to enter a
file name. The input is limited to twelve
characters (FILENAME.EXT), and it is automatically converted to uppercase so that it
may be readily compared to, say, a list of file
names. The attribute, 112, causes the string
to be echoed in reverse image.

```
Filename := InputLine(40,11,112,12,'U');
```

Function InputRight(Col,Row,Color,MaxLen: integer; CharCase: char): stype;

FILE NAME: INPRIGHT.PAS   (288 code bytes)

PURPOSE: *InputRight* receives up to a specified number of characters from the keyboard and assigns them to a string variable. The input is displayed in the given attribute beginning at *Col* and *Row* and moving to the left so that, with each added character, the entire string moves one column to the left. A carriage return ends input. Both the Backspace and Delete keys eliminate the last character entered and cause the string to shift to the right. The Escape key erases all that has been entered and starts over. Other control codes (ASCII 0–31) and extended codes are rejected.

PARAMETERS: *Col* and *Row* set the initial cursor position from which the input is echoed to the left. The cursor remains at this position throughout input. Columns are counted from 1 to 80, rows from 1 to 25.

Color is the attribute in which characters are displayed. It is a number from 0 to 255, where 7 is "normal" white-on-black. *Color* may be a global variable set by routines in Chapter 6. Backspacing clears characters in this attribute.

MaxLen is the maximum number of characters allowed in the string, from 1 to 80. The string will not wrap around to a new line from the left edge of the screen. Once a string reaches the left edge, additional keystrokes are discarded, and the speaker beeps. This occurs even when *MaxLen* has not yet been reached.

CharCase flags whether all alphabetic characters should be converted to upper- or lowercase, or whether no conversion should be made. Use "U" or "u" to cause all characters to be converted to uppercase, and "L" or "l" for lowercase. Any other character results in no conversion taking place. The case conversion is made to both the characters echoed on the display and the characters returned in the string.

NOTES:

1. *InputRight* beeps the system speaker when characters arrive after *MaxLen* is reached. These additional characters are discarded, allowing you to limit user input to a particular region of the screen. You must see to it that *MaxLen* does not exceed *stype.*

2. Characters are deleted from the string by both the Del key and the Backspace key. Both keys cause the speaker to beep if they are used when the string is zero-length.

3. The function returns null when the cursor coordinates are out of range, or when MaxLen is zero.

4. Avoid using underlining as an attribute with this routine, since the spaces cleared by backspacing will be filled with underlined blanks.

EXAMPLE:

This example enters strings at opposite ends of the top row of the screen. First *InputLine* (also in this section) receives a 30-character string on the left. Then *InputRight* right-justifies the second, 40-character string against the right margin of the screen. Both are displayed in intense image (ASCII 15 on a monochrome monitor). The first string is converted to uppercase; the second is not altered.

```
Name := InputLine(1,1,15,30,'U');
CompanyName := InputRight(80,1,15,40,'X');
```

Function WrapInput(Row,LeftCol,RightCol,Color,MaxLen: integer): stype;

FILE NAME: WRAPINP.PAS   (397 code bytes)

PURPOSE: *WrapInput* inputs a string from the keyboard, performing word-wrap as the charac-
ters are echoed on the screen. Striking the
carriage return ends input. The function sets
the left and right columns between which the
string is displayed. The length of the string
may be restricted to any length less than or
equal to the size of the string returned by the
function. The Backspace key is operative, and
the Escape key cancels the input operation so
that a null string is returned.

PARAMETERS: *Row* is the row on which display begins, the
first character appearing at *LeftCol,Row*.
Rows are counted from 1 to 25.

LeftCol and *RightCol* are the left and right
columns forming the area in which the input
is displayed. The columns are counted from
1 to 80.

Color is the attribute in which characters are
displayed. It is a number from 0 to 255,
where 7 is "normal" white-on-black. *Color*
may be a global variable set by routines in
Chapter 6.

MaxLen is the maximum number of characters of input that are accepted. It must never
be greater than *stype*. This feature helps
with error-checking and stops careless input
from overwriting parts of the screen that will
not then be cleared. The speaker beeps when
additional input is attempted and the keystrokes are discarded. *MaxLen* reflects the
number of characters in the string returned
by the function; the extra spaces used by the

word-wrap, which have no bearing, should be considered when allotting display space.

NOTES:

1. The rightmost column, ordinarily occupied by space characters, holds some other character only when no space appears anywhere in the line and the "word" is broken.

2. The speaker beeps when you backspace from the starting cursor position.

3. All control codes (ASCII 0–31) are ignored except the carriage return and backspace. This means that the tab key is inoperative. All extended codes are also rejected.

4. The routine checks that **RightCol** is actually to the right of **LeftCol**. A null string is returned when it is not; this also happens when any of the row or column positions are out of range. You must ensure that **Row** is high enough on the screen to allow space below for the longest possible string (there is no automatic scrolling).

5. The Escape key signals that input it canceled without backspacing the string to zero length. While Esc causes **WrapInput** to return a null string, it does not erase the screen image. Typically, a program would check if the return string is null, and if so it would clear the area between the two input columns and then recall **WrapInput** for another try.

EXAMPLE:

This example inputs a string of up to 80 characters between columns 20 and 50. The string, which begins on row 3, is written in intense image (assuming a monochrome display):

```
Strg := WrapInput(3,20,50,15,80);
```

Procedure InputInteger(Col,Row,Color,MaxLen: integer);

FILE NAME:	INPINT.PAS (283 code bytes)
PURPOSE:	*InputInteger* inputs a string of numerals from the keyboard and returns it as an *integer* or *real* value. The input is displayed beginning from the **Col,Row** position and moving to the left so that, with each additional character, the entire string moves one column to the left. A carriage return ends input. Both the Delete and Backspace keys eliminate the last character entered and cause the string to shift to the right. Non-numeric keystrokes other than the minus sign are discarded. *InputInteger* contains the Turbo Pascal *Val* procedure, which converts the character string to numeric form. You must set up the three variables required by *Val*.
PARAMETERS:	*Col* and *Row* are the column and row position at which the rightmost character of the string is displayed. The cursor remains at this position throughout input. Columns are counted from 1 to 80, and rows are counted from 1 to 25.
	Color is the attribute in which characters are displayed. It is a number from 0 to 255, where 7 is "normal" white-on-black. *Color* may be a global variable set by routines in Chapter 6. Characters are cleared in this attribute when the input string is backspaced.
	MaxLen is the maximum number of characters accepted for the string. Once *MaxLen* is reached, additional keystrokes are discarded and the speaker beeps.
	NumberString is a string variable into which the string is placed. It must be at least as long as *MaxLen*.

InputValue is the numeric value of the string. As such, it is the "result" of this procedure. It may be of either *integer* or *real* type. The input string must be between 32767 and −32768 when this variable is declared as an *integer*. When *InputValue* is made *real*, very long integers are allowed.

InputError is an integer used by the *Val* procedure to report errors. It is **0** when there is no conversion error; otherwise, it is the position of the first character in error in *NumberString*.

NOTES:

1. A negative sign is accepted only at the start of the string. Input is allowed in integer format only; floating-point input is not accepted even when *InputValue* is declared as *real*.

2. The Delete key is the proper choice for eliminating characters in this format. The Backspace is also made operative because users are accustomed to using it in normal left-to-right entry.

EXAMPLES:

This example enters a string starting at, and to the left of, column 20, row 1. The string is written in normal image (ASCII 7), and it is restricted to three digits.

```
Var
   InputValue : integer;
   InputError : integer;
   NumberString : stype;

InputInteger(20,1,7,3);
```

A much longer integer may be entered by changing *InputValue* to *real*. Here, up to twelve digits are accepted:

```
Var
   InputValue : real;
   InputError : integer;
   NumberString : stype;

InputInteger(20,1,7,12);
```

Procedure InputReal(Col,Row,Color,MaxLeft,MaxRight: integer);

FILE NAME:	INPREAL.PAS	(550 code bytes)

PURPOSE:

InputReal inputs a string of characters from the keyboard and returns it as a value of *real* type. The routine begins by writing a decimal point at **Col,Row**. The subsequent input is displayed around this fixed point. Input first appears to the left of the point, each successive character causing the prior characters to shift one column to the left. Once the Period key or Decimal Point key (up-shifted Del) is struck, input is directed in similar fashion to the right of the decimal point. A carriage return signals the end of input. Both the Delete and Backspace keys remove the prior character and make the appropriate screen adjustments. Backspacing is allowed from the right to the left side of the string. Exponential notation is supported, and inbuilt error-checking ensures that characters may only be entered in an acceptable order. **InputReal** contains the Turbo Pascal **Val** procedure, which converts the character string to numeric form. You must set up the three variables required by **Val**, as explained below.

PARAMETERS:

Col and **Row** are the column and row position at which the fixed decimal point is displayed. Columns are counted from 1 to 80, rows from 1 to 25.

Color is the attribute in which characters are displayed. It is a number from 0 to 255, where 7 is "normal" white-on-black. **Color** may be a global variable set by routines in Chapter 6. Characters are cleared in this attribute when the input string is backspaced.

MaxLeft and *MaxRight* are the numbers of characters allowed to the left and right of the decimal point. *MaxLeft* doesn't require an extra character for a minus sign; both **333.3** and **−333.3** may be entered when *MaxLeft* is **3**. *MaxRight*, on the other hand, must be large enough to accommodate every character in the right portion of the string, including "e," "+," and "−." Additional keystrokes are ignored, and the speaker beeps, when *MaxLeft and MaxRight* are reached.

NumberString is a string variable into which the string is placed. It must be at least as long as *MaxLeft* plus *MaxRight*, *plus two more* for the decimal point and a leading minus sign.

InputValue is the numeric value of the string. As such, it is the "result" of this procedure. It must be of type *real*.

InputError is an integer used by the *Val* procedure to report errors. It is **0** when there is no conversion error; otherwise, it is the position of the first character in error in *NumberString*.

NOTES:

1. The routine accepts only numerals, the "+" and "−" signs, "e" and "E," the decimal point (or period), and Del and Backspace. All other keystrokes are discarded.

2. The cursor remains at the column to the left of the decimal point while the left side of the string is entered. When the right side is written, the cursor moves a column to the right after each keystroke.

EXAMPLE:

This example inputs a real number with up to eight digits to the left of the decimal and six digits to the right. The number is written in normal attribute (ASCII 7) with the decimal point placed at column 20, row 12.

```
Var
   InputValue : real;
   InputError : integer;
   NumberString : stype;

InputReal(20,12,7,8,6);
```

Once executed, **NumberString** holds the input string and **InputValue** holds the numeric representation.

Section 3: Monitor/control the shift and toggle keys

This section contains routines that change or report the status of the shift and toggle keys. The shift keys include the Ctrl, Alt, and left and right alphabet shift keys. The toggle keys are the NumLock, ScrollLock, CapsLock, and Ins keys. These routines can change the setting of any of the toggle keys from "on" to "off" or the reverse. They can report the current setting of a toggle key. And they can tell whether any shift or toggle key is held down at the moment the routine is executed.

One reason toggle-key settings are made by software is to help along the program user. When a spreadsheet program expects the user to enter data, it can set the NumLock status to "on." You may also wish to set the toggle keys when a program is loaded. For example, an editor may need to start up in *insert* rather than *overwrite* mode. When loaded, the program should set the insert-key status to "on" to ensure that it is correct.

Reading the status of the toggle and shift keys helps with a number of odd jobs. The most obvious is to be able to inform the user of the current status of the keys. These keys may also be used to communicate with the computer under special circumstances. They offer the advantage that they do not place a character in the keyboard buffer (the Ins key is an exception). While a program is sending data to the printer, for example, it can repeatedly check whether the Scroll Lock key is down as a signal to discontinue printing; type-ahead characters in the buffer are left untouched. Another peculiarity of the shift and toggle keys is that they are not governed by the typematic rate. As a result, they can effectively enter thousands of keystrokes per second, responding instantly to the user's touch. This feature may be applied to video games, graphics-drawing programs, and so on.

Function CapsLockOn: boolean;
Function NumLockOn: boolean;
Function ScrollLockOn: boolean;
Function InsKeyOn: boolean;

FILE NAMES: CAPSLKON.PAS   (24 code bytes)
                          NUMLKON.PAS   (24 code bytes)
                          SCRLLKON.PAS   (24 code bytes)
                          INSKEYON.PAS   (24 code bytes)

PURPOSE: These functions return TRUE when the respective toggle keys are set "on" and FALSE when they are "off."

NOTES: 1. The functions use a BIOS function to read the keyboard status byte at 0040:0017.

EXAMPLE: Sometimes it is desirable to display the status of one or more toggle keys. The status of a key can change at any time since the keyboard interrupt will break in and change the status setting at 0040:0017 no matter what a program is doing. It is possible to constantly monitor and update the status information, but this approach is difficult to implement as a freestanding subroutine. The four functions here can in most cases do nearly as good a job simply by placing them in a keyboard input loop that cycles around and around while waiting for a keystroke, checking the toggle status many times each second.

In this example, Turbo's **KeyPressed** function tells whether a keystroke has arrived. If not, **NumLockOn** checks to see if the NumLock status is set to "on." If so, the routine writes **NumLock ON** at the bottom of the screen (in reverse image); otherwise, it writes **NumLock OFF**. The message is displayed by the **Display** procedure, found in

Chapter 6. Its parameters are first the string, then the column, row, and attribute.

```
while not KeyPressed do
  begin
    if NumLockOn then
      Display(' NumLock ON  ',5,25,112);
    else
      Display(' NumLock OFF ',5,25,112);
  end;
Read(kbd,Ch);
```

Function AltKeyDown: boolean;
Function CtrlKeyDown: boolean;
Function RightShiftDown: boolean;
Function LeftShiftDown: boolean;

Function CapsLockDown: boolean;
Function NumLockDown: boolean;
Function ScrollLockDown: boolean;
Function InsKeyDown: boolean;

FILE NAMES:	ALTDOWN.PAS	(29 code bytes)
	CTRLDOWN.PAS	(29 code bytes)
	RGHTDOWN.PAS	(29 code bytes)
	LEFTDOWN.PAS	(29 code bytes)
	CAPSDOWN.PAS	(35 code bytes)
	NUMDOWN.PAS	(35 code bytes)
	SCRLDOWN.PAS	(35 code bytes)
	INSDOWN.PAS	(35 code bytes)

PURPOSE: These eight routines report whether a toggle or shift key is held down at the moment the function is called.

NOTES: 1. The routines use the keyboard status word found at 0040:0017. A BIOS function fetches the information for the four shift keys, but since it cannot do the same for the toggle keys, a direct memory access is made in those cases.

EXAMPLE: This example uses the left and right shift keys as buttons to control a video game. Because they are not governed by the keyboard typematic rate, these keys exactly register up and down motions. Here, a sprite is moved to the left or right each time the procedures *SpriteLeft* and *SpriteRight* are called. They are placed within a loop that continues until a normal keystroke is received. The *Delay* procedure follows each move to control the speed of play.

```
while not KeyPressed do
  begin
    if LeftShiftDown then
      begin
        SpriteLeft;
        Delay(DelayTime);
      end;
    if RightShiftDown then
      begin
        SpriteRight;
        Delay(DelayTime);
      end;
  end;
```

Procedure SetCapsLock;
Procedure SetNumLock;
Procedure SetScrollLock;
Procedure SetIns;

Procedure ClrCapsLock;
Procedure ClrNumLock;
Procedure ClrScrollLock;
Procedure ClrIns;

FILE NAMES:

SETCAPLK.PAS	(25 code bytes)
SETNUMLK.PAS	(25 code bytes)
SETSCRLK.PAS	(25 code bytes)
SETINS.PAS	(25 code bytes)
CLRCAPLK.PAS	(25 code bytes)
CLRNUMLK.PAS	(25 code bytes)
CLRSCRLK.PAS	(25 code bytes)
CLRINS.PAS	(25 code bytes)

PURPOSE: The first four routines set the status of the respective keys to "ON" and the second four set the status to "OFF."

NOTES: 1. These routines work by direct access to the keyboard status bytes (there is no BIOS function to set these values).

2. The status indicators on the PC AT keyboard change when these functions alter the current setting for the CapsLock, NumLock, or ScrollLock.

EXAMPLE: In this example, setting the NumLock status to "OFF" anticipates cursor key input. Of course, the user could strike NumLock before typing a cursor key, but fewer errors are likely to occur when this measure is taken.

```
Writeln('Move the bar cursor using the cursor keys');
ClrNumLock;
Read(kbd,ch);
```

6
Screen Output

Section 1: Control the monitor

This chapter is in four parts. The first is concerned with controlling some special aspects of video hardware while the second gives advanced control over the cursor. The third eases setting and changing screen colors. And the fourth supplies various procedures that write on the screen.

This first section gives you control over a miscellany of video features unsupported by Turbo Pascal. First, *GetMode* and *SetMode* let you find or set any screen mode. While Turbo Pascal has four procedures for setting screen modes, it does not give access to the advanced EGA modes. These routines do.

Next are the *GetPage* and *SetPage* routines. They report or set the *current page*, that is, the page of video memory currently in view. Turbo Pascal can only write on page 0, and it can only display this page. But the screen-output routines in this chapter and others allow you to write on pages that are out of view. *SetPage* lets you switch the display to these pages.

Another valuable feature is control over the blink attribute. Ordinarily, in color modes only eight colors may be used as a character's background color because the highest bit in attribute bytes flags whether a character is blinking. This bit instead can serve as an intensity bit for the background color so that sixteen colors are possible, exactly as for foreground colors. *ClearBlink* and *SetBlink* control this feature.

185

Finally, this section provides two routines for direct memory-mapping to the video buffer. Because of inferior design, the IBM Color Graphics Adaptor (and some imitations) are likely to produce "snow" when characters are written directly to the video buffer. The interference is avoided by writing to the buffer during precise intervals. Only assembly language is fast enough. **MemoryMapByte** writes a character and **MemoryMapWord** writes a character and attribute byte.

Procedure SetMode(ModeNumber: integer);
Function GetMode: integer;

FILE NAMES: SETMODE.PAS   (21 code bytes)
                       GETMODE.PAS   (23 code bytes)

PURPOSE: *SetMode* sets the screen to one or the text or graphics modes. (Turbo Pascal comes with four procedures to set screen modes— *TextMode*, *GraphColorMode*, *GraphMode*, and *HiRes*—but there is no provision for the new EGA modes.) *GetMode* returns the current screen mode.

PARAMETERS: *ModeNumber* is a mode number taken from the following table:

0. 40x25 black-and-white alphanumeric (CGA,EGA)
1. 40x25 color alphanumeric (CGA,EGA)
2. 80x25 black-and-white alphanumeric (CGA,EGA)
3. 80x25 color alphanumeric (CGA,EGA)
4. 320x200 4-color graphics (CGA,EGA)
5. 320x200 black-and-white graphics (CGA,EGA)
6. 640x200 black-and-white graphics (CGA,EGA)
7. 80x25 black-and-white alphanumeric (MDA,EGA)
13. 320x200 16-color graphics (EGA)
14. 640x200 16-color graphics (EGA)
15. 640x350 4-color graphics (EGA)
16. 640x350 16-color graphics (EGA)

GetMode returns a number from the table.

NOTES: 1. Depending on the hardware, an incorrect value for *ModeNumber* could throw the video system into an unsupported mode or the code could be ignored altogether.

2. There is, of course, much more to operating in a video mode than simply getting BIOS to set the mode. You need a way to write on the screen. If you use **SetMode** to run one of the advanced EGA graphics modes, you may need to write directly to the video buffer. This process is much more complicated with the EGA than with the CGA. Consult the author's *Programmer's Problem Solver* to learn how it is done.

EXAMPLES: To set the EGA for 640x350 16-color graphics:

```
SetMode(16);
```

To find the current screen mode:

```
Write('The current mode is number '+GetMode);
```

Procedure SetPage(PageNumber: integer);
Function GetPage: integer;

FILE NAMES:	SETPAGE.PAS	(21 code bytes)
	GETPAGE.PAS	(25 code bytes)

PURPOSE: *SetPage* sets the *current page*, that is, the page of video memory currently displayed. *GetPage* reports the current page.

PARAMETERS: *PageNumber* is the page number. It may be from 0 to 3 on the Color Graphics adaptor, or from 0 to 7 on the EGA. The monochrome card has only one page.

GetPage returns a value from 0 to 7.

NOTES: 1. The screen output commands in Turbo Pascal write only to page 0, the lowest in the video buffer. But routines in this chapter and the next can write to any page. Use *SetPage* to make the screen display any of the other pages, either before or while they are written upon.

EXAMPLES: These examples write a message on page 2 and then switch the page into view. First the display (set to page 0) is cleared, and a delay is made so that you can see what is happening. Afterward, page 0 is reset. The examples use the *Display* and *DisplayB* procedures, which write a string, setting its column, row, and color. *Display* memory-maps while *DisplayB* uses the BIOS. The memory-mapping code is given first. Note how the value of VideoBuffer is set to $B800 + $0200 = $BA00 to point the routine to page 2.

```
ClrScr;
VideoBuffer := $B800;
Display('Here is page 0',35,10,7);
VideoBuffer := $BA00;
Display('Here is page 2',35,10,7);
```

```
Delay(2000);
SetPage(2);
Delay(2000);
SetPage(0);
```

Here is the BIOS version:

```
ClrScr;
VideoPage := 0;
DisplayB('Here is page 0',5,10,7);
VideoPage := 2;
DisplayB('Here is page 2',5,10,7);
Delay(2000);
SetPage(2);
Delay(2000);
SetPage(0);
```

Procedure ClearBlink(Code: integer);
Procedure SetBlink(Code: integer);

FILE NAMES:	CLRBLINK.PAS	(44 code bytes)
	SETBLINK.PAS	(44 code bytes)

PURPOSE: *ClearBlink* and *SetBlink* set the status of the blink feature for color text display. Ordinarily, only eight background colors are available when working in sixteen-color text mode, since the highest bit of the four describing the background color controls whether the character is blinking. *ClearBlink* causes this bit instead to function as an *intensity* bit, so that the eight basic colors may be shown in either high or low intensity. Thus, the same sixteen colors for foreground color are made available to the background color. *SetBlink* returns the blink bit to its usual function.

PARAMETERS: *Code* tells the type of video adaptor. Use **2** for the CGA and **3** for the EGA. These numbers correspond to those returned by the *CurrentAdaptor* function in Section 1 of Chapter 2.

NOTES: 1. Most programs use blinking text very little, usually to announce an error. Even with the blink feature turned off, creating blinking text for such occasions is simple. Just keep writing and overwriting the text, making a delay, while waiting for the responding keystroke. Or the line can be cleared or written in different colors. Use *KeyPressed* to check for a keystroke after each write operation.

2. Nothing happens if **Code** is a number other than 2 or 3.

EXAMPLE: In this example, the Color Graphics Adaptor displays a string in red on dark blue with the blink bit set. The bit pattern for red is **0100**, and for blue, **0001**. These combine to form **00010100** and, with the high bit turned on to enable blinking, the bit pattern becomes **10010100**. This equals the decimal value **148**, which the *Display* procedure uses to write the message (*Display* is discussed in Section 4 of this chapter). After the string is written and a delay is made, *ClearBlink* turns off the blink feature so that the high bit changes the background to high intensity—that is, to light blue. Following a second delay, the blink feature is restored and the background color reverts to dark blue.

```
Display('To blink or not to blink',12,12,148);
Delay(2000);
ClearBlink;
Delay(2000);
SetBlink;
```

Procedure MemoryMapByte(Character: char; Offset: integer);
Procedure MemoryMapWord(Character: char; Color,Offset: integer);

FILE NAMES: MEMMAP8.PAS   (66 code bytes)
                MEMMAP16.PAS   (69 code bytes)

PURPOSE: Snow may appear on the screen when video
                data is sent directly to the video buffer of the
                color graphics adaptor (CGA). This problem
                is avoided by watching a register on the
                video controller chip and writing to the
                buffer only during retrace intervals. While
                Turbo Pascal can access the video register, it
                is not fast enough to send a character before
                the retrace interval ends; only assembly lan-
                gage can do the job. *MemoryMap8* writes a
                single character to the buffer, and
                MemoryMap16 writes a character and its
                attribute.

PARAMETERS: *Character* is the ASCII character written in
                video memory.

                Color is the attribute byte written after the
                character.

                Offset is a number from 0 to 3999 corre-
                sponding to a position in the buffer (assum-
                ing an 80 by 25 text screen). Characters are at
                even-numbered positions, their attribute
                bytes at the following odd-numbered posi-
                tion. The character at row 1, column 1 is at
                offset **0**, and its attribute is at offset **1**. The
                character at row 2, column 1 is at offset
                160, and so on. In general, **Offset
                :=160*(ROW-1)+2*(COL-1)** (counting rows
                from 1 to 25 and columns from 1 to 80).

                VideoBuffer is a global variable that holds
                the segment (memory location) of the video
                adaptor. This value is usually **$B000** for the
                monochrome card, **$B800** for the color

graphics card, or either of these values for the EGA, depending on the screen mode. See the discussion in Chapter 1.

NOTES:

1. *MemoryMapByte* can change a character's attribute without changing the character itself by making *Character* the ASCII equivalent of an attribute value, writing it to an odd-numbered offset.

2. In memory mapping, no characters are interpreted. Tabs, carriage-returns, and so on, are displayed as ASCII symbols.

3. These routines work in graphic modes as well, although the mapping is more complicated.

4. Note that all memory-mapping routines in this collection contain code to guard against CGA interference.

EXAMPLE:

This example uses *MemoryMapWord* to write a string directly into the video buffer of a Color Graphics Adaptor, positioning it at column 10, row 5, and writing it in reverse image (ASCII 112);

```
VideoBuffer := $B800;
Strg := 'A boring sample string';
Column := 10;
Row := 5;
BufferOffset := 160*(Row-1)+2*(Column-1);
for I := 1 to length(Strg) do
  begin
   MemoryMapWord(Copy(Strg,I,1),112,BufferOffset);
   BufferOffset := BufferOffset+2;
  end;
```

Section 2: Control the cursor

GotoXY is the only Turbo Pascal command for controlling the cursor. Sophisticated programs require much more. Most important, you must be able to turn the cursor on and off. Turning the cursor "off" merely hides it; it continues to operate as a screen pointer that positions output. The cursor really needs to appear only during keyboard entry; at other times, it may be a distraction. Here two routines, *CursorOn* and *CursorOff*, switch it on and off.

Next comes *Locate*, which sets the cursor position, much as *GotoXY*, but it locates the cursor on any video page (Chapter 1 discusses paging). This capability is useful for procedures that can write on any video page using the cursor, such as the *Wrt* and *Wrtln* procedures found in Section 4 of this chapter.

GetShape and *SetShape* report and set the shape of the cursor. This is done by setting the cursor's *startline* and *stopline*—the horizontal scan lines at which the cursor starts and ends. By setting these two values you can create a number of variations including a block cursor, a two-part cursor, and no visible cursor at all.

Finally, four routines make *relative* cursor moves: *CursorUp*, *CursorDown*, *CursorLeft*, and *CursorRight*. These move the cursor a specified number of rows or columns from its current position.

Procedure CursorOn;
Procedure CursorOff;

FILE NAMES: CURSON.PAS   (39 code bytes)
                  CURSOFF.PAS   (37 code bytes)

PURPOSE: *CursorOn* and *CursorOff* turn the cursor on and off. This means just that the cursor becomes invisible; it continues to function as a screen pointer so that *GotoXY* positions output on the display. These routines work properly only with normal underline cursors.

NOTES: 1. To ensure compatability with all graphics cards, these routines rely upon operating system calls rather than direct access to video controller chips. Unfortunately, the BIOS doesn't provide a function that turns the cursor on and off. But the cursor can be obscured by setting both the start- and stoplines (scan lines) to a value higher than the actual range. On 350-line screens, the scan lines number 0 to 13 for each character, and on 200-line screens, they number 0 to 7. In the first case, a "normal" cursor starts at line 11 and stops at line 12, and, in the second, it starts on line 6 and stops at line 7.

                  2. *CursorOff* checks whether the current startline is 12 and, if so, it sets the startline to 14 and the stopline to 0, effectively turning the cursor off. When the initial startline is not 12, the routine assumes that it is 6 and instead sets the startline to 8. *CursorOn* reverses this process, checking whether the current startline is 14 and setting the start- and stoplines for a visible cursor accordingly. When you use the *GetShape* and *Set-*

Shape routines (also in this section) to set the cursor to a nonstandard form, *CursorOn* and *CursorOff* become confused. To turn the cursor on and off in this case, you need to set the scan lines yourself using *SetShape*.

3. When your program terminates, be sure to turn the cursor on again. DOS does not automatically restore the cursor when it resumes control. You may wish to use *SetShape* to ensure that a normal cursor is in force when your program starts up.

EXAMPLE: This example demonstrates how the cursor continues to function as a screen pointer even when it is "turned off." A series of delays show the normal cursor, the obscured cursor, the cursor writing text, and the cursor returned to view.

```
ClrScr;
Delay(2000);
CursorOff;
Delay(2000);
GotoXY(20,12);
Write('I may be invisible, but I am still here!');
Delay(2000);
CursorOn;
```

Procedure Locate(Col,Row: integer);

FILE NAME: LOCATE.PAS   (64 code bytes)

PURPOSE: *Locate* sets the cursor position, just as *GotoXY* does, but it allows you to choose the video page (every video page has its own cursor pointer). *Locate* is required whenever *SetPage* has been used to make a page other than page 0 the *current page*.

PARAMETERS: *Col* and *Row* are the new cursor position. Columns are counted from 1 to 80 and rows from 1 to 25.

                VideoPage is a global integer variable that determines the page for which the cursor is set.

NOTES: 1. The routine returns without doing anything when *Col* or *Row* are out of range. No check is made on the video page number.

EXAMPLE: This example uses *Locate* with *Wrte*, the memory-mapping equivalent of the Pascal *Write* statement (found in Section 4), to format three strings on page 2. Page 0 is the initial *current page*, and after a delay, *SetPage* brings page 2 into view so that you can see the result. The routine then returns the display to page 0.

```
ClrScr;
VideoBuffer := $BA00;
VideoPage := 2;
Color := 112  {write in reverse-image}
Locate(5,5);Wrte('One');
Locate(10,10);Wrte('Two');
```

```
Locate(15,15);Wrte('Three');
Delay(2000);
SetPage(2);
Delay(2000);
SetPage(0);
```

Procedure GetShape;
Procedure SetShape(StartLine,Stopline: integer);

FILE NAMES: GETSHAPE.PAS   (78 code bytes)
                   SETSHAPE.PAS   (24 code bytes)

PURPOSE: *SetShape* and *GetShape* set and report the *scan line* positions at which the cursor starts and stops. Under the color graphics adaptor, the box in which a character is written consists of eight horizontal scan lines numbered downward from 0 to 7. There are 350 lines on a monochrome or high-resolution color screen, and a character box has 14 scan lines, numbered from 0 to 13. Although the cursor ordinarily covers only one or two lines, it may be set to any thickness. The *StartLine* is the scan-line number at which the cursor starts, and the *StopLine* is the line number at which it stops. *GetShape* places the current scan-line values in two predefined variables, *StartLine* and *StopLine*.

PARAMETERS: *StartLine* and *StopLine*, as parameters for *SetShape*, are the scan line numbers from 0 to 7 or 0 to 13. For *GetShape*, however, *StartLine* and *StopLine* are two integer variables in which the current values are placed. No other names may be used for these variables without altering the routine.

NOTES: 1. The stopline may be a higher number than the startline. In this case, a two-part cursor extends from the startline to the bottom of the character box, and from the top of the box to the stopline.

2. You can "turn off" the cursor (make it invisible) by setting the stopline to **0** and the startline to a value one higher than the highest scan line. Thus, for a 200-line screen, the startline would be **8** and the

stopline **0**, while for a 350-line screen, the values would be **14** and **0**.

3. Be sure to restore a normal cursor before program termination. DOS doesn't automatically reset the cursor when it regains control. On a 350-line screen, a normal cursor starts on line 11 and ends on line 12 (counting from 0 to 13). On a 200-line (ordinary graphics) screen, the startline is 6 and the stopline is 7.

EXAMPLES:

The following examples assume a monochrome display or high resolution color monitor with the EGA. First, to create a full-height block cursor:

```
SetShape(0,13);
```

To restore a normal cursor:

```
SetShape(11,12);
```

To turn the cursor off:

```
SetShape(14,0);
```

To find the shape of the current cursor:

```
GetShape;
Writeln('The startline is ',StartLine);
Writeln('The stopline is ',StopLine);
```

Procedure CursorUp(Rows: integer);
Procedure CursorDown(Rows: integer);
Procedure CursorLeft(Columns: integer);
Procedure CursorRight(Columns: integer);

FILE NAMES:	CURSUP.PAS	(58 code bytes)
	CURSDOWN.PAS	(58 code bytes)
	CURSLEFT.PAS	(58 code bytes)
	CURSRGHT.PAS	(58 code bytes)

PURPOSE: These four routines move the cursor from its current position by the specified number of columns or rows. They are useful for formatting screens and for drawing character graphics.

PARAMETERS: *Rows* and *Columns* are the number of rows or columns that the cursor is displaced. The cursor is moved to the edge of the display when the displacement would take it offscreen.

VideoPage is a global integer variable that determines the video page in which the cursor is moved. The normal value is **0**. Paging is discussed in Chapter 1.

NOTES: 1. Section 4 of this chapter has routines that write strings and then automatically move the cursor to a location relative to the starting point.

2. Use these routines with the *FormatLeft* and *FormatRight* routines (Section 4 of this chapter) which make relative cursor moves after displaying strings. They make it easy to format and edit lists and tables, since all cursor moves are made relative to one starting point.

EXAMPLE: This example repeatedly writes the string -*- across row 13, dividing the screen in two. *CursorLeft* adds spaces by shifting the cursor leftward by four columns each time the string is printed.

```
GotoXY(1,13);
for I := 1 to 12 do
  begin
    Write('-*-');
    CursorRight(4);
  end;
```

Section 3: Set character attributes

This section contains two kinds of routines. First are those that set the attributes for the screen-oriented routines in this collection. All such routines require that you supply an integer parameter specifying the attribute in which characters are written. For example, the *Display* procedure writes a string at a particular position in a particular attribute. The parameters are listed starting with the string, then the column and row, and then the attribute. To display a string at the top left corner of the screen in normal attribute (ASCII 7), you would write **Display('This is the string',1,1,7)**. You could as easily write **Display('This is the string',1,1,Color)**, where *Color* is a global integer variable. The routines in this section that set the screen color do so by adjusting the value held in this predefined variable.

One set of routines is specialized for the monochrome display. It contains procedures like *UnderLine* and *BlinkOn* that make changes in *Color* that underline characters, cause characters to blink, and so on. The values created by these routines work perfectly well with a color adaptor, but the colors are mostly limited to black and white. Other routines—*Foreground* and *Background*—are provided to give you complete access to all colors. Be sure to read Chapter 1 if you aren't familiar with the logic behind setting screen colors.

The second kind of routine in this section changes attributes on the screen without changing what is written. *SetColor* does this for single positions, *RowColor* and *RowColorB* do it for rows, *ColumnColor* and *ColumnColorB* do it for columns, and *BoxColor* and *BoxColorB* do it for rectangular areas of the screen. Except for *SetColor*, each routine comes in memory-mapping and BIOS versions (the latter shown by the B suffix). Use these routines to highlight areas of the screen, make bar cursors, and so on. You also find here the *GetColor* procedure, which reports the current attribute at any screen position.

Procedure Normal;
Procedure UnderLine;
Procedure Reverse;
Procedure IntenseOn;
Procedure IntenseOff;
Procedure BlinkOn;
Procedure BlinkOff;

FILE NAMES:	NORMAL.PAS	(51 code bytes)
	UNDERLN.PAS	(51 code bytes)
	REVERSE.PAS	(51 code bytes)
	INTENSON.PAS	(48 code bytes)
	INTENSOF.PAS	(48 code bytes)
	BLINKON.PAS	(48 code bytes)
	BLINKOFF.PAS	(48 code bytes)

PURPOSE: These seven procedures provide a convenient way of setting text attributes in programs designed for a monochrome display. They operate on the value held in the variable **Color**. **Color** may be set up as a global variable used by the screen-oriented routines in this collection, all of which require an integer argument that sets the color in which characters are displayed.

NOTES: 1. *Normal*, *Underline*, and *Reverse* cancel each other out. They don't affect the current setting for blinking and intensity, and vice versa. It is easiest to set the initial attribute by number: Color := 7.

2. These routines may just as easily be used with a color display, but the selection of colors is uninteresting. "Normal" is white on black, and "reverse" is black on white. "Underline" is blue on black. "Intense" switches the foreground color between normal and bright white, or dark and light blue. "Blink" turns blinking on and off if blinking is enabled (see the proce-

dures in Section 1 of this chapter that disable blinking), or else it switches the background color between dark and light intensities of white and black.

EXAMPLE: This example writes the line, "It is a *very* good idea." It uses the **Wrt** procedure, which works just like Pascal's **Write** except that it memory-maps and it sets the text color (**Wrt** is found in Section 4 of this chapter).

```
Normal;
Wrt('It is a',Color);
Underline;
Wrt('very',Color);
Normal;
Wrt('good idea.',Color);
```

Procedure Foreground(Code: char);
Procedure Background(Code: char);

FILE NAMES: FOREGRND.PAS   (120 code bytes)
                BACKGRND.PAS   (124 code bytes)

PURPOSE: These routines provide a convenient way of
                constructing the **Color** parameter for rou-
                tines in this collection that write on the dis-
                play, which assume that you have declared a
                global integer variable called **Color**. **Fore-
                ground** changes the bits in **Color** that set the
                foreground color of a character; **Background**
                does the same for background color. A char-
                acter code specifies the color. The code is the
                first letter of the name of the color, except for
                black, where the final letter ("k") distin-
                guishes it from blue. Uppercase letters set
                the color to intense image; lowercase letters
                make it normal image, as follows.

k	black	**K**	light black (grey)
b	blue	**B**	light blue
g	green	**G**	light green
c	cyan	**C**	light cyan
r	red	**R**	light red
m	magenta	**M**	light magenta
y	dark yellow (brown)	**Y**	yellow
w	white	**W**	bright white

                In normal use, uppercase letters turn blink-
                ing on when they are used as a background
                color. To select sixteen background colors in-
                stead, see the **ClearBlink** routine in Section 1
                of this chapter.

PARAMETERS: **Code** is a character code from the preceding
                table. The routines return without altering
                Color when the code doesn't match one of
                the sixteen letters.

NOTES:

1. The colors apply to a monochrome display as well. Use the following codes for the ten possible monochrome attributes:

	foreground	background
Normal	'w'	'k'
Intense	'W'	'k'
Normal underlined	'b'	'k'
Intense underlined	'B'	'k'
Reverse image	'k'	'w'
Blinking normal	'w'	'K'
Blinking intense	'W'	'K'
Blinking normal underlined	'b'	'K'
Blinking intense underlined	'B'	'K'
Blinking reverse image	'k'	'W'

Note there are many other combinations; it can be time-consuming to choose attributes that look good in both monochrome and color.

EXAMPLES:

The **Wrt** procedure (found in Section 4 of this chapter) is a memory-mapping version of the Pascal's **Write** command; it is given the attribute as a second parameter. To write light blue characters on a white background, you may either calculate the value of the attribute's bit pattern:

```
Wrt('Here is the string',121);
```

or you can use **Foreground** and **Background**:

```
Foreground('B');
Background('w');
Wrt('Here is the string',Color);
```

Note that there is no need to set both the foreground and background each time a change is made in **Color**. To write red on white and then green on white:

```
Background('w');
Foreground('r');
Wrt('This is red on white',Color);
Foreground('g');
Wrt('This is green on white',Color);
```

Function GetColor(Col,Row: integer): integer;
Procedure SetColor(Col,Row,Color: integer);

FILE NAMES:

GETCOLOR.PAS   (80 code bytes)
SETCOLOR.PAS   (78 code bytes)

PURPOSE:

SetColor changes the attribute at a single position on a text screen without affecting the character found there. *GetColor* reports the attribute of a specified screen position. Chapter 1 explains how to decode the value returned to learn the foreground and background colors. Both routines rely on the BIOS.

PARAMETERS:

Col and *Row* are the column and row positions from which the attribute is read. Columns are counted from 1 to 80 and rows from 1 to 25.

Color, the attribute to which the screen position is changed, is a number from 0 to 255, where 7 is "normal" white-on-black. *Color* may be a global variable set by routines also found in this section.

NOTES:

1. Making repeated calls to *SetColor* to change the attribute of large areas of the display is inadvisable. The combination of the inherent sluggishness of the BIOS routines (three BIOS calls per character) and the overhead of Turbo Pascal's stack operations would make this approach painfully slow. Use other routines found in this section instead.

2. Both routines check that the cursor position is in range and return without doing anything if it is not. *GetColor* returns zero when this error occurs. While zero could itself be a screen attribute, it is highly unlikely that it would be returned

under normal circumstances, since it causes nothing to be displayed at all (black-on-black).

EXAMPLES: To set column 5, row 3 to reverse image on a monochrome display (ASCII 112):

```
SetColor(5,3,112);
```

If you were then to check the attribute at this position:

```
Attribute := GetColor(5,3);
```

Attribute would equal 112. With the routines in Chapter 3, you can easily test the contents of particular bit fields within the bit pattern that 112 represents. For example, *IntegerField* retrieves the value of a specified number of bits taken from an integer; this value is itself returned as an integer. Since bit 7 is set when a value is blinking, you can test if the character at **5,3** is blinking by writing the following expression, where **7** sets the bit position and the following **1** tells how many bits to read:

```
if IntegerField(GetColor(5,3),7,1) = 1 then Blnk := TRUE;
```

Procedure RowColor(Col,Row,Width,Color: integer);
Procedure RowColorB(Col,Row,Width,Color: integer);
Procedure ColumnColor(Col,Row,Depth,Color: integer);
Procedure ColumnColorB(Col,Row,Depth,Color: integer);

FILE NAMES:

ROWCOLOR.PAS	(103 code bytes)
ROWCOLRB.PAS	(101 code bytes)
COLCOLOR.PAS	(107 code bytes)
COLCOLRB.PAS	(95 code bytes)

PURPOSE:

These routines change the attribute of one or more positions along a row or column of text. No change is made to what is written at those positions. Use the routines for highlighting or decorating parts of the screen and for creating bar cursors. **RowColor** and **ColumnColor** work by memory-mapping; **RowColorB** and **ColumnColorB** uses BIOS calls.

PARAMETERS:

Col and **Row** are the column and row at which the attribute change begins, extending downward. Columns are counted from 1 to 80 and rows from 1 to 25.

Width and **Depth** give the number of columns or rows in which the attribute is changed.

Color, the attribute in which characters are displayed, is a number from 0 to 255, where 7 is "normal" white-on-black. **Color** may be a global variable set by routines also found in this section.

VideoBuffer, a global integer variable required by **RowColor** and **ColumnColor**, holds the segment (memory location) of the video adaptor. This value is usually **$B000** for the monochrome card, **$B800** for the color graphics card, or either of these values for the EGA, depending on the screen mode. See the discussion in Chapter 1.

VideoPage, a global integer variable required by *RowColorB* and *ColumnColorB*, determines which video page the routine writes upon. The normal value is **0**. Chapter 1 gives details.

NOTES:

1. The routines return without doing anything when *Col*, *Row*, *Width*, or *Depth* are out of range. In the case of *RowColor* and *RowColorB*, when *Width* is too long to fit between the starting point and the edge of the display, the new attribute wraps around to the next line below. For *ColumnColor* and *ColumnColorB*, on the other hand, there is no wrap-around; no matter how large *Width* is, the attribute change ends on row 25.

EXAMPLES:

This example draws text across all 25 screen lines and then moves a bar cursor across them. It assumes a monochrome monitor and uses ASCII 112 for reverse image. The bar cursor is "erased" (before being redrawn at an adjacent row) by reapplying the routine using ASCII 7. First write some text using the *Display* procedure and *Intstrg* to convert the line number to string form:

```
for I := 1 to 25 do
  begin
    Display('Text line number'+Intstrg(I),10,I,7);
  end;
```

Now move a bar cursor down the screen:

```
for I := 1 to 15 do
  begin
    RowColor(1,I,80,112);
    Delay(600);
    RowColor(1,I,80,7);
  end;
```

Watch how ASCII 0 may be used to obscure text from view without erasing it:

```
for I := 1 to 15 do
  begin
    RowColor(1,I,80,112);
    Delay(600);
    RowColor(1,I,80,0);
  end;
```

To restore the text:

```
for I := 1 to 15 do
  begin
    RowColor(1,I,80,112);
    Delay(600);
    RowColor(1,I,80,7);
  end;
```

ColumnColor may be used to highlight vertically written strings (see the *WriteVertical* procedures in the next section). Screen graphics are another application. Here, *ColumnColor* divides a monochrome screen by underlining the spaces making up column 40:

```
ColumnColor(40,1,25,1);
```

Procedure BoxColor(Col,Row,Width,Depth,Color: integer);
Procedure BoxColorB(Col,Row,Width,Depth,Color: integer);

FILE NAMES: BXCOLOR.PAS   (152 code bytes)
               BXCOLORB.PAS   (114 code bytes)

PURPOSE: *BoxColor* and *BoxColorB* change the attribute of a rectangular area of the screen without altering the text written in that area. They are useful for highlighting areas of the screen. *BoxColor* is the memory-mapping version. *BoxColorB* uses the BIOS; for large boxes it is slow, but not unacceptably so.

PARAMETERS: *Col* and *Row* are the column and row position of the top left corner of the box. Columns are counted from 1 to 80, rows from 1 to 25.

Width is the number of columns in the horizontal dimension of the box.

Depth is the number of rows in the vertical dimension of the box.

Color is the attribute in which characters are displayed. It is a number from 0 to 255, where 7 is "normal" white-on-black. *Color* may be a global variable set by routines also found in this section.

VideoBuffer is a global integer variable required by *BoxColor*. It holds the segment (memory location) of the video adaptor, which is usually **$B000** for the monochrome card, **$B800** for the color graphics card, or either of these values for the EGA, depending on the screen mode. See the discussion in Chapter 1.

VideoPage is a global integer variable required by *BoxColorB*. It determines which video page the routine writes upon. The normal value is **0**. Chapter 1 gives details.

NOTES:

1. These routines can change the attributes of rectangular areas that are only one column wide or one row deep; thus, they can change the attribute of one character. In fact, they can do the work of several other routines in this section, but the flexibility comes at the cost of additional code space and speed.

2. The routines return without doing anything when **Row**, **Col**, **Width**, or **Depth** are out of range. They do not, however, check to see that there is room to accommodate the box between **Col** and **Row** and the screen edge. When **Width** and **Depth** are too large, the image wraps around in unpredictable ways.

3. One application of these routines is temporarily to obscure screen information from view. Simply use ASCII 0 as **Color**, or, on color displays, match the foreground and background colors. The characters disappear from view but remain in the video buffer. Return them to view by reapplying the routine with a "visible" attribute. Of course, the screen area must not be written upon while the characters are out of view, or they are erased. See the **SaveBox** and **RestoreBox** procedures in Chapter 7 to save an area of the screen, write over it, and then restore the original contents.

EXAMPLES:

On a monochrome display, this example uses reverse-image to highlight the 40-column-by-10-row area with its top-left corner at column 20, row 10. First, a box is drawn with **DrawBox** (Chapter 7) and labeled with

Display (Section 4 of this chapter). Then, between delays, the original attribute of the box is changed and restored.

```
DrawBox('D','D',20,10,40,10,7);
Display('This text is unchanged',14,16,7);
Delay(2000);
BoxColor(20,10,40,10,112);
Delay(2000);
BoxColor(20,10,40,10,7);
```

Or apply the routine twice to encircle an area of the screen in reverse image or in another color. First, change the attribute in a box as large as the encirclement. Then immediately rewrite a slightly smaller box in the center of the area with the original attribute. The temporary change of color at the center of the box is too quick to notice, particularly with the memory-mapping versions of these routines.

```
BoxColor(20,10,40,10,112);
BoxColor(22,11,36,8,7);
```

Section 4: Write strings

Turbo Pascal gives you the standard *Write* and *Writeln* procedures for writing data on the screen. They use the operating system (BIOS) to display each character, which makes them quite slow. Screen positions are set through the *GotoXY* command, and attributes are set with *Color* or related commands. Ornate formatted screens require a lot of code, and the results are less than snappy, particularly on a slower 8088 machine.

This section contains a wide selection of screen output choices. Many have built-in cursor and attribute control, letting one statement do the work of three. Most are given in memory-mapped and BIOS versions. The memory-mapped versions are extremely fast; the BIOS versions are much slower, but they still manage to perform at more than double Turbo Pascal's speed. All of these routines have the disadvantage that they can not write numeric values without first converting them to string form (conversions functions are given in Section 3 of Chapter 4). They also are limited to taking a single string argument—multiple strings must be joined by ' + ' signs rather than by commas, as in *Write* or *Writeln*.

First come *Display* and *DisplayB*, which simply write a string in a given color at a specified screen position. Next are *Wrt* and *Wrtln*, which behave exactly as Turbo Pascal's *Write* and *Writeln* procedures except that they write directly to the video buffer, and consequently operate many times faster. The string is written starting from the current cursor position, as set by *GotoXY*, and scrolling occurs when row 25 is filled. These routines may be substituted in an existing Turbo Pascal program to speed up screen operations. A second version of the routines, *Wrte* and *Wrteln*, uses the global variable *Color* to set character colors rather than repeatedly specify the color, as *Wrt* and *Wrtln* require.

Four routines perform relative cursor moves to let you easily format lists and tables. *FormatLeft* and *FormatLeftB* write a string in normal fashion and then move the cursor by a specified offset to the right or below the initial cursor location. *FormatRight* and *FormatRightB* do the same, but they write the strings leftward from the starting cursor position, right-justifying them.

Next come three pairs of routines that write strings in special ways. **WriteEnd** and *WriteEndB* write a string and then clear all remaining positions in a line. They make it easy to write one string over another without remnants of the prior string remaining at the end of the line. *WriteCenter* and *WriteCenterB* center a string between any two columns and clear all positions to the left and right. And *WriteVertical* and *WriteVerticalB* write a string vertically—something useful for labeling and decoration.

Finally, *Wrapln* and *WraplnB* automatically word-wrap a string as it is written between any two columns. They keep track of the current cursor position so that a series of strings may be effortlessly displayed. These procedures are ideal for handling short text objects or for creating dialog boxes (Chapter 4 provides *WrapString* for setting up large word-wrapped text arrays).

Procedure Display(Strg: stype; Col,Row,Color: integer);
Procedure DisplayB(Strg: stype; Col,Row,Color: integer);

FILE NAMES: DISPLAY.PAS   (155 code bytes)
                DISPLAYB.PAS   (99 code bytes)

PURPOSE: *Display* and *DisplayB* write strings on the
                screen. Unlike Pascal's *Write* and *Writeln*
                statements, these routines set the screen po-
                sition and attribute of the string. *Display*
                writes directly to the video buffer while *Dis-*
                playB uses the BIOS. Note that these state-
                ments lack the flexibility of the standard
                Pascal statements, since they accept only
                string arguments.

PARAMETERS: *Strg* is the string that is displayed.

                Col and *Row* are the column and row at
                which display begins. Columns are counted
                from 1 to 80 and rows from 1 to 25.

                Color, the attribute in which characters are
                displayed, is a number from 0 to 255, where
                7 is "normal" white-on-black. *Color* may be
                a global variable set by routines provided in
                Section 3.

                VideoBuffer, a global integer variable re-
                quired by *Display*, holds the segment (mem-
                ory location) of the video adaptor. This value
                is usually **$B000** for the monochrome card,
                $B800 for the color graphics card, or either of
                these values for the EGA, depending on the
                screen mode. See the discussion in Chapter
                1.

                VideoPage, a global integer variable required
                by both routines, determines which video
                page the routine writes on. The usual value
                is **0**. Chapter 1 gives details.

NOTES:

1. *Display* is extremely fast. With a 6-MHz PC AT and a monochrome adaptor, it can write a full screen of 80-character lines nearly forty times a second. *DisplayB* is limited in its performance by the inherent sluggishness of the BIOS. Still, it writes at about two-and-a-half times the rate of the combined Turbo Pascal *GotoXY* and *Write* commands.

2. These routines check that the screen coordinates are in range and return without writing anything if there has been an error.

3. Both routines leave the cursor at the screen position following the last character of the string. When the string ends at column 80, the cursor wraps to the next row. There is no upward scroll when the routines write at the bottom right corner of the display.

EXAMPLES:

To display a string at column 5, row 10, using reverse image on a monochrome display:

```
Display('Here is the string',5,10,112);
```

You may instead set the color using the global variable *Color* to set the attribute:

```
Reverse;  {changes the value in Color}
Display('Here is the string',5,10,Color);
```

To display numeric values, use the *IntStr* or *RealStr* functions found in Section 3 of Chapter 4.

```
NumKong := 13;
Display('He interviewed '+IntStr(NumKong)+' Gorillas.');
```

The result:

```
He interviewed 13 Gorillas
```

Procedure Wrt(Strg: stype; Color: integer);
Procedure WrtIn(Strg: stype; Color: integer);
Procedure Wrte(Strg: stype);
Procedure Wrteln(Strg: stype);

FILE NAMES:	WRT.PAS	(224 code bytes)
	WRTLN.PAS	(231 code bytes)
	WRTE.PAS	(241 code bytes)
	WRTELN.PAS	(252 code bytes)

PURPOSE:

Wrt and *WrtIn* display strings at the current cursor position, just as the Pascal **Write** and **Writeln** statements, but they *memory-map* the data rather than send it character by character through the BIOS. *Wrt* leaves the cursor at the column following the last character of the string, while *WrtIn* positions it at the first column of the next row. Both routines scroll the screen when output to the bottom of the screen requires it. *Wrte* and *Wrteln* are alternate versions in which the screen attribute is automatically taken from the global variable *Color* rather than set by a parameter.

PARAMETERS:

Strg is the string that is displayed.

Color, the attribute in which characters are displayed, is a number from 0 to 255, where 7 is "normal" white-on-black. For *Wrte* and *Wrteln*, *Color* must be a global variable set by routines provided in Section 3. The *Wrt* and *WrtIn* routines can use the global variable as an argument.

VideoBuffer, a global integer variable required by all four routines, holds the segment (memory location) of the video adaptor. This value is usually **$B000** for the monochrome card, **$B800** for the color graphics card, or either of these values for the EGA, depending on the screen mode. See the discussion in Chapter 1.

VideoPage, a global integer variable, determines which video page provides the cursor setting for the routines. The normal value is 0. *VideoPage* does *not* in itself set the page to which the string is written; *VideoBuffer* must be adjusted as well, as explained in Chapter 1.

NOTES:

1. Use these routines to retrofit existing Turbo Pascal programs so that screen operations become instantaneous. In some cases, you need only to include the two files and change every instance of **Write** to **Wrte**, and every instance of **Writeln** to **Wrteln**. But keep in mind that these routines accept only string arguments; numeric values must be converted to string form. Section 3 of Chapter 4 contains four functions (**IntStr**, **IntStrg**, **RealStr**, and **RealStrg**) that return numeric values as strings. Another limitation is that these routines display only one string at a time; they cannot take multiple arguments separated by commas.

2. Vacated lines are cleared in "normal" attribute (ASCII 7) when scrolling occurs.

3. These routines are very fast—they write roughly 850 80-character lines per second with a 6-MHz PC AT and a monochrome display (but only about one-tenth that when scrolling occurs). Hence, they operate at about fifty-five times the speed of the Turbo Pascal commands.

EXAMPLES:

To assemble a sentence from fragments, underlining one word:

```
GotoXY(1,5);
Wrt('A name like ',7);
Wrt('Algonquin',1);
Wrt(' is hard to live down.',7);
```

or, without the underline:

```
Name := 'Algonquin';
GotoXY(1,5);
Wrt('A name like '+Name+' is hard to live down.',7);
```

To use a numeric value:

```
Age := 150;
Wrtln('He must be at least '+IntStr(Age)+' years old.',7);
```

Use *Wrteln* to use the current value of *Color*
as the attribute:

```
IntenseOn;    {write in intense image}
Wrteln('He must be at least '+IntStr(Age)+' years old.');
```

Procedure FormatLeft(Strg: stype; Distance,Color: integer);
Procedure FormatLeftB(Strg: stype; Distance,Color: integer);
Procedure FormatRight(Strg: stype; Distance,Color: integer);
Procedure FormatRightB(Strg: stype; Distance,Color: integer);

FILE NAMES:

FORMLF.PAS	(162 code bytes)
FORMLFB.PAS	(116 code bytes)
FORMRT.PAS	(167 code bytes)
FORMRTB.PAS	(118 code bytes)

PURPOSE:
These four routines write a string starting from the current cursor position and then forward the cursor to a position that is a specified distance to the right of, or below, the starting position. This feature makes them ideal for formatting complicated lists and tables. *FormatLeft* and *FormatLeftB* write the string in normal fashion to the right of the initial cursor position. *FormatRight* and *FormatRightB* write the string to the left of the initial cursor position, leaving the final character at the starting position, right-justifying the string. *FormatLeft* and *FormatRight* write directly to the video buffer while *FormatLeftB* and *FormatRightB* use the BIOS.

PARAMETERS:
Strg is the string that is written.

Distance is the number of columns or rows between the starting cursor position and return cursor position. When *Distance* is a positive value, the cursor is offset to the right of the initial position. When it is a negative number, the cursor is moved to a position directly below its starting point.

Color, the attribute in which characters are displayed, is a number from 0 to 255, where 7 is "normal" white-on-black. *Color* may be a global variable set by routines provided in Section 3 of this chapter.

VideoBuffer, a global integer variable required by *FormatLeft* and *FormatRight*, holds the segment (memory location) of the video adaptor. This value is normally **$B000** for the monochrome card, **$B800** for the color graphics card, or either of these values for the EGA, depending on the screen mode. See the discussion in Chapter 1.

VideoPage is a global integer variable required by all four routines. It determines which video page the routine writes on; the normal value is **0**. Chapter 1 gives details.

NOTES:

1. If *Distance* attempts to forward the cursor beyond the edge of the screen, the cursor is left at column 80 or row 25; it does not wrap around.

2. Memory-mapping routines do not ordinarily require that *VideoPage* be set. Here, however, the page value is required to find the current cursor position.

3. These routines tend to force you to lay out data starting from the top left corner of the display. To move back to the top or left of the screen, use the relative cursor-move routines in Section 2 of this chapter.

EXAMPLES:

This example uses *FormatLeft* to write out a five-by-five table of numbers, converting them to string form with *IntStr* (found in Section 3 of Chapter 4). The numbers are written in intense image (ASCII 15) in ten-column fields.

```
for I := 1 to 5 do
  begin
    GotoXY(10,3+I);
    for J := 1 to 5 do
      begin
        FormatLeft(IntStr(Table[I,J]),10,15);
      end;
  end;
```

The result:

24	465	849584	365	879
12	35	499504	1254	98
367	344	84959	333	2233
77	2100	488859	2311	88
61	39	11456	998	430

When *FormatRight* is used instead:

24	465	849584	365	879
12	35	499504	1254	98
367	344	84959	333	2233
77	2100	488859	2311	88
61	39	11456	998	430

Here, *FormatLeft* writes out a menu, double-spacing the lines:

```
for I := 1 to MenuLines do
  begin
    FormatLeft(Menu[I],-2,7);
  end;
```

Procedure WriteEnd(Strg: stype; Col,Row,Length,Color: integer);
Procedure WriteEndB(Strg: stype; Col,Row,Length,Color: integer);

FILE NAMES: WRTEND.PAS   (150 code bytes)
                  WRTENDB.PAS   (130 code bytes)

PURPOSE: *WriteEnd* and *WriteEndB* write a string starting from a specified screen position and then clear characters following the string until a given line length is met. *WriteEnd* writes directly to the video buffer while *WriteEndB* uses the BIOS.

PARAMETERS: *Strg* is the string that is written.

Col and *Row* define the screen position at which the string is written. Rows are counted from 1 to 25, columns from 1 to 80.

Length is the line length—that is, the number of columns written upon or cleared.

Color, the attribute in which characters are displayed, is a number from 0 to 255, where 7 is "normal" white-on-black. *Color* may be a global variable set by routines in Section 3 of this chapter.

VideoBuffer, a global integer variable required by *WriteEnd*, holds the segment (memory location) of the video adaptor. This value is normally **$B000** for the monochrome card, **$B800** for the color graphics card, or either of these values for the EGA, depending on the screen mode. See the discussion in Chapter 1.

VideoPage is a global integer variable required by *WriteEndB*. It determines which video page the routine writes on; the normal value is **0**. Chapter 1 gives details.

NOTES: 1. These routines help expedite writing preformatted text strings of varying length. They save the time it takes to clear each line before writing. When the length of the string exceeds **Length**, it is written in its entirety, spilling over the right margin and possibly wrapping around to the next column.

2. When **Strg** is null, columns are cleared from the starting position to the point specified by **Length**. Hence, these procedures can clear lines.

EXAMPLE: This example writes a full screen of text on top of the same, automatically clearing fragments of prior strings.

```
for J := 1 to 25 do
  begin
    WriteEnd(Text[LinePtr + J],1,J,80,7);
  end;
```

Procedure WriteCenter(Strg:stype;Col,Row,Length,LnColor,StrgColor:integer);
Procedure WriteCenterB(Strg:stype;Col,Row,Length,LnColor,StrgColor:integer);

FILE NAMES: WRTCNTR.PAS   (175 code bytes)

                    WRTCNTRB.PAS   (157 code bytes)

PURPOSE: *WriteCenter* and *WriteCenterB* display a string, automatically centering it in the line starting at *Col* and *Row* and extending to *Length*. The positions surrounding the string are cleared. The attributes (colors) of the string and the surrounding cleared area are specified separately, allowing underlined titles, reverse-image labels, and so on. *WriteCenter* writes directly to video memory while *WriteCenterB* uses the BIOS services.

PARAMETERS: *Strg* is the string centered and displayed.

Col and *Row* are the column and row positions at which the string begins. Columns are counted from 1 to 80, rows from 1 to 25.

Length is the number of columns written upon, in which the string is centered and the remaining positions are cleared.

LnColor and *StrgColor* are the attributes in which the string and fill characters are displayed, respectively. They are numbers from 0 to 255, where 7 is "normal" white-on-black. Either value (or both) may be a global variable set by routines provided in Section 3 of this chapter.

VideoBuffer, a global integer variable required by *WriteCenter*, holds the segment (memory location) of the video adaptor. This value is usually **$B000** for the monochrome card, **$B800** for the color graphics card, or either of these values for the EGA, depending on the screen mode. See the discussion in Chapter 1.

VideoPage is a global integer variable required by *WriteCenterB*; it determines which video page the routine writes upon. The normal value is **0**. Chapter 1 gives details.

NOTES:

1. By clearing outward to the boundary columns, these routines effectively erase the line before writing to it, although each screen position is written upon only once.

2. Nothing is written when *Col* or *Row* are out of range, or when *Length* is greater than 80. The entirety of *Strg* is displayed when *Length* is less than the length of *Strg*. When *Strg* is null, the entire area set by *Length* is cleared.

3. When *Length* minus the length of *Strg* is an odd number, the extra fill character appears on the left of the string.

EXAMPLE:

This example writes "Title" midway between the left edge of the screen and column 40. The word "Title" is underlined (using ASCII 1), and the surrounding columns from 1 to 40 are cleared in normal attribute (ASCII 7).

```
WriteCenter('Title',1,1,40,7,1);
```

Procedure WriteRight(Strg: stype; Col,Row,Color: integer);
Procedure WriteRightB(Strg: stype; Col,Row,Color: integer);

FILE NAMES: WRTRGHT.PAS   (120 code bytes)
                 WRTRGHTB.PAS   (106 code bytes)

PURPOSE: *WriteRight* and *WriteRightB* write a string justified against a specified column and row position. For example, if the column and row are **70,5**, the string is written to the left so that its last character falls at **70,5**. *WriteRight* writes directly to video memory, while *WriteRightB* uses the BIOS.

PARAMETERS: *Strg* is the string that is displayed.

                 Col and *Row* define the screen position at which the last character of the string is written. Rows are counted from 1 to 25, columns from 1 to 80.

                 Color, the attribute in which characters are displayed, is a number from 0 to 255, where 7 is "normal" white-on-black. *Color* may be a global variable set by routines provided in Section 3 of this chapter.

                 VideoBuffer, a global integer variable required by *WriteRight*, holds the segment (memory location) of the video adaptor. This value is usually **$B000** for the monochrome card, **$B800** for the color graphics card, or either of these values for the EGA, depending on the screen mode. See the discussion in Chapter 1.

                 VideoPage, a global integer variable required by *WriteRightB*, determines which video page the routine writes upon. The usual value is **0**. Chapter 1 gives details.

NOTES: 1. When *Strg* is longer than the number of columns between *Col* and the left edge of the screen, characters from the string are omitted. The string does not wrap around to the row above.

EXAMPLE: This example displays five strings, each of a different length, justifying them against column 60:

```
Line[1] := 'This routine';
Line[2] := 'is much more convenient';
Line[3] := 'than';
Line[4] := 'fooling around with';
Line[5] := 'GOTOXY and LENGTH instructions';
Row := 7;
for I := 1 to 5 do
   begin
     WriteRight(Line[I],60,Row+I,7);
   end;
```

The result:

```
                             This routine
                   is much more convenient
                                      than
                       fooling around with
            GOTOXY and LENGTH instructions
```

Procedure WriteVertical(Strg: stype; Col,Row,Color: integer);
Procedure WriteVerticalB(Strg: stype; Col,Row,Color: integer);

FILE NAMES:

WRTVERT.PAS   (131 code bytes)
WRTVERTB.PAS   (99 code bytes)

PURPOSE:

WriteVertical and *WriteVerticalB* write a string vertically on the screen. Vertical strings are useful as labels, dividers, and decorations. *WriteVertical* directly writes to video memory, while *WriteVerticalB* uses the BIOS services.

PARAMETERS:

Strg is the string written vertically.

Col and *Row* are the column and row positions at which the string begins. The string is written downward from this point. Columns are counted from 1 to 80, rows from 1 to 25.

Color, the attribute in which characters are displayed, is a number from 0 to 255, where 7 is "normal" white-on-black. *Color* may be a global variable set by routines provided in Section 3 of this chapter.

VideoBuffer is a global integer variable required by *WriteVertical*. It holds the segment (memory location) of the video adaptor. This value is usually **$B000** for the monochrome card, **$B800** for the color graphics card, or either of these values for the EGA, depending on the screen mode. See the discussion in Chapter 1.

VideoPage, a global integer variable required by *WriteVerticalB*, determines which video page the routine writes upon. The normal value is **0**. Chapter 1 gives details.

NOTES:

1. The string wraps around to a nonadjacent column on the screen when is it overlong. BIOS becomes confused about the current

cursor position when this occurs with *WriteVerticalB*.

2. *WriteVerticalB* leaves the cursor at the bottommost character of the string. *WriteVertical* doesn't affect the cursor.

EXAMPLES: Labels on a monochrome display often look best written in reverse image (112). Here the top-left edge of the screen is labeled "ERRORS":

```
WriteVertical(' ERRORS ',1,3,112);
```

This example divides the screen down the middle with a zigzag line:

```
WriteVertical('/\/\/\/\/\/\/\/\/\/\/\/\/',40,1,7);
```

Procedure Wrapln(Strg: stype; var Col,Row: integer; Left,Right,Color: integer);
Procedure WraplnB(Strg: stype; var Col,Row: integer; Left,Right,Color: integer);

FILE NAMES: WRAPLN.PAS   (345 code bytes)
               WRAPLNB.PAS   (329 code bytes)

PURPOSE: *Wrapln* and *WraplnB* automatically word-wrap strings as they write them between two specified columns. *Wrapln* directly memory-maps the output, while *WraplnB* uses the BIOS services. The routines write one string each time they are called. Writing begins from the current setting of *Col* and *Row*, and once the string is written, the routines change *Col* and *Row* so that these variables point to the screen position following the last character written. Hence, only an initial setting for *Col* and *Row* is made, and then a series of strings may be output. The routines stop writing when they reach the final column on row 25; thereafter they do nothing until *Col* and *Row* are reset.

PARAMETERS: *Strg* is the string that is written.

    Col and *Row* are variables that hold the current screen position from which writing begins. **Col** is counted from 1 to 80, **Row** from 1 to 25.

    Left and *Right* are the columns forming the left and right boundaries of the area in which the strings are written. The columns are included in this area; they are counted from 1 to 80.

    Color, the attribute in which characters are displayed, is a number from 0 to 255, where 7 is "normal" white-on-black. *Color* may be a global variable set by routines provided in Section 3 of this chapter.

VideoBuffer, a global integer variable required by *Wrapln*, holds the segment (memory location) of the video adaptor. This value is usually **$B000** for the monochrome card, **$B800** for the color graphics card, or either of these values for the EGA, depending on the screen mode. See the discussion in Chapter 1.

VideoPage, a global integer variable required by *WraplnB*, determines which video page the routine writes upon. The usual value is 0. Chapter 1 gives details.

NOTES:

1. These routines are not intended for word-wrapping large text files. They are most useful for writing messages in dialogue boxes and the like or for filling the screen with small segments of text that don't require scrolling, such as in card-file programs. If you want to set up a large text file for bidirectional scrolling, refer to the *WrapString* function in Section 4 of Chapter 4. This routine can reformat a text array into a word-wrapped array. Section 2 of Chapter 7 contains a vertical scrolling procedure.

2. The routines clear to the end of the line—that is, they clear all characters from the last word they write on a line up to (and including) the position set by *Right*. This means that you don't need to clear the area of the screen written on so long as the new output covers as many rows as the prior output. Use the *CharBox* procedure in Section 1 of Chapter 7 to clear a rectangular area of the screen.

3. The routines check that *Col*, *Row*, *Left*, and *Right* are in range, and they return without writing anything when there is an error. This is also the case when *Left* is greater than *Right*, or when *Strg* is null.

4. The routines handle "words" longer than the distance between *Left* and *Right* by breaking them into two or more lines.

5. Spaces that would fall at the beginning of a line are eliminated so that all lines will be flush with the left margin. This rule does not apply, however, when there are more than three spaces in a row. As a result, you can create indentations at the start of paragraphs by outputting a string of at least three characters.

6. The routines don't interpret tabs, carriage returns, line feeds, or any other control characters. Instead, they print the associated ASCII symbols. Use the routines in Chapter 4 to ferret out special characters in the text. Carriage returns and line feeds may be accommodated by finding the codes, eliminating them, and adjusting *Col* and *Row* to new starting positions.

EXAMPLES:

This example writes a series of five strings from a text array, word-wrapping them between columns 20 and 60, beginning from row 5. The strings are written in "normal" attribute (ASCII 7).

```
Col := 20;
Row := 5;
for I := 1 to 5 do
  begin
    Wrapln(Text[I],Col,Row,20,60,7);
  end;
```

To indent the first line by five characters:

```
Col := 20;
Row := 5;
Wrapln('       ',Col,Row,20,60,7);
for I := 1 to 5 do
  begin
    Wrapln(Text[I],Col,Row,20,60,7);
  end;
```

7

Text Graphics

Section 1: Draw text graphics

The *Turbo Graphix Toolbox* gives Turbo Pascal tremendous facility in dot-addressable graphics. But the fact remains that most computers have no dot graphics capability. Since most programs are character-oriented, they tend to be bland to look at. This chapter describes a number of text-oriented graphics routines. For the most part, what they do is simple. But with imagination, they can be combined to create striking visual effects with little code overhead.

Turbo Pascal provides the standard **Write** and **Writeln** commands for writing on the screen. These use the operating system functions (BIOS), making them far too slow for character-oriented animation. Another limitation is that either command causes the display to scroll upward when it writes at the bottom right corner, making full-screen graphics impossible. The solution to these limitations is "memory-mapping"—using the **Mem[]** or **MemW[]** statements to write directly to the video buffer; memory-mapping is discussed in Chapter 1. Because of the considerable overhead that accompanies repeated calls to **Mem**, even direct memory-mapping is unacceptably slow in many applications.

The routines found here overcome these problems—they are both fast and flexible. As in the prior chapter, most come in both memory-mapped and BIOS versions. The latter are intended for those who are concerned about upward compatability with new hardware and operating environments. The BIOS versions are written in a way that makes them significantly faster than when the same service is performed through *Write* or *Writeln*. The memory-mapped versions are virtually instantaneous.

The first section of this chapter contains routines that draw lines and boxes. *DrawBox* draws boxes with block characters, and *HorizontalLine* and *VerticalLine* draw lines within the boxes, automatically inserting the correct block characters at their end-points and at intersections with other lines. These routines let you effortlessly draw and edit complicated screens. *CharLine* and *CharBox* draw lines or solid rectangles of a single character. When that character is a space, these procedures can clear selected areas of the display. Note that routines in Section 3 of Chapter 6 let you change underlying screen attributes (colors) of rows, columns, and rectangles without altering the text. Finally, *StringLine* creates horizontal or vertical lines made up of the repetition of a string. Placed in a loop, this routine can fill the entire screen with a decorative backdrop.

Procedure DrawBox(HrzChar,VrtChar:char;TopX,TopY,Width,Depth,Color:integer);
Procedure DrawBoxB(HrzChar,VrtChar:char;TopX,TopY,Width,Depth,Color:integer);

FILE NAMES: DRAWBOX.PAS   (293 code bytes)
               DRAWBOXB.PAS   (296 code bytes)

PURPOSE: *DrawBox* and *DrawBoxB* draw a rectangle on the screen using the single- and double-line block characters (ASCII 179-218). *DrawBox* directly maps the routines into the video buffer, whereas *DrawBoxB* uses the BIOS facilities. The verticals and horizontals are independently set for single- or double-line characters, making four box designs possible.

PARAMETERS: *HrzChar* and *VrtChar*, respectively, determine whether the verticals and horizontals are drawn using single- or double-line block characters. The characters "**D**" and "**d**" specify double lines. "**S**" or "**s**" should be used for single lines, although any character other than "**D**" and "**d**" results in single lines.

TopX and *TopY* are the column and row positions of the top left corner of the box. Columns are counted from 1 to 80, rows from 1 to 25.

Width gives the horizontal dimension of the box, measured in columns.

Depth gives the vertical dimension of the box, measured in rows.

Color, the attribute in which characters are displayed, is a number from 0 to 255, where 7 is "normal" white-on-black. *Color* may be a global variable set by routines in Chapter 6.

VideoBuffer, a global integer variable required by *DrawBox*, holds the segment (memory location) of the video adaptor. This value is normally **$B000** for the monochrome card, **$B800** for the color graphics card, or either of these values for the EGA, depending on the screen mode. See the discussion in Chapter 1.

VideoPage, a global integer variable required by *DrawBoxB*, determines which video page the routine writes upon. The usual value is 0. Chapter 1 gives details.

NOTES:

1. Both routines check that the screen coordinates are in range. When the values for *Width* or *Depth* are less than 2, the routines quit with a partial box displayed. When these values are too large, no error recovery is made; a haphazard design is displayed but the machine won't crash.

2. The area inside the box is unaffected. To fill the box with a reverse-image background, use *CharBox* to clear the area and set a new attribute or use *BoxColor* to change only the attribute bytes.

3. The next group of routines in this section draw vertical and horizontal lines within boxes. They automatically place the correct block characters at points where they meet the box edges or where they intersect other lines.

EXAMPLES:

This example draws a 40-column by 12-row box with its top-left corner at column 20, row 5. The horizontals are double lines and the verticals are single lines. The attribute (7) is "normal."

```
DrawBox('D','S',20,5,40,12,7);
```

You can build a more attractive box by placing a normal-image, double-line box immediately inside an intense-image, single-line
box. Leave an extra column between the verticals, as in this example:

```
DrawBox('S','S',20,5,40,12,15);
DrawBox('D','D',22,6,36,10,7);
```

Also consider using **DrawBox** to build three-
dimensional images. In this example, seven
boxes are drawn, each overlapping the prior
box and each somewhat larger, creating the
illusion of an approaching column of boxes.
Hidden lines are removed by using *CharBox*
to clear the interior of each box after it is
drawn. Note that **DrawBoxB** and **CharBoxB**
function too slowly for this example to work
well.

```
for I := 1 to 7 do
  begin
DrawBox('D','D',I*3,I,30+I,10+I,7);
    CharBox(' ',I*3+1,I+1,28+I,8+I,7);
  end;
GotoXY(31,15);
Write('Here is a message');
```

Procedure HorizontalLine(HrzChar:char;LeftCol,LeftRow,Width:integer);
Procedure HorizontalLineB(HrzChar:char;LeftCol,LeftRow,Width:integer);

Procedure VerticalLine(VrtChar:char;TopCol,TopRow,Depth:integer);
Procedure VerticalLineB(VrtChar:char;TopCol,TopRow,Depth:integer);

FILE NAMES:	HRZLINE.PAS	(282 code bytes)
	HRZLINEB.PAS	(217 code bytes)
	VRTLINE.PAS	(291 code bytes)
	VRTLINEB.PAS	(219 code bytes)

PURPOSE: These two pairs of procedures draw horizontal and vertical lines, respectively, using the single- and double-line block characters (ASCII 179-218). **HorizontalLine** and **VerticalLine** memory-map the characters, while **HorizontalLineB** and **VerticalLineB** use the BIOS facilities. The routines automatically fill in the appropriate characters at the endpoints of the line; they also insert cross characters when the line intersects a perpendicular block character. A line should begin and end at perpendiculars, although these need not be at the side of a box. Horizontal lines are drawn to the right from the starting point, and vertical lines are drawn down. The attribute found at the starting point is used for the entire line.

PARAMETERS: **HrzChar** and **VrtChar** specify whether the lines are drawn in single- or double-line block characters. "**D**" and "**d**" set double-line characters. "**S**" and "**s**" should be used for single-line characters, although any character other than "**D**" or "**d**" results in single lines.

LeftCol or **TopCol** set the column position of the starting point, counting from 1 to 80.

LeftRow or *TopRow* set the row position of the starting point, counting from 1 to 25.

Width or *Depth* are the length of the line in characters. The smallest value allowed is **2**, in which case only two end-characters are drawn, with no straight segments between.

VideoBuffer, a global integer variable required by *HorizontalLine* and *VerticalLine*, holds the segment (memory location) of the video adaptor. This value is usually **$B000** for the monochrome card, **$B800** for the color graphics card, or either of these values for the EGA, depending on the screen mode. See the discussion in Chapter 1.

VideoPage, a global integer variable required by *HorizontalLineB* and *VerticalLineB*, determines which video page the routine writes upon. The normal value is **0**. Chapter 1 gives details.

NOTES:

1. The procedures check for a double-line perpendicular at the starting point and any other character is interpreted as a single-line perpendicular. When no perpendicular is found at the other end of the line, a straight segment is drawn.

2. Since the routines check the perpendiculars at *both* ends of the line, a line may begin from a double-line perpendicular and end at a single-line perpendicular, or the reverse.

3. The routines check that the starting position is a valid screen coordinate. There is no error-check on the width or depth of the lines. Overlarge values make a mess of the screen, but the machine won't crash.

4. Use **CharLine** to draw just a simple dividing line across the screen with a single
character. **StringLine**, which does the
same, builds the line by writing repeatedly a string instead of one character.

EXAMPLE:

This example sets up a form for a calendar. A
large box is drawn and divided into five rows
of seven columns. All horizontal lines are
single, and all verticals are double. **DrawBox**
draws the 21-row-by-77-column box starting
from the top left corner of the screen:

```
DrawBox('S','D',1,1,77,21,7);
```

Next, the three horizontals are drawn:

```
J := 5
while J < 21 do
  begin
    HorizontalLine('S',1,J,77);
    J := J + 4;
  end;
```

Finally, the verticals:

```
J := 11;
while J < 77 do
  begin
    VerticalLine('D',J,1,21);
    J := J + 11;
  end;
```

Procedure CharLine(Ch,Dir: char; Col,Row,Length,Color: integer);
Procedure CharLineB(Ch,Dir: char; Col,Row,Length,Color: integer);

FILE NAMES:	CHRLINE.PAS	(128 code bytes)
	CHRLINEB.PAS	(121 code bytes)

PURPOSE: *CharLine* and *CharLineB* display horizontal or vertical lines made up of a single character. The line is cleared when the character is a space. These procedures are useful for drawing dividing lines using block-graphic characters. *CharLine* writes directly to video memory; *CharLineB* uses the BIOS services.

PARAMETERS: *Ch* is the character used in the string.

Dir flags the direction of the line. When it is "V" or "v" the line is vertical and is drawn downward from the coordinate set by *Col* and *Row*. Horizontal lines should be signaled by "H" or "h," although any character other than "V" or "v" results in horizontal lines, which are drawn to the right from the specified coordinate.

Col and *Row* are the column and row positions at which the line begins. The line is written to the left or downward from this point. Columns are counted from 1 to 80 and rows from 1 to 25.

Length is the length of the line in columns or rows.

Color, the attribute in which characters are displayed, is a number from 0 to 255, where 7 is "normal" white-on-black. *Color* may be a global variable set by routines provided in Chapter 6.

VideoBuffer, a global integer variable required by *CharLine*, holds the segment (memory location) of the video adaptor. This value is normally **$B000** for the monochrome card, **$B800** for the color graphics card, or either of these values for the EGA, depending on the screen mode. See the discussion in Chapter 1.

VideoPage is a global integer variable required by *CharLineB*. It determines which video page the routine writes upon. The normal value is **0**. Chapter 1 gives details.

NOTES:

1. The routines check that the column and row are in range. There is no checking on the line length. Overlong horizontal strings wrap around to the next line in both the memory-mapping and BIOS versions, and a very large value fills the whole screen. Do not, however, use *CharLine* to fill large screen areas when a color graphics adaptor is in use, since snow appears on the display; use *CharBox* instead. When a vertical line is overlarge, the wrap occurs at nonadjacent columns.

2. The BIOS routine is faster than most when it draws horizontal lines, because only one function call draws the whole string. Still, the memory-mapping routine is about five times faster.

3. *CharLineB* leaves the cursor at the first character of the string when it writes horizontally or at the last character of the string when it writes vertically. *CharLine* doesn't affect the cursor position.

EXAMPLES:

To draw a simple dividing line across the middle of the screen:

```
CharLine(chr(196),'H',1,13,80,7);
```

This line draws the equivalent vertical line in intense-image:

```
CharLine(chr(179),'V',40,1,25,15);
```

This loop draws a large diamond made up of diamond characters (ASCII 4):

```
for I := 0 to 12 do
  begin
CharLine(Chr(4),'H',40-I*2,I+1,I*4+1,7);
    CharLine(Chr(4),'H',40-I*2,25-I,I*4+1,7);
  end;
```

Procedure StringLine(Strg: stype; Dir: char; Col,Row,Length,Color: integer);
Procedure StringLineB(Strg: stype; Dir: char; Col,Row,Length,Color: integer);

FILE NAMES:	STRLINE.PAS	(152 code bytes)
	STRLINEB.PAS	(136 code bytes)

PURPOSE: *StringLine* and *StringLineB* display a horizontal or vertical line made up of the repetition of a string. For example, if the input string is **––END**, when a twelve-character line is drawn, it will be **––END––END––**. Besides drawing dividing lines on the screen, these procedures can create decorative patterns. *StringLine* writes directly to video memory; *StringLineB* uses the BIOS services.

PARAMETERS: *Strg* is the string repeated within the line. When the line length isn't an even multiple of the string length, part of the string is used at the end of the line.

Dir flags the direction of the line. When it is "V" or "v" the line is vertical and is drawn downward from the coordinate set by *Col* and *Row*. Horizontal lines should be signaled by "H" or "h," although any character other than "V" or "v" results in horizontal lines, which are drawn to the right from the specified coordinate.

Col and *Row* are the column and row positions at which the string begins. From this point, the string is written downward or to the right. Columns are counted from 1 to 80, rows from 1 to 25.

Length is the number of rows or columns occupied by the string.

Color, the attribute in which characters are displayed, is a number from 0 to 255, where 7 is "normal" white-on-black. *Color* may be a global variable that is set by routines provided in Chapter 6.

VideoBuffer, a global integer variable required by *StringLine*, holds the segment (memory location) of the video adaptor. This value is usually **$B000** for the monochrome card, **$B800** for the color graphics card, or either of these values for the EGA, depending on the screen mode. See the discussion in Chapter 1.

VideoPage, a global integer variable required by *StringLineB*, determines which video page the routine writes upon. The normal value is **0**. Chapter 1 gives details.

NOTES:

1. The routines check that the column and row are in range. There is no checking on the line length. Overlong horizontal lines wrap around to the next row in both the memory-mapping and BIOS versions, and a very large value fills the whole screen. Do not, however, use **StringLine** to fill large screen areas when a color graphics adaptor is in use, since snow occurs on the display; use **CharBox** instead. When a vertical line is overlong, the wrap occurs at nonadjacent columns.

2. *StringLineB* leaves the cursor at the last character of the line when it writes either horizontally or vertically. *StringLine* doesn't affect the cursor position.

EXAMPLES:

This example draws a zigzagged vertical divider:

```
StringLine('/\','V',40,1,25,7);
```

Use a loop to fill the entire screen with a backdrop of repeated characters. Here, diamonds (ASCII 4) are distributed at every tenth column on even-numbered rows, with alternating rows offset by five columns. The string consists of the diamond character followed by nine spaces.

```
J := 0;
for I := 1 to 12 do
  begin
    StringLine(chr(4)+'         ','H',J+1,I*2,74,7);
    if J = 0 then J := 5 else J := 0;
  end;
```

Procedure CharBox(Ch: char; Col,Row,Width,Depth,Color: integer);
Procedure CharBoxB(Ch: char; Col,Row,Width,Depth,Color: integer);

FILE NAMES:	CHARBOX.PAS	(148 code bytes)
	CHARBOXB.PAS	(104 code bytes)

PURPOSE: *CharBox* and *CharBoxB* fill a rectangular area of the screen with a specified character. The area is cleared when the fill character is a space.

PARAMETERS: *Ch* is the character used in the box.

Col and *Row* are the column and row positions of the top left corner of the box. Columns are counted from 1 to 80 and rows from 1 to 25.

Width is the number of columns the box occupies.

Depth is the number of rows the box occupies.

Color, the attribute in which characters are displayed, is a number from 0 to 255, where 7 is "normal" white-on-black. *Color* may be a global variable set by routines provided in Chapter 6.

VideoBuffer, a global integer variable required by *CharBox*, holds the segment (memory location) of the video adaptor. This value is normally **$B000** for the monochrome card, **$B800** for the color graphics card, or either of these values for the EGA, depending on the screen mode. See the discussion in Chapter 1.

VideoPage, a global integer variable required by *CharBoxB*, determines which video page the routine writes upon. The normal value is 0. Chapter 1 gives details.

NOTES: 1. The width or depth may be **1**, in which
                case a portion of a single row or column is
                filled.

EXAMPLES: To erase the left half of the screen:

```
CharBox(' ',1,1,40,25,7);
```

This line creates a decorative pattern across
the center of the screen using superimposed
boxes written in different fill characters:

```
Row := 11;
Col := 1;
Ch  := chr(176);
For I := 1 to 38 do
  begin
    CharBox(Ch,Col,Row,3,2,7);
    If Ch = chr(176) then
      begin
        Ch := chr(177);
        Row := 12;
      end else
      begin
        Ch := chr(176);
        Row := 11;
      end;
    Col := Col+2;
  end;
```

Section 2: Scroll and page

Turbo Pascal supports primitive vertical scrolling. *InsLine* inserts an empty line at the cursor position and scrolls everything below downward. *DelLine* deletes a line and pulls everything below upward, clearing the bottom line. These procedures operate on the whole screen. But you can use the *Window* statement to define a window that, for example, doesn't contain the bottom line of the screen; then only the top twenty-four rows scroll. The *ScrollVert* and *ScrollHorz* routines in this section are much more flexible. They not only scroll a window of any size, but also you can specify the attribute for cleared lines and the number of lines to scroll. The routines also can clear any window.

Scrolling is associated with text processing, but scrolling is also useful for text-oriented animation. You can easily draw a box at the left of the screen and zip it over to the right by defining a horizontal scroll area the height of the box and the width of the screen. Similarly, you can jiggle or bounce text objects or even break them in two. Usually, the best way to approach this sort of animation is always to scroll by one row or two columns, which are about the same distance. Place the scroll routines within loops and make a single shift followed by a delay to control the timing (use the Turbo *Delay* procedure).

Paging keeps multiple screen images in memory at the same time. In 80-column modes, the color graphics adaptor supports four pages of color or black-and-white text (numbered 0–3), and the EGA allows eight (0–7). The monochrome adaptor has but one page (number 0). Turbo's *Write* and *Writeln* statements always write on page 0, which is always the one displayed. However, any of the routines in this chapter and Chapter 6 can write on any page (Chapter 1 tells how), and the *SetPage* procedure lets you display any page you choose. So you can easily create screens "backstage" and then instantly bring them to view. *ClearPage* clears pages other than the one currently in view. And *PageSwap* swaps the contents of a page and a 4000-byte buffer that you set up in memory. This routine effectively lets you add paging to the monochrome card.

Procedure ScrollVert(Dir: char; TopX,TopY,Width,Depth,Lines,Color: integer);

FILE NAME: SCRLVERT.PAS   (63 code bytes)

PURPOSE: *ScrollVert* scrolls a defined area of the screen either up or down. The area scrolled away from is cleared in the specified attribute. The entire scroll area is cleared when the number of lines to scroll is set to 0.

PARAMETERS: *Dir* flags the direction. When it is "D" or "d" the scroll is made downwards. "U" or "u" should be used to indicate an upward scroll, but it results from any value other than "D" or "d."

TopX and *TopY* are the column and row positions of the top left corner of the scroll area. Columns are counted from 1 to 80 and rows from 1 to 25.

Width is the number of columns in the scroll area.

Depth is the number of rows in the scroll area.

Lines is the number of rows each line is shifted. The scroll is made by this many rows in one jump, not as a succession of single-line shifts.

Color, the attribute used to clear empty rows, is a number from 0 to 255, where 7 is "normal" white-on-black. *Color* may be a global variable set by routines provided in Chapter 6.

NOTES: 1. *ScrollVert* uses a BIOS function to make the scroll. Most screen output performed through the BIOS is slow because a procedure call is made for each character, and a good deal of housekeeping is performed each time. The scroll operation, however, can shift all 2000 screen positions by just one function call—it's very fast.

2. The global *VideoPage* variable is not required for this routine. It always scrolls page 0.

EXAMPLES:

This line scrolls the top twenty-four rows up by three lines, clearing the bottom three rows in "normal" attribute (ASCII 7):

```
ScrollVert('U',1,1,80,24,3,7);
```

The next example exchanges the contents of the top and bottom halves of the screen. First, **DrawBox** draws two boxes and labels them. Then the *SaveBox* procedure saves the contents of rows 1 through 12. After a delay, *ScrollVert* rolls the entire screen up by twelve lines. Finally, *RestoreBox* rewrites the saved image at the bottom of the display. (*SaveBox* and *RestoreBox* are found in Section 3 of this chapter.)

```
DrawBox('S','S',20,1,40,12,15);
GotoXY(38,7);Write('BOX 1');
DrawBox('D','D',1,13,80,12,7);
GotoXY(38,19);Write('BOX 2');
Delay(2000);
SaveBox(BoxCopy,1,1,80,12);
ScrollVert('U',1,1,80,24,12,7);
RestoreBox(BoxCopy,1,13,80,12);
```

Procedure ScrollHorz(Dir: char; TopX,TopY,Width,Depth,Cols,Color: integer);

FILE NAME: SCRLHORZ.PAS   (201 code bytes)

PURPOSE: *ScrollHorz* scrolls a defined area of the screen to either the right or left. The area that is scrolled away from is cleared in the specified attribute. The entire scroll area is cleared when the number of lines to scroll is set to 0.

PARAMETERS: *Dir* flags the direction. When it is "**L**" or "**l**," the scroll is made to the left. "**R**" or "**r**" should indicate a scroll to the right, but any value other than "L" or "l" produces this result.

TopX and *TopY* are the column and row positions of the top left corner of the scroll area. Columns are counted from 1 to 80 and rows from 1 to 25.

Width is the number of columns in the scroll area.

Depth is the number of rows in the scroll area.

Cols is the number of columns each line is shifted. The scroll is made by this many columns in one jump and not as a succession of single-column shifts.

Color, the attribute used to clear emptied columns, is a number from 0 to 255, where 7 is "normal" white-on-black. *Color* may be a global variable set by routines provided in Chapter 6.

VideoBuffer, a global integer variable, holds the segment (memory location) of the video adaptor. This value is normally **$B000** for the monochrome card, **$B800** for the color graphics card, or either of these values for the EGA, depending on the screen mode. See the discussion in Chapter 1.

NOTES:

1. Unlike **ScrollVert**, **ScrollHorz** doesn't use a BIOS routine (none is available). It operates by direct memory-mapping. No version is given here that uses character-by-character BIOS calls because it would be too slow.

2. Like the BIOS vertical scrolling routine, **ScrollHorz** clears the screen (or portion thereof) when **Cols** is zero. The scroll area is also cleared when **Cols** is greater than **Width**.

3. The routine checks that the row and column are in range. Odd things happen on the screen when inappropriate values are given for **Width** and **Depth**, but the machine won't crash.

EXAMPLE:

This example scrolls the entire display five columns to the left. Then it fills in the right edge of the screen, writing the eighty-first through eighty-fifth characters (if they exist) of 25 lines from a text array.

```
ScrollHorz('L',1,1,80,25,5,7);
For I := 0 to 24 do
   begin
     LineLen := Length(TextLines[LnPtr+I]);
     if LineLen > 80 then
        begin
          GotoXY(76,I+1);
          Num := LineLen - 80;
          if Num > 5 then Num := 5;
          Write(Copy(TextLines[LnPtr+I],81,Num));
        end;
   end;
```

Procedure ClearPage(PageNumber,Color: integer);

FILE NAME: CLRPAGE.PAS   (35 code bytes)

PURPOSE: *ClearPage* clears a page of video memory. A program may then write on the page and switch it into view. The screen is cleared when this procedure is applied to the *current page*.

PARAMETERS: *PageNumber*, the number of the 80-column page that will be cleared, is from 0 to 3 on the color graphics adaptor, and from 0 to 7 on the enhanced graphics adaptor in either color or monochrome modes. *PageNumber* may be used to clear the page that is currently displayed; that is, it can clear the screen.

Color, the attribute in which the page is cleared, is a number from 0 to 255, where 7 is "normal" white-on-black. *Color* may be a global variable set by routines provided in Chapter 6.

NOTES: 1. This routine assumes an 80-column page. The monochrome card has only one page. There is no reason to use this routine with it, although no harm would result.

2. The routine leaves the cursor at the top-left corner of the page. (Every page has its own cursor pointer. Use *Locate*—found in Chapter 6—to set the cursor on any other page.)

3. The *SetPage* and *GetPage* routines in Section 1 of Chapter 6 let you switch the display to a different page or find out which page is currently selected.

EXAMPLES: This example uses two other routines found in this book—*DrawBox* and *Wrt*—to write a message on an off-screen page. The page is number 1, and its buffer address is **$B900**. First the page is cleared in normal white-on-black attribute (ASCII 7) using ***ClearPage***. Then ***DrawBox*** draws a box at the center of the page and ***Display*** labels it. Finally, after a delay, ***SetPage*** makes page 1 the *current page*, so that it is displayed on the screen.

```
VideoBuffer := $B900;    {address used by GrabBox}
ClearPage(1,7);
DrawBox('D','D',20,10,40,7,15);
Display('This is page 1',23,13,15);
Delay(3000);
SetPage(1);
```

Procedure PageSwap(var Box: boxtype; PageNumber: integer);

FILE NAME: PAGESWAP.PAS   (92 code bytes)

PURPOSE: *PageSwap* exchanges the contents of a page of video memory and a byte array in memory. It always moves 4000 bytes—the memory required to hold the character and attribute for each of the 2000 screen positions in 80-column mode. When the page of video memory is the *current page* (the page currently displayed) the memory contents are swapped directly onto the screen.

PARAMETERS: *Box* is a data array for storing the video image; *boxtype* is always an **array [1..4000] of byte**.

PageNumber is the number of the video page with which the array contents are exchanged. Page numbers range from 0 to 3 on a color graphics card and from 0 to 7 on an EGA. Always use 0 with the monochrome card.

VideoBuffer is a global integer variable holding the segment (memory location) of the video adaptor. This value is usually **$B000** for the monochrome card, **$B800** for the color graphics card, or either of these values for the EGA, depending on the screen mode. See the discussion in Chapter 1.

NOTES: 1. *PageSwap* writes directly to video memory. There is no BIOS version. Always set the value for *VideoBuffer* to the beginning of the buffer ($B000 or $B800); the routine calculates the offset to the specified page.

2. The routine contains code that checks the status of the color graphics adaptor and waits until it can write without creating

snow. The check is made regardless of the video page currently displayed.

EXAMPLES: To declare the byte array:

```
Type boxtype
  pagetype = array[1..4000] of byte;
Var
  ExtraPage : boxtype;
```

Then to trade contents with the screen using a monochrome monitor:

```
VideoBuffer := $B000);
PageSwap(ExtraPage,0);
```

To exchange the buffer contents with page 2 of the color graphics adaptor:

```
VideoBuffer := $B800;
PageSwap(ExtraPage,2);
```

Section 3: Windows

Turbo Pascal has a built-in windowing facility. Although it's very useful in some circumstances, in others it can be unwieldly and wasteful of memory. This section presents routines that create the illusion of windowing without incurring the usual overhead. The routines, which are ideal for making pop-down menus and dialog boxes, may be used to move information from one part of the screen to another. *SaveBox* saves a defined area of the screen in a byte array; *GrabBox* does the same and also clears the area. You can then write any information you choose at the saved area and later restore the former contents using *RestoreBox*. All three routines come in both memory-mapped and BIOS versions. Consider using these routines in tandem with the vertical and horizontal scrolling procedures in Section 2 of this chapter. For example, you can make a menu scroll down from offscreen by saving the overlaid area without clearing it, writing the bottom line of the menu at the top of the area, scrolling it down one line, writing the next line, and so on—all the while adding delays to control the speed of animation.

This section also presents four routines that are a lot of fun—*BoxUp*, *BoxDown*, *BoxLeft*, and *BoxRight*. These move the contents of an area of the screen from one place to another while completely preserving the screen contents beneath. It is as if the image were floating above the screen. The move is made row by row or column by column at any desired speed. An imaginative combination of these routines, the *SaveBox* and *RestoreBox* routines, and the scroll routines can result in striking, dynamic presentations—all achieved with little labor and little extra code.

Procedure SaveBox(var Box: boxtype; TopX,TopY,Width,Depth: integer);
Procedure SaveBoxB(var Box: boxtype; TopX,TopY,Width,Depth: integer);

FILE NAMES: SAVEBOX.PAS   (141 code bytes)
               SAVEBOXB.PAS   (131 code bytes)

PURPOSE: *SaveBox* and *SaveBoxB* copy the contents of a specified area of the screen (a "box") into a byte array in memory; the attributes (colors) as well as the characters are saved. *SaveBox* directly writes to memory, and *SaveBoxB* uses the BIOS functions. The screen area may then be overwritten with dialog boxes, pop-down menus, or whatever, without loss of screen contents. The *RestoreBox* procedure (also found in this section) restores the original image to the screen.

PARAMETERS: *Box* is a byte array large enough to hold the box (it may be larger). Allocate two bytes for every row and column position. For a 10 by 10 box, **boxtype = array[1..200] of byte**.

TopX and *TopY* are the column and row positions of the top left corner of the box. Columns are counted from 1 to 80 and rows from 1 to 25.

Width is the number of columns the box occupies.

Depth is the number of rows the box occupies.

VideoBuffer, a global integer variable required by *SaveBox*, holds the segment (memory location) of the video adaptor. This value is usually **$B000** for the monochrome card, **$B800** for the color graphics card, or either of these values for the EGA, depending on the screen mode. See the discussion in Chapter 1.

VideoPage, a global integer variable required by *SaveBoxB*, determines which video page the routine writes on. The usual value is **0**. Chapter 1 gives details.

NOTES:

1. These routines don't check that the coordinates are in range or that the width and depth are appropriate. If you give the procedure the wrong coordinates, there will be no indication until you use *RestoreBox*. On the other hand, an overlarge value for the width or depth causes the routine to write outside the *Box* array, destroying adjacent data.

EXAMPLES:

To declare the byte array for a 10 by 20 box (equaling 400 bytes):

```
Type
  boxtype = array[1..400] of byte;
Var
  BoxCopy : boxtype;
```

This line saves a window 20 columns wide and 10 rows deep, with its top left column at column 40, row 5:

```
SaveBox(BoxCopy,40,5,20,10);
```

Later, to restore the box at the same position:

```
RestoreBox(BoxCopy,40,5,20,10);
```

You can use *SaveBox* to save part of a screen while erasing everything else:

```
SaveBox(BoxCopy,40,5,20,10);
Clrscr;
RestoreBox(BoxCopy,40,5,20,10);
```

Procedure GrabBox(var Box:boxtype;TopX,TopY,Width,Depth,Color:integer);
Procedure GrabBoxB(var Box:boxtype;TopX,TopY,Width,Depth,Color:integer);

FILE NAMES: GRABBOX.PAS   (170 code bytes)
                GRABBOXB.PAS   (143 code bytes)

PURPOSE: *GrabBox* and *GrabBoxB* copy the contents of
                a specified area of the screen (a "box") into a
                byte array in memory and then clear the area
                in a given attribute. *GrabBox* is exactly like
                SaveBox, but it clears the area it saves. The
                RestoreBox procedure (also found in this
                section) restores the image to the screen.
                GrabBox directly writes to memory, and
                GrabBoxB uses the BIOS functions.

PARAMETERS: *Box* is a byte array large enough to hold the
                box (it may be larger). Allocate two bytes for
                every row and column position. For a 10 by
                10 box, **boxtype = array[1..200] of byte**.

                TopX and *TopY* are the column and row po-
                sitions of the top left corner of the box. Col-
                umns are counted from 1 to 80, and rows
                from 1 to 25.

                Width is the number of columns the box
                occupies.

                Depth is the number of rows the box
                occupies.

                Color, the attribute used when the box is
                cleared after it is saved, is a number from 0
                to 255, where 7 is "normal" white-on-black.
                Color may be a global variable set by rou-
                tines provided in Chapter 6.

                VideoBuffer, a global integer variable re-
                quired by *GrabBox*, holds the segment
                (memory location) of the video adaptor. This
                value is usually **$B000** for the monochrome
                card, **$B800** for the color graphics card, or ei-

ther of these values for the EGA, depending on the screen mode. See the discussion in Chapter 1.

VideoPage, a global integer variable required by *GrabBoxB*, determines which video page the routine writes on. The usual value is **0**. Chapter 1 gives details.

NOTES:

1. These routines don't check that the coordinates are in range or that the width and depth are appropriate. If you give the procedure the wrong coordinates, there won't be any indication until you use *RestoreBox*. On the other hand, an overlarge value for the width or depth causes the routine to write outside the *Box* array, destroying adjacent data.

EXAMPLES:

This example creates a "dialog box" in reverse image. First, declare a byte array for a 5 by 40 box (equaling 400 bytes):

```
Type
   boxtype = array[1..400] of byte;
Var
   BoxCopy : boxtype;
```

Use *CharBox* to fill the screen with a character, giving an image to write over, then make a delay:

```
CharBox(Chr(206),1,1,80,20,7);
Delay(2000);
```

Next, save the area at which the dialog box appears, clearing it in reverse-image:

```
GrabBox(BoxCopy,25,5,40,5,112);
```

You may wish to surround the dialog box with lines. The first routine in this chapter, **DrawBox**, does the job:

```
DrawBox('S','S',25,5,40,5,112);
```

The message comes next, along with a wait for the answering keystroke. Use the *Display* procedure found in Chapter 6 to write in reverse image at **28,7**.

```
Display('Quit without saving file?  Yes/No',28,7,112);
```

Now wait for a keystroke in reply:

```
Read(kbd,ch);
```

then erase the box by restoring the original screen contents:

```
RestoreBox(BoxCopy,25,5,40,5);
```

Procedure RestoreBox(var Box:boxtype;TopX,TopY,Width,Depth:integer);
Procedure RestoreBoxB(var Box:boxtype;TopX,TopY,Width,Depth:integer);

FILE NAMES: RSTORBX.PAS   (151 code bytes)
                     RSTORBXB.PAS   (137 code bytes)

PURPOSE: *RestoreBox* and *RestoreBoxB* restore to the screen an image saved in a byte array by *SaveBox* or *GrabBox*. *RestoreBox* writes directly to the video buffer, while *RestoreBoxB* uses the BIOS services.

PARAMETERS: *Box* is a byte array large enough to hold the box (it may be larger). Allocate two bytes for every row and column position. For a 10 by 10 box, **boxtype = array[1..200] of byte**.

TopX and *TopY* are the column and row positions of the top left corner of the box. Columns are counted from 1 to 80, and rows from 1 to 25.

Width is the number of columns the box occupies.

Depth is the number of rows the box occupies.

VideoBuffer, a global integer variable required by *RestoreBox*, holds the segment (memory location) of the video adaptor. This value is normally **$B000** for the monochrome card, **$B800** for the color graphics card, or either of these values for the EGA, depending on the screen mode. See the discussion in Chapter 1.

VideoPage, a global integer variable required by *RestoreBoxB*, determines which video page the routine writes on. The usual value is **0**. Chapter 1 gives details.

NOTES: 1. The byte array keeps its contents after *RestoreBox* or *RestoreBoxB* is called. By changing the *Col* and *Row* positions at which the box is positioned, an image can be duplicated at many places on the screen.

EXAMPLES: To see **RestoreBox** in normal use, refer to the examples for the **SaveBox** and **GrabBox** procedures. Here, **GrabBox** moves the top-left quarter of the screen to the bottom-right quarter. The top-left quarter is cleared, but the other two quarters are unaffected (scrolling, of course, cannot achieve this result). Boxes are first drawn in all quarters but the bottom-right, and a delay is made, so that you can see what is happening.

First, draw the boxes and delay:

```
DrawBox('D','D',1,1,40,12,15);
GotoXY(12,6);Write('This box will move');
DrawBox('S','S',41,1,40,12,7);
DrawBox('S','S',1,13,40,12,7);
Delay(2000);
```

Next, save the 40-column by 12-row area with its top-left corner at **1,1**, clearing the area in normal attribute (ASCII 7):

```
GrabBox(BoxCopy,1,1,40,12,7);
```

Then restore the box to the screen with its top-left corner at column 41, row 13:

```
RestoreBox(BoxCopy,41,13,40,12);
```

Procedure BoxUp(var Box:boxtype;var Col,Row:integer;Width,Depth:integer);
Procedure BoxDown(var Box:boxtype;var Col,Row:integer;Width,Depth:integer);
Procedure BoxLeft(var Box:boxtype;var Col,Row:integer;Width,Depth:integer);
Procedure BoxRight(var Box:boxtype;var Col,Row:integer;Width,Depth:integer);

FILE NAMES:

BOXUP.PAS	(328 code bytes)
BOXDOWN.PAS	(296 code bytes)
BOXLEFT.PAS	(354 code bytes)
BOXRIGHT.PAS	(351 code bytes)

PURPOSE:

These four procedures shift an area on the screen by one row or two columns. The routines are intended to be placed inside a loop with a delay made after each call. The two variables that set the position of the top-left corner of the area are automatically adjusted by the routines each time they are called. Thus, a succession of calls causes the box to move smoothly across the display. The delay made after the call sets the speed.

The routines exchange data with a byte array holding the contents of the overlay area. Ordinarily, an area of the screen is first saved with the **SaveBox** or **GrabBox** routines (found in this section). Then the information that will be shifted across the screen is written into the area. When the area is shifted, say, up one row, the newly overlaid part of a row is saved, the shift is made, and the contents of the prior bottom row are restored. When the cross-screen shift is complete, the **RestoreBox** function may restore the prior screen contents of the new position. The net result is that the image appears, floats across the screen, and then disappears.

PARAMETERS:

Box is a byte array that temporarily holds screen contents in memory. *It must be larger than the array usually allocated for* **SaveBox** *or* **GrabBox**.) For horizontal moves, add four times the box depth to the usual array size. For vertical moves, add two times the box width. When both kinds of motion are made, add the larger number to the array size. A box five rows deep and twenty columns across needs two hundred bytes plus an extra forty for both vertical and horizontal moves, or only twenty extra for horizontal moves alone.

Col and *Row* are the column and row positions of the top left corner of the box. Columns are counted from 1 to 80, and rows from 1 to 25. These variables are adjusted by the routine as the box travels across the screen.

Width, the number of columns the box occupies, must be at least two columns.

Depth, the number of rows the box occupies, may be as little as one row.

VideoBuffer is a global integer variable that holds the segment (memory location) of the video adaptor. This value is usually **$B000** for the monochrome card, **$B800** for the color graphics card, or either of these values for the EGA, depending on the screen mode. See the discussion in Chapter 1.

NOTES:

1. There is no requirement that *RestoreBox* be used to eliminate the image after the shift is made. For example, starting with a cleared screen you might want to introduce a block of text midscreen, move it to the top right, then introduce another block midscreen, move it to the bottom right, and so on. Although no prior screen contents need to be saved, the routines still must make the data exchange with a byte array. So you must still use *SaveBox*, which saves the *blank* area at

midscreen to ensure that there is data to replace the vacated rows and columns as the box is moved. Once the box is shifted to the new position, your code restores the original midscreen *Row* and *Col* positions, *SaveBox* is called again, the next text block is written and moved, and so on until the entire screen is assembled.

2. In the description above, a program saves an area, writes something else, then moves what is freshly written across the display. But something already on the display can be shifted as well. This is done by using *SaveBox* at some point to make a copy of a blank region of the screen of the same dimensions as the area to be moved. The copy is placed in a buffer later used as *Box*. This strategy can be taken a step further by having several buffers, each with an image that was at some point copied from the screen. One of these buffers is used as *Box* when the initial image is moved away from the screen area, exposing the hitherto undisplayed image beneath. The process may be repeated, giving the impression of a stack of pages being removed one by one. This is illustrated in the second example given on page 284.

3. The horizontal shifts are made two columns at a time since this distance is about the same as the height of one row. The routines return without doing anything when the box reaches the border of the screen. For example, if the top left corner is **1,1**, then neither *BoxUp* nor *BoxLeft* has any effect. Since two-column shifts aren't made, you must start a box at an odd-numbered column if you want it

shifted all the way to the left or right edge of the display.

4. *SaveBox*, *GrabBox*, and *RestoreBox* (and the related BIOS routines) can handle a box only one column wide. But the minimum box width for these four routines is two columns. A ''box'' one column wide makes a mess of the screen.

5. Use Turbo Pascal's *Delay* procedure to time intervals precisely between moves; otherwise, varying CPU speeds will change the animation speed. To operate on any hardware, you will need two sets of delays, one for monochrome screens and one for color. The routines operate *much* more slowly on color adaptors, thanks to the CGA screen interference problem. In fact, it is impractical to move large blocks on a 4MHz IBM PC using a CGA mode.

6. The routines check that the row and column coordinates, as well as the width and depth, are in range. They cannot ascertain, however, whether the width and depth coordinates correspond to the amount of data contained in the *Box* buffer. You must ensure that the same dimensions are used with *SaveBox*, *BoxUp* (and so on), and *RestoreBox*. A mismatch can result in damage to data adjacent in memory to *Box*.

7. There are no BIOS versions of these routines since the BIOS is simply not fast enough to handle them.

EXAMPLES: The first example uses *GrabBox* to save part of the screen and clear it. *CharBox* first fills the screen with a graphics character to provide an image for the box to cross over. A

box is drawn around the saved area and a label is written. A delay is made, then the box
is propelled from left to right across the display using a tenth-second delay between
shifts. After a final delay, the box is erased
by **RestoreBox**.

```
Type
   boxtype = array[1..220] of byte;
Var
   BoxCopy : boxtype;
```

Draw a backdrop for the box to travel over,
then delay:

```
CharBox(chr(206),1,1,80,25,7);
Delay(1000);
```

Draw the box:

```
Col := 10;
Row := 10;
GrabBox(BoxCopy,Col,Row,20,5,112);
DrawBox('D','D',Col,Row,20,5,112);
Display('Message',Col+7,Row+2,15);
Delay(1000);
```

Now shift the box across the screen:

```
for I := 1 to 20 do
  begin
    BoxRight(BoxCopy,Col,Row,20,5);
    Delay(100);
  end;
```

Finally, return to the original screen:

```
Delay(1000);
RestoreBox(BoxCopy,Col,Row,20,5);
```

The second example, which is much more complicated, disassembles a "stack of images," as described in note 2. The images are rectangles of a single character (the heart, diamond, club, and spade) drawn by *CharBox*. Initially, the box of spaces appears at center screen. It is shifted to the top left, revealing another image beneath, which in turn is shifted to the top right, revealing yet another image, and so on. The fourth image moves to the bottom left, leaving the center screen blank.

To achieve this effect, four byte arrays are required. Three hold images for hearts, diamonds, and clubs, and the fourth is filled with spaces so that it can clear the center screen when the last image is shifted. These arrays must first be filled, and this is done by quickly writing the images at the top-left corner of the screen and saving them with *SaveBox*. The screen is immediately cleared, and the whole process happens so quickly that it can hardly be noticed. The images are fifteen characters wide and eight high, requiring $15*8*2 = 240$ bytes. The extra array space required for the vertical movements is $15*2 = 30$ bytes, and for horizontal movements it is $8*4 = 32$ bytes. The larger value plus 240 makes for a 272-byte array:

```
Type
  boxtype = array[1..272] of byte;
Var
  BoxCopy : array[1..4] of boxtype;
```

To fill the arrays:

```
for I := 1 to 3 do
  begin
    CharBox(chr(I+2),1,1,15,8,7);
```

```
        SaveBox(BoxCopy[I],1,1,15,8);
   end;
ClrScr;
SaveBox(BoxCopy[4],1,1,15,8);
```

Now the preparations are complete. Set the column, row, and shift delay, draw the initial image, pause for a moment, then make the four shifts. Note how the starting column and row must be reset after each shift.

```
Col := 32;
Row := 10;
Speed := 100;
CharBox(chr(6),Col,Row,15,8,7);
Delay(2000);

for I := 1 to 8 do
  begin
    BoxLeft(BoxCopy[1],Col,Row,15,8);
    BoxUp(BoxCopy[1],Col,Row,15,8);
    Delay(Speed);
  end;

Col := 32;Row := 10;
for I := 1 to 8 do
  begin
    BoxRight(BoxCopy[2],Col,Row,15,8);
    BoxUp(BoxCopy[2],Col,Row,15,8);
    Delay(Speed);
  end;

Col := 32;Row := 10;
for I := 1 to 8 do
  begin
    BoxRight(BoxCopy[3],Col,Row,15,8);
    BoxDown(BoxCopy[3],Col,Row,15,8);
    Delay(Speed);
  end;
```

```
Col := 32;Row := 10;
for I := 1 to 8 do
  begin
    BoxLeft(BoxCopy[4],Col,Row,15,8);
    BoxDown(BoxCopy[4],Col,Row,15,8);
    Delay(Speed);
  end;
```

8

File Operations

Section 1: Disk operations

This section contains routines that give special control over disk drives and disks. The first two routines, *GetVolume* and *SetVolume*, let your program find out or change a disk's volume label. They may be useful for checking that the proper diskette is present, keeping track of backup diskettes, and so on.

Next come *FreeSpace* and *FreeSpacePlus*, which report the amount of room available on a disk. Disk space is usually needed in integer form, but integers in Turbo Pascal range only up to 32767. So *FreeSpace* returns the remaining disk space in kilobytes. *FreeSpacePlus* does the same but also writes the remaining fraction of a kilobyte in an integer variable for a very accurate reading.

DOS can be made to double-check its write operations to ensure that crucial data was correctly transferred to disk by including the VERIFY command in the CONFIG.SYS file, or the feature may be turned on and off from within programs. *SetVerify* performs this service, and *GetVerify* reports the current verification status.

This section ends with *ReadSector* and *WriteSector*, which read and write absolute disk sectors. *Writing* sectors is seldom done, and it can be risky. But there are occasions when the ability to *read* particular disk locations is essential, as, for example, when a program needs to trace through the disk's file allocation table. These routines use the DOS system of *logical sector numbers*, where every sector is assigned a unique number.

Function GetVolume(Spec: integer): stype;
Procedure SetVolume(NewLabel: stype; Spec: integer);

FILE NAMES:	GETVOLUM.PAS (134 code bytes)
	SETVOLUM.PAS (131 code bytes)

PURPOSE:

GetVolume and *SetVolume* report and change, respectively, a disk's volume label. (The volume label, a disk identifier held in the disk's main directory, can be created when DOS formats the disk. The label may have up to eleven characters.) When no volume label is present, *SetVolume* can add a label to the disk.

PARAMETERS:

Spec is the disk drive specifier, where **0** is the current drive, and the numbers **1, 2, 3,** . . . refer to drives **A:, B:, C:,** . . . .

NewLabel is a character string holding no more than eleven bytes.

WorkArea, a global variable, is an **array of byte[1..44]** used by the routines. The contents of the array is of no concern.

GetVolume returns a volume label up to eleven bytes long.

NOTES:

1. When *NewLabel* is null, the volume label is deleted (if one exists).

2. If *NewLabel* is too long, the first eleven characters of the string are used for the new volume label.

3. These routines work through operating-system functions.

4. The *FirstFile* function in Section 2 of this chapter also can read the volume label.

EXAMPLES:

To report the volume label of the diskette in drive A:

```
Var
  WorkArea : array[1..44] of byte;

Write('The diskette in drive A is: ');
Writeln(GetVolume(1));
```

To set the volume label of the current drive to "BACKUP23":

```
SetVolume(0,'BACKUP23');
```

Function FreeSpace(Spec: integer): integer;
Function FreeSpacePlus(Spec: integer): integer;

FILE NAMES: FREESPC.PAS   (36 code bytes)
FREESPC&.PAS   (63 code bytes)

PURPOSE: *FreeSpace* returns the number of *kilobytes* of disk space available at a specified drive. This value is truncated and there may be an appreciable fraction of a kilobyte available as well. *FreeSpacePlus* is a modified version of **FreeSpace**, which also returns the number of bytes in the remaining fraction, should that degree of exactitude be required.

PARAMETERS: *Spec* is a number representing a disk drive, where 1 = A:, 2 = B:, and so on. When Spec = 0, the available space on the default drive is returned.

ExtraSpace is an integer variable accessed by *FreeSpacePlus*. After the function is executed, it contains the number of bytes in the fraction of one kilobyte not counted in the value returned by the function.

NOTES: 1. The numbers are returned in two parts because Turbo Pascal does not have *long* integers, and a conversion to real form would not be practical. When writing out the combined value of *FreeSpacePlus* and *ExtraSpace*, always allocate three digits for the latter, as in the example that follows.

                    2. *FreeSpace* rounds down so that the amount of available space will never be over-reported.

EXAMPLES: To find out the number of kilobytes available on drive C:

```
Writeln(FreeSpace(3),' kilobytes of disk space free');
```

To display the exact number of bytes available on drive C, use the *IntStr* function
found in Section 3 of Chapter 4 to convert
the numbers returned by *FreeSpacePlus* to
string form. Use *PadLeft* (also in Chapter 4)
to pad the value returned in *ExtraSpace* to
three digits.

```
Write('Available disk space: ',FreeSpacePlus);
TempString := IntStr(ExtraSpace);
PadLeft(TempString,3,'0');
Writeln(TempString);
```

Procedure SetVerify(Setting: boolean);
Function GetVerify: boolean;

FILE NAMES:	SETVERFY.PAS	(23 code bytes)
	GETVERFY.PAS	(21 code bytes)

PURPOSE: When *SetVerify = TRUE*, DOS automatically checks after every disk write operation that the data was transferred without errors. A FALSE value for *SetVerify* turns verification off. **GetVerify** returns the current verification setting.

PARAMETERS: *Setting* is TRUE when the verify switch is "on," and FALSE when it is "off."

NOTES: 1. The *verify* state can also be activated (or deactivated) at the DOS command level or when DOS is booted.

EXAMPLES: To find out the verification status:

```
Write(GetVerify);
```

To turn it on:

```
SetVerify(TRUE);
```

Function ReadSector(Segment,Offset,Drive,Sector,Number:integer):integer;
Function WriteSector(Segment,Offset,Drive,Sector,Number:integer):integer;

FILE NAMES:	RDSECTOR.PAS	(50 code bytes)
	WRSECTOR.PAS	(50 code bytes)

PURPOSE:

ReadSector transfers the 512 bytes kept in a particular disk sector to a buffer set up in memory. **WriteSector** does the reverse, writing the data to disk. More than one sector may be transferred in a single operation. The data is read from, or written to, a byte array set up in Turbo Pascal's data segment or heap.

PARAMETERS:

Segment is the segment of the array from which data is taken or to which it is directed. Use Turbo Pascal's **Seg** function to obtain this value.

Offset is the offset of the data array in **Segment**. Use TURBO's **Ofs** function to obtain this value.

Drive is the number of the disk drive, where 1 = A:, 2 = B:, and so on.

Sector is the *logical sector number* of the first (and possibly only) sector read or written to. See the note below about calculating a logical sector number.

Number is the number of sectors read starting from **Sector**. The sectors are laid down in sequence in memory, so you must be sure that the byte array is large enough.

ReadSector and **WriteSector** return an integer error code. When the read or write operation is successful the value is 0. Otherwise a non-zero error code is returned. Most codes indicate a hardware failure, but several are useful for error messages:

2 = disk-formatting problem
3 = attempted write to write-protected disk
4 = requested a nonexistent sector number
128 = drive-door open

NOTES:

1. These routines are useful for reading root directories and file allocation tables, giving you access to obscure directory information. Advanced programmers can track down subdirectories, a service not provided by the DOS functions. The data needed for these operations is available in the DOS technical reference manual, or in the author's *Programmer's Problem Solver for the IBM PC, XT & AT*.

2. DOS assigns a unique logical sector number to every sector on a disk. The numbers are counted from 0 upward starting from the outside rim of the disk. The counting method applies to disks of any size or kind. The logical sector count begins from side 0, track 0, sector 1 (by convention, sides and tracks are counted from 0 but sectors are counted from 1). The count continues to side 1, track 0, then goes on to side 0, track 1, etc. On multiplatter fixed disks, the entire outside *cylinder* is counted first. Depending on how the disk is formatted, the logical sector number increases by a certain amount with every track. For a 360K floppy, each track (taking both sides) adds 18 to the number. But the calculation is slightly complicated by the fact that the numbering begins from 0. Thus, the first sector of track 3 on side 1 might at first seem to be 3*18 for tracks 0–2, plus 9 for side 0 of track 3, plus 1 to point to the first sector of

track 3 on side 1. This equals 64. The logical sector number is 1 less than this number.

3. Be very, very careful about using **WriteSector**. One wrong move can fatally damage a disk's directory or file allocation table, resulting in the loss of *all* data on the disk. Always first use **ReadSector** in place of **WriteSector** to see that the proper sector(s) are accessed.

EXAMPLE: This example reads the first directory sector of a floppy disk formatted for 360K.

```
Var
  Dir : array[1..512] of byte;

I := ReadSector(Seg(Dir),Ofs(Dir),1,3,1);
if I <> 0 then DiskError;
```

To see the file names for the first sixteen entries, read the first eleven bytes at 32-byte intervals:

```
ArrayPtr := 0;
for I := 1 to 16 do
  begin
    Name := '';
    for J := 0 to 10 do
      begin
        Name := Name + chr(Dir[ArrayPtr+J]);
      end;
    Writeln(Name);
    ArrayPtr := ArrayPtr + 32;
  end;
```

Section 2: Directory access

This section provides routines that inform your programs about files. *SeekFile* searches for a file and tells a program whether it will be there if the program tries to open it. It can tell your program whether the file is missing or the path string is bad. Next come *FirstFile* and *NextFile*, two routines that let your programs search for files by name or by the DOS global file name characters (? and *). They can make systematic directory searches, and they let your programs display any directory.

FileBytes and *FileKilobytes* report a file's size in two formats. *FileKilobytes* is the simpler of the two routines. It returns a single integer value giving the number of kilobytes in a file, where all values are rounded up, so that a file of 1001 bytes would be reported as having 2K. This routine is adequate for rough estimates. *FileBytes*, on the other hand, gives a value accurate to the byte. Because Turbo Pascal does not allow large integers, the routine returns the value in two parts: an (unrounded) kilobyte value and a second integer holding the remainder.

Finally, six routines report special directory information. File attributes, such as "read-only" or "hidden," are set or reported by *SetFileAttribute* and *GetFileAttribute*. And the time and date of a file's creation may be found or changed by means of *GetFileTime*, *SetFileTime*, *GetFileDate*, and *SetFileDate*.

Function SeekFile(Path: stype): integer;

FILE NAME: SEEKFILE.PAS   (82 code bytes)

PURPOSE: *SeekFile* tests that a file and its (optional) subdirectory path exists. The routine takes a string that contains a file name, with or without a subdirectory path. It returns **0** if the file is found. Otherwise, it returns a code that will be **2** when the file wasn't found (but its directory was) and **3** when the subdirectory path was invalid.

PARAMETERS: *Path* is the file name and/or subdirectory path, both in standard DOS format.

NOTES: 1. *SeekFile* may return **4** when too many files are open or **5** when there is some other problem. DOS 2.1 often returns **2** or **bad path**. These results occur because *SeekFile* looks for a file by attempting to open it.

                2. To test for the existence of a file path alone, use a phony file name; global characters (* or ?) don't work. Use a (nearly) impossible name, perhaps all spaces except for a leading character: 'X   . .

EXAMPLE: This example tests for a file and alerts the computer user to any problem:

```
I := SeekFile('B:\MAMMALS\PRIMATES\GIBBONS.MS');
if I <> 0 then case I of
   2: Write('Bad File Name');
   3: Write('Bad Subdirectory Path');
   4: Write('Too Few File Buffers');
   5: Write('Disk Drive Problem');
end;
```

Function FirstFile(Path: stype; FType: integer): stype;
Function NextFile: stype;

FILE NAMES:	FRSTFILE.PAS	(136 code bytes)
	NEXTFILE.PAS	(72 code bytes)

PURPOSE: These two routines search a directory and report all matches to a given file or subdirectory name, where the name may incorporate the global characters **?** and *****. The file name **TRYAGAIN.PAS** would result in one match at most, while ***.PAS** would return all files with **.PAS** extensions and ***.*** would return a complete directory listing. *FirstFile* returns the name of the first match in the directory. Once *FirstFile* has been used, a program can repeatedly call **NextFile** to find out the names of subsequent matches. The routines return a null string when no (further) match can be made.

PARAMETERS: *Path* is the file name and/or subdirectory path in standard DOS format.

FType is the *attribute* of the directory entry, telling whether it is a normal file, a hidden file, a subdirectory, etc. The values for *FType* are:

0	normal file
1	read-only file
2	hidden file
4	system file
8	volume label
16	subdirectory
32	written to since backup

These values refer to bit settings in the attribute byte. They may be combined. Use routines in Chapter 2 to set and read bit patterns.

WorkArea is an **array[1..43] of byte** that DOS requires to perform this service. The routines look for the array in memory—it is not passed as a parameter. Your program doesn't access it directly. *NextFile* uses the data left in *WorkArea* by *FirstFile* to seek subsequent matches.

NOTES:

1. For files, these routines return file names only. To obtain other parts of a directory listing—the file size, date, and time—apply other routines in this chapter once you have learned each file's name.

2. Use * or ???????? for subdirectories, *.* for volume labels (labels over 8 characters will have a period inserted).

3. The machine will crash if a program calls *NextFile* without first using *FirstFile*.

EXAMPLES:

To display the first twenty normal files listed in a directory:

```
Var
  WorkArea : array[1..43] of byte;

Writeln(FirstFile('C:\BADCODE\*.*',0));
for I := 1 to 19 do
  begin
    Writeln(NextFile);
  end;
```

To display the names of the first five subdirectories:

```
Writeln(FirstFile('C:*',16));
for I := 1 to 4 do
  begin
    Writeln(NextFile);
  end;
```

Function FileBytes(Path: stype): integer;
Function FileKilobytes(Path: stype): integer;

FILE NAMES:

FILEBYTE.PAS   (131 code bytes)
FILEKILO.PAS   (111 code bytes)

PURPOSE:

FileBytes and *FileKilobytes* report the size of a file, the first returning the exact number of bytes in the file, and the second returning the file size in kilobytes. Because Turbo Pascal cannot handle integer values over 32767, *FileBytes* must return the exact file size in two parts, returning the number of kilobytes as the function value and also setting a global variable to give the remaining fraction of a thousand. *FileKilobytes* returns only the function value, rounding up any remainder from 1 to 999, so that a 1001-byte file is reported as being 2K.

PARAMETERS:

Path is the file name and/or subdirectory path in standard DOS format.

FileRemainder is an integer variable in which *FileBytes* deposits the value held in the low three digits (decimal) of the file size.

NOTES:

1. Both routines return 0 when the file is not found.

EXAMPLES:

To find a file's size in kilobytes:

```
Size := FileKilobytes('A:\ROUTINES\BYTE2BIN.PAS');
```

This example displays the exact number of bytes in a file. After writing the kilobyte value, *FileRemainder* is converted to string form by *IntStr* (found in Chapter 4), lengthened to three digits by *PadLeft* (also from Chapter 4), and printed adjacent ot the kilobyte reading.

```
Var
  FileRemainder: integer;

Write('The file size is: ');
Write(FileBytes('A:\ROUTINES\BYTE2BIN.PAS'));
TempString := IntStr(FileRemainder);
PadLeft(TempString,3,'0');
Write(TempString);
```

Function GetFileAttribute(FilePath: stype): integer;
Function SetFileAttribute(FilePath: stype; Attribute: integer): integer;

FILE NAMES: GETFATTR.PAS   (78 code bytes)
                      SETFATTR.PAS   (81 code bytes)

PURPOSE: *GetFileAttribute* and *SetFileAttribute* report and set the attribute byte in a file's directory entry. Values for the attribute byte include **0** for normal files, **1** for read-only files, **2** for hidden files, **4** for system files, and **32** for files that have been accessed since the last use of the DOS BACKUP command. These values may be added together in any combination when more than one attribute applies. Both functions return −1 when unable to locate the file; otherwise, they return the attribute set or found.

PARAMETERS: *FilePath* is the file name and/or subdirectory path in standard DOS format.

                Attribute is an attribute code or combination of attribute codes.

NOTES: 1. The *hidden file* and *system file* attributes are generally used only in systems programming. These routines are most useful for changing files between read-only and read-write status or for finding out that status.

           2. The attribute values correspond to bit settings for bits 0 (read-only), 1 (hidden), 2 (system), and 5 (archive). When *GetFileAttribute* returns a value, you may want to use a routine from Chapter 3 such as *Bytefield* to find out the setting of any particular bit.

EXAMPLES: When a file is read-only, the attribute byte is an odd number (bit 0 is set). This example tests the read-only status:

```
Attri := GetFileAttribute('B:DONTREAD.ME');
if Attri mod 2 <> 0 then ReadOnly := TRUE;
```

To set a normal file to read-only:

```
ErrorCheck := SetFileAttribute('B:DONTREAD.ME',1);
if ErrorCheck = (1 then WriteErrorMessage;
```

Procedure GetFileTime(FilePath: stype);
Procedure SetFileTime(FilePath: stype);

FILE NAMES:

GETFTIME.PAS   (132 code bytes)
SETFTIME.PAS   (160 code bytes)

PURPOSE:

GetFileTime reports a file's time and *SetFile-Time* sets it. The hours are counted from 0 to 23 (0 = midnight), and the minutes and seconds from 0 to 59. DOS keeps the time as three bit fields packed into an integer in the file's directory entry. The routines return or receive the time as three integer variables, *FileTime.Hour*, *FileTime.Minutes*, and *File-Time.Seconds*. A file must be *closed* when these routines are used.

PARAMETERS:

FilePath is a file's name and directory path written in standard DOS format.

FileTime is the name of a record set up as follows:

```
Type
  TimeType = record
               Hour : integer;
               Minutes : integer;
               Seconds : integer;
               end;
Var
  FileTime : TimeType;
```

Before calling *SetFileTime*, the values for hour, minutes, and seconds must be assigned to *FileTime.Hour*, *FileTime.Minutes*, and *FileTime.Seconds*. Conversely, *GetFileTime* places new values in these variables. Of course, the record must either be local to the block that calls these routines or it must be global (that is, it must be declared in the body of the program).

NOTES:

1. When the routine cannot open the file (usually on account of a bad file name or path name) it sets the value of *File-Time.Hour* to **100** and returns. The other variables are left unchanged.

2. These routines open the file, read or change the time, and then close the file. They cannot be used with an already opened file; when an attempt is made, they set *FileTime.Hour* to **100**.

3. *SetFileTime* checks the range of the input data. If it finds a value outside of the acceptable range, it places **100** in *File-Time.Seconds* and returns.

4. The routines look up the address of *File-Time* by that name and access the three integers as offsets from the address. Thus, you can name the components of the record any way you please without changing the routines. But the order of the record elements must not be altered.

5. To fit the value for seconds into five bits, DOS actually stores the number of *2-second* periods. The routines automatically make the conversion to and from single seconds.

EXAMPLES:

First set up the record:

```
Type
  TimeType = record
             Hour : integer;
             Minutes : integer;
             Seconds : integer;
             end;
Var
  FileTime : TimeType;
```

Now get the time:

```
FilePath := 'a:\OVERDUE\ACCOUNTS.EXT';
GetFileTime(FilePath);
Write('The file was written ',FileTime.Hour,':',FileTime.Minutes);
```

Next, set the file time to 2:15 PM:

```
FileTime.Hour := 14;
FileTime.Minutes := 15;
FileTime.Seconds := 0;
SetFileTime(FilePath);
```

Check for errors:

```
If FileTime.Hour = 100 then PathNameError;
If FileTime.Seconds = 100 then ParameterError;
```

Procedure GetFileDate(FilePath: stype);
Procedure SetFileDate(FilePath: stype);

FILE NAMES: GETFDATE.PAS   (128 code bytes)
                 SETFDATE.PAS   (165 code bytes)

PURPOSE: *GetFileDate* reports a file's date, and
                 SetFileDate sets it. The year is counted from
                 1980 to 2099. The month is counted from 1 to
                 12, and the day from 1 to 31. DOS keeps the
                 date as three bit fields packed into an integer
                 in the file's directory entry. The routines re-
                 turn or receive the date as three integer vari-
                 ables, *FileDate.Hour*, *FileDate.Minutes*,
                 and *FileDate.Seconds*. A file must be *closed*
                 when these routines are used.

PARAMETERS: *FilePath* is a file's name and directory path
                 written in standard DOS format. It may con-
                 sist of nothing more than a file name, or it
                 may include a subdirectory path and/or an
                 initial drive specifier.

                 FileDate is the name of a record set up as
                 follows:

```
Type
  DateType = record
               Year : integer;
               Month : integer;
               Day : integer;
               end;
Var
  FileDate : DateType
```

                 Before calling *SetFileDate*, the values for
                 year, month, and day must be assigned to
                 FileDate.Year, *FileDate.Month*, and *File-
                 Date.Day*. Conversely, *GetFileDate* places
                 new values in these variables.

NOTES:

1. When the routine cannot open the file (usually because of a bad file- or path name), it sets the value of *FileDate.Year* to **100** and returns. The other variables are left unchanged.

2. These routines open the file, read or change the date, and then close the file. They cannot be used with an already opened file; if an attempt is made, they set *FileDate.Year* to **100** and return.

3. *SetFileDate* checks the range of the input data. If it finds a value outside the acceptable range, it places **100** in *FileDate.Day* and returns.

4. DOS stores the year as a 7-bit field that holds an offset (0–119) from 1980. The routines make the conversions.

5. The routines look up the address of *File-Date* by that name and access the three integers as offsets from the address. Thus, you can name the components of the record any way you please without changing the routines. But the order of the record elements must not be altered.

EXAMPLES:

First set up the record:

```
Type
   DateType = record
                Year : integer;
                Month : integer;
                Day : integer;
                end;
Var
   FileDate : DateType;
```

Now get the date:

```
FilePath := 'a:\MAMMALS\PRIMATES\GORILLAS.EXT';
GetFileDate(FilePath);
Write('The file was written on
',FileDate.Month,'-',FileDate.Day);
```

Next, change the file time to June 21, 1987:

```
FileDate.Year := 7;
FileDate.Month := 6;
FileDate.Day := 21;
SetFileDate(FilePath);
```

Check for errors:

```
If FileDate.Year = 100 then PathNameError;
If FileDate.Day = 100 then ParameterError;
```

9
Printer Output

Section 1: Printer operation

This section provides routines that give you extra control over the printer and simplify programming for printer output. The first routine, ***ChangePrinter***, allows a program to switch between two printers connected to the machine. ***PrinterReady*** reports whether a printer is ready to receive data.

Next come two routines that simply send strings to the printer. Turbo Pascal does this with the statements **Write(lst,OutputData)** or **Writeln(lst,OutputData)**. When the printer isn't ready or when it is shut off during output, Turbo Pascal doesn't recover. Instead, a DOS error message comes on the screen. The message may confuse the program user, and after recovery the program has no way of knowing that an error has occurred so that it can restart printing from the top of the page rather than from the start of the document. ***Print*** and ***Println*** avoid the DOS printer-output functions; they constantly check that the printer remains on line, and if there is a problem, they set an error code and return. Your program may continuously monitor the error code to see that everything is all right.

Two related routines, ***Prt*** and ***Prtln***, have an added feature: they interpret *embedded control codes*. These codes are ASCII characters in the range 128-159 that may be embedded within the output strings. They are arbitrarily assigned a meaning such as "underline ON" or "subscript OFF". When the routines encounter one of these codes in a string, they look up the contents of a corresponding position in an array of multi-character control sequences. That control sequence is sent to the printer instead of the single-character code. To support a different printer, you need merely change the control sequences in the array.

There are two other minor routines. *CRLF*, which outputs a given number of carriage-return/line-feed pairs, is used to end lines of text and to forward the printer paper. The second routine, *PrtSc*, invokes the BIOS PrtSc routine that dumps the screen image onto the printer. PtrSc can copy both text and graphics images.

Procedure ChangePrinter;

FILE NAME: CHGPRTR.PAS   (34 code bytes)

PURPOSE: **ChangePrinter** makes LPT1 become LPT2 and vice-versa. Each time the routine is called, it toggles the choice of printer that receives output from Turbo Pascal statements or from the routines provided here.

NOTES: 1. This routine changes the first two parallel port *base addresses* in the BIOS data area.

          2. Don't lose track of which printer is which. A program should restore the original printer choice when it terminates.

EXAMPLE: To change from LPT1 to LPT2:

```
ChangePrinter;
```

Repeat the statement to change back to LPT1.

Function PrinterReady: boolean;

FILE NAME:	PRTREADY.PAS (37 code bytes)
PURPOSE:	*PrinterReady* returns TRUE when the printer (LPT1) is ready for output.
NOTES:	1. The routine returns FALSE when bit 3 in the printer port status register is 0.
	2. Printer output routines in this chapter (*Print*, *Println*, and so on) constantly make this test so that they can detect when a printer goes off line during operation. Any of those routines can substitute for this one.
EXAMPLE:	To alert the user to an off-line printer:

```
if not PrinterReady then Writeln('Printer not ready');
```

Procedure Print(Strg: stype);
Procedure Println(Strg: stype);

FILE NAMES:	PRINT.PAS (99 code bytes) PRINTLN.PAS (122 code bytes)
PURPOSE:	*Print* and *Println* send output to the printer in the usual fashion, but they check for a printer error after each character is sent, setting an error-status variable when they finish. *Println* adds a carriage-return and line-feed after each string; *Print* does not.
PARAMETERS:	*Strg* is the output string. Unlike similar Turbo Pascal *Write* statements, all data must be in string form, and only one argument may be listed.
	PrinterOK is a global Boolean variable that is TRUE when the routines have successfully printed the entire string or FALSE when the printer goes off line (or never was on line).
NOTES:	1. This routine does *not* use the DOS printer-output functions and, in this way, avoids the DOS critical-error handler, which issues the message "No paper error writing LPT1/Abort, Retry, Ignore?". Besides fouling the display, this message can confuse inexperienced users.
	2. All output is directed to LPT1.
EXAMPLE:	This example writes a string and then checks that the operation was successful:

```
Var
  PrinterOK : Boolean;
Print('Not for all the gold in the world');
if not PrinterOK then write('Printer error!');
```

Procedure Prt(Strg: stype);
Procedure Prtln(Strg: stype);

FILE NAMES: PRT.PAS   (167 code bytes)
               PRTLN.PAS   (189 code bytes)

PURPOSE: *Prt* and *Prtln* perform exactly as the *Print* and *Println* procedures discussed earlier in this section: they output strings to the printer, constantly checking for printer errors, and they return an error code. *Prtln* adds a carriage-return and line-feed after each string. What sets these two routines apart is that they make use of a scheme for *embedded control codes*. In this scheme, a string array of up to 32 elements is created to hold control-code sequences, such as **ESC "M,"** which may be written as **chr(27) + chr(77)**. ASCII codes 128–159 are used to flag these array elements. For example, when ASCII character 128 is encountered in the printer-output string, the character is discarded, and instead the control sequence contained in the first array element is output to the printer. ASCII 129 would flag the second array element. Through this technique, you need only change the contents of the array to make the print output file compatible with different printers.

PARAMETERS: *Strg* is the output string. Unlike similar Turbo Pascal *Write* statements, all data must be in string form, and only one argument may be listed.

               PrinterCodes, a global variable, is a string array holding the control-code sequences. It is an **array[1..32] of stringtype** where **stringtype** is **string[5]**.

PrinterOK is a global Boolean variable that is TRUE when the routines have successfully printed the entire string or FALSE when the printer goes off line (or never was on line).

NOTES:

1. The code array must be sized for five-byte strings. The routines expect to find the start of each subsequent entry at a position six bytes higher than the last (five bytes plus the string descriptor).

2. There are few printer-control sequences that won't fit into five bytes. When one arises, it must be output to the printer separately from this scheme.

3. The 32 ASCII codes may be used independently. Since the routines can handle a string only one character long, by outputting just one code, a whole control sequence can be sent to the printer. For example, if the first array element contains **ESC "M"**, then writing **Prt(chr(246),CodeArray)** sends **ESC "M"** to the printer.

4. The *PrinterCodes* array doesn't have to be 32 elements long if fewer code strings are required. If there are fewer than 32 array elements and an ASCII code is used that is out of range, random data will be sent to the printer.

5. ASCII codes 128–159 were chosen because in most printer-code sequences they are redundant with codes 0–31.

EXAMPLE:

This example writes a string with one word written in italics. It is set up to operate on an Epson printer, where **ESC "4"** turns italics on, and **ESC "5"** turns italics off. First, declare the code array:

```
Type
  stringtype = string[5];
Var
  CodeArray : array[1..32] of stringtype;
```

Now initialize the first two elements of the array:

```
CodeArray[1] := chr(27)+'4';
CodeArray[2] := chr(27)+'5';
```

Here is the string (the ASCII codes are un-wieldly when inserted as shown here, but a program's formatting routines can handle them easily):

```
S := "What a "+chr(246)+"great"+chr(247)+" idea, Bonzo.";
```

To print it and make a carriage return:

```
Prtln(S);
```

Afterward, check the *PrinterOK* error code:

```
if not PrinterOK then PrinterError;
```

Here is the result:

```
What a great idea, Bonzo.
```

Procedure CRLF(NumLines: integer);

FILE NAME:	CRLF.PAS (100 code bytes)
PURPOSE:	**CRLF**, which stands for "carriage-return/line-feed," returns the printhead to the left and advances the paper by a specified number of lines. Like other routines in this chapter, **CRLF** constantly checks that the printer is on line and returns the value FALSE in the global Boolean variable **PrinterOK** when an error occurs.
PARAMETERS:	**NumLines** is the number of lines the paper is advanced.
	PrinterOK is a global Boolean variable that is TRUE when the routine successfully prints the entire string or FALSE when the printer goes off line (or never was on line).
NOTES:	1. You may use **CRLF** to end a line after a number of line fragments have been output with Turbo Pascal's **Write(lst,OutputVar)** or with the **Print** or **Prt** procedures in this section. If text may reach to the right edge of the paper, you need to keep track of the printhead's position because most printers automatically make a CR/LF after printing at the 80th (or 132nd) column of a line. Using **CRLF** results in a double line-feed when a line of text ends exactly at column 80.
EXAMPLES:	This example uses the **Print** procedure in this section to output three parts of a line, and then **CRLF** for a carriage-return and line-feed.

```
Print(Strg1);
Print(Strg2);
Print(Strg3);
CRLF(1);
```

To forward the page by six lines:

```
CRLF(6);
```

Procedure PrtSc;

FILE NAME:	PRTSC.PAS (16 code bytes)
PURPOSE:	**PrtSc** invokes the same BIOS routine that operates when the Shift-PrtSc key combination is typed.
NOTES:	1. DOS version 2.0 and later can print graphics screens by the PrtSc feature, providing the required code has been loaded with the **GRAPHICS** command. The PrtSc routine automatically uses this feature when the screen is in a graphics mode.
EXAMPLE:	To dump the screen onto the printer:

```
PrtSc;
```

Section 2: Formatting

This section has routines that help format printer output. Usually, print is formatted by interspersing strings of spaces between character strings. To help with this approach, **PrintChar** outputs strings of spaces or any other character. However, if you have room to spare in your programs, you will find other routines here that perform spacing automatically. **IndentIn** and **Indentline** automatically add a left margin before printing a string. **PrintForward** and **PrtForward** print a string and then forward the print head to a specified distance from the starting point. **PrintCenter** and **PrtCenter** center a string between any two columns, and they can surround the string with any border character. The second routine of all three pairs uses the system of embedded control codes described in the discussion of the **Prt** procedure in Section 1 of this chapter.

The other two routines don't actually send output to the printer. Rather, they format strings for output. The **WrapPrint** function returns as much of a string as can fit on a line of given length when the string is word-wrapped. The remainder of the source string, which is returned separately, may be added to the next string variable that is in turn processed by the function. **JustifyPrint** does the same, but it adds space characters so that the string is right-justified. Both routines ignore embedded control codes when they calculate line length.

Procedure PrintChar(Ch: char; Number: integer);

FILE NAME:	PRNTCHAR.PAS (188 code bytes)
PURPOSE:	*PrintChar* prints a string of specified length made up of the same character. It is useful for page formatting, especially for making the spacing between strings. Like other routines in this chapter, it constantly checks that the printer is on line and returns the value FALSE in the global Boolean variable *PrinterOK* when an error occurs.
PARAMETERS:	*Ch* is the character printed.
	Number is the number of times the character is printed.
	PrinterOK is a global Boolean variable that is TRUE when the routine successfully prints all of the characters or FALSE when the printer goes off line (or never was on line).
NOTES:	1. This routine is for convenience and clarity. You can instead use the *CharString* function in Section 1 of Chapter 4 to make a string of a single character, placing the result in an ordinary print output procedure: *Write(lst, CharString(' ',50));*
EXAMPLE:	This example prints a chapter name and page number with a line of periods between, fitting it onto a 50-character line:

```
Chapter := 'Chapter 3: Cybernetic Hysteria';
Page := '37';
Print(Chapter);
```

```
PrintChar('.',50-Length(Chapter)-Length(Page));
Print(Page);
if not PrinterOK then PrinterError;
```

The result:

```
Chapter 3: Cybernetic Hysteria.................37
```

Procedure Indentln(Strg: stype; Margin: integer);
Procedure Indentline(Strg: stype; Margin: integer);

FILE NAMES: INDENTLN.PAS   (140 code bytes)
                      INDTLINE.PAS   (212 code bytes)

PURPOSE: *Indentln* prints a string and makes a carriage-return/line-feed, inserting a specified number of space characters at the start of a line to create a left margin. *Indentline* works in the same way, but it supports the system of embedded control codes described for the *Prt* and *Prtln* procedures in Section 1 of this chapter. Both routines constantly check for printer errors and returns FALSE in the global Boolean variable *PrinterOK* when an error has occurred.

PARAMETERS: *Strg* is the output string. Unlike similar Turbo Pascal *Write* statements, all data must be in string form, and only one argument may be listed.

                     Margin is the number of spaces inserted at the start of the string.

                     PrinterCodes, a global variable, is a string array accessed by *IndentLine* that holds the control-code sequences. It is an **array[1..32]of stringtype** where **stringtype** is **string[5]**.

                     PrinterOK is a global Boolean variable that is TRUE when the routines have successfully printed the entire string, or FALSE when the printer went off line (or never was on line).

NOTES: 1. See the notes for *Prt* and *Prtln* if you use *Indentline*. The system of embedded control codes works in exactly the same way.

2. *Margin* can be made very large (say, 90) to double-space text. This approach may slow down some printers.

EXAMPLES: To write a string offset from the left edge of the paper by 15 spaces (plus whatever small margin is beyond the printhead's reach):

```
Indentln('This is the string',15);
```

The next example does the same, but the word "string" is boldfaced. ASCII 130 represents "boldface ON" and ASCII 131, "boldface OFF". The corresponding codes placed in the array are those for Epson printers—Esc-G and Esc-H. First set up the array:

```
Type
   stringtype = string[5];
Var
   Codes : array [1..20] of stringtype;
Codes[3] := chr(27)+'G';
Codes[4] := chr(27)+'H';
```

Now, write the string:

```
Indentln('I '+chr(130)+'think'+chr(131)+' not',15);
```

The result:

```
                    I think not
```

Procedure PrintForward(Strg: stype; FieldSize: integer);
Procedure PrtForward(Strg: stype; FieldSize: integer);

FILE NAMES: PRNTFRWD.PAS   (140 code bytes)
                  PRTFRWD.PAS   (245 code bytes)

PURPOSE: *PrintForward* and *PrtForward* send a string to the printer and then forward the print head to a specified position. For example, when **Strg := '12345'** and **FieldSize := 15**, the string is printed and the print head is then forwarded ten characters. The routines simplify printing tables and headings. They constantly check for printer errors and return FALSE in the global Boolean variable *PrinterOK* when an error has occurred. *PrtForward* differs from *PrintForward* in that it supports the system of embedded control codes described for the *Prt* and *Prtln* procedures in Section 1 of this chapter.

PARAMETERS: *Strg* is the output string. Unlike similar Turbo Pascal *Write* statements, all data must be in string form, and only one argument may be listed.

FieldSize is the number of printer columns occupied by the string and the spaces following it.

PrinterCodes, a global variable, is a string array accessed by *PrtForward* that holds the control-code sequences. It is an **array[1..32] of stringtype** where **stringtype** is **string[5]**.

PrinterOK is a global Boolean variable that is TRUE when the routines have successfully printed the entire string and trailing spaces, or FALSE when the printer went off line (or never was on line).

NOTES: 1. See the notes for *Prt* and *Prtln* if you use *PrtForward*. The system of embedded control codes works in exactly the same way.

2. When the length of **Strg** exceeds **Field-Size**, the routines print only as much of **Strg** as can fit. **PrtForward** does not count embedded control codes in setting the field size.

EXAMPLES:

To print a table of twenty-five numbers in five rows, spacing them twelve columns apart:

```
for I := 1 to 5 do
  begin
    for J := 1 to 5 do
      begin
PrintForward(IntStr(Number[I,J]),12);
      end;
    CRLF(1);   {make carriage-return}
  end;
```

The result:

35	465	143	79	623
27	69	994	2	908
354	465	112	68	697
66	332	98	29	112
49	446	39	60	834

IntStr, a function from Section 3 of Chapter 4, converts the number to string form. To right-justify the numbers, use the **PadLeft** procedure (also in Chapter 4) to extend the string to a specified length:

```
for I := 1 to 5 do
  begin
    for J := 1 to 5 do
      begin
        TempStrg := IntStr(Number[I,J]);
        PadLeft(TempStrg,' ',5);
        PrintForward(TempStrg,12);
```

```
              end;
           CRLF(1);
         end;
```

The result:

35	465	143	79	623
27	69	994	2	908
354	465	112	68	697
66	332	98	29	112
49	446	39	60	834

Procedure PrintCenter(Strg:stype; FieldSz:integer; Ch:char);
Procedure PrtCenter(Strg:stype; FieldSz:integer; Ch:char);

FILE NAMES: PRNTCNTR.PAS   (185 code bytes)
                      PRTCNTR.PAS   (284 code bytes)

PURPOSE: *PrintCenter* and *PrtCenter* print a string, centering it within a specified line length. No carriage-return/line-feed is made, leaving the print head at the position following the defined field. *PrtCenter* differs in that it interprets embedded control codes, as explained for the *Prt* and *Prtln* procedures in Section 1 of this chapter. Both routines constantly check for printer errors and return FALSE in the global Boolean variable *PrinterOK* when an error has occurred.

PARAMETERS: *Strg* is the string that is printed.

FieldSz is the length of the line in which the string is centered.

Ch is the character filling the field to the left and right of the string. Use a space or, to print a border, use characters like "−," "=," or "*."

PrinterCodes, a global variable, is a string array accessed by *PrtCenter* that holds the control-code sequences. It is an **array[1..32] of stringtype** where **stringtype** is **string[5]**.

PrinterOK is a global Boolean variable that is TRUE when the routine successfully prints the entire string or FALSE when the printer goes off line (or never was on line).

NOTES: 1. See the notes for *Prt* and *Prtln* if you use *PrtCenter*. The system of embedded control codes works in exactly the same way.

2. When the string is longer than the space allotted, as much of the string is printed as there is room.

3. When the number of spaces (or border characters) to the left and right of the string cannot be equal, the left side is made shorter.

4. *FieldSz* need not reach from one side of the page to the other. You could call **PrintCenter** twice in a row, centering two strings in adjacent 40-column fields, and then making a carriage-return.

EXAMPLES: To place a string dead center on a page:

```
PrintCenter('Very Dramatic Title',80,' ');
```

When bordering the string, it usually looks best to leave a space or two on either side of the string so that the border won't touch it. Here, a string is surrounded by the character " – ":

```
PrintCenter(' Chapter 3 ',50,'-');
```

The result:

```
-------------------- Chapter 3 --------------------
```

Function WrapLine(Strg: stype; LineLen: integer): stype;

FILE NAME	WRAPLINE.PAS (198 code bytes)
PURPOSE:	*WrapLine* formats a string for output to the printer in word-wrapped form. The function returns as many characters from *Strg* as fit in *LineLen*. The remaining characters in *Strg* are copied to a variable named *Remainder*. This remnant is to be combined with the next string from the text array that is printed. By repeated calls to *WrapLine* and a printer output procedure, an entire array may be printed in word-wrapped format. WrapLine ignores embedded control codes; the line length is correct no matter the number of codes.
PARAMETERS:	*Strg* is a string variable from which a word-wrapped line is extracted.
	LineLen, the maximum number of characters returned, is the line length when the word-wrapped strings are printed.
	Remainder is a string variable that is at least as large as **Length(Strg) − LineLen**. It receives whatever remains of Strg after a word-wrapped line has been extracted.
NOTES:	1. Be sure that the string sent to *WrapLine* is at least as long as *LineLen*. This rule does not apply, of course, when the routine is sent the last fragment of a paragraph.
EXAMPLE:	To extract up to 50 word-wrapped characters from an element of an array named *Text:*

```
PrintLine[PrtCounter] := WrapLine(Text[TextPtr],50);
```

The remainder of *Text[TextPtr]*, if any, now resides in *Remainder*. To continuously for-

mat a series of strings taken from a text array, see the example given for *WrapString* in
Section 4 of Chapter 4. It is similar to this
routine, but it does not make allowances for
imbedded control codes.

Function JustifyLine(Strg: stype; LineLen: integer): stype;

FILE NAME: JUSTLINE.PAS   (320 code bytes)

PURPOSE: *JustifyLine* formats a string for output to the
                    printer in right-justified, word-wrapped
                    form. The function returns a string that has
                    as many characters as *LineLen*. These char-
                    acters include as much of *Strg* as could fit on
                    a word-wrapped line, plus additional space
                    characters spread across the line to right-jus-
                    tify it. The remaining characters in *Strg* are
                    copied to a variable named *Remainder*. This
                    remnant is to be combined with the next
                    string from the text array that is output. By
                    repeated calls to *JustifyLine* and a printer
                    output procedure, an entire array may be
                    printed right-justified. JustifyLine ignores
                    embedded control codes; the line length is
                    correct no matter the number of words.

PARAMETERS: *Strg* is a string variable from which a right-
                    justified, word-wrapped line is created.

                    LineLen, the length of a justified line, is the
                    number of characters returned by the func-
                    tion, providing there were at least that many
                    characters in *Strg*. When *Strg* is shorter than
                    LineLen, the routine returns an unjustified
                    line, which prevents the last few words of a
                    paragraph from being spread across the
                    width of the page.

                    Remainder is a string variable that is at least
                    as large as **length(Strg) – LineLen**. It receives
                    whatever remains of Strg after a word-
                    wrapped line has been extracted.

EXAMPLE: This example creates an 80-column, right-
                    justified line from an element of an array
                    named *Text*:

```
PrintLine[PrtCounter] := JustifyLine(Text[TextPtr],80);
```

The remainder of *Text[TextPtr]*, if any, now resides in *Remainder*. The example given for the *WrapString* function in Section 4 of Chapter 4 shows how to continuously format a series of strings.

10

Writing Your Own Assembly Language Subroutines

This chapter explains how to write your own assembly language routines for Turbo Pascal. Although you must know some assembly language to understand the discussion here, you need not know a lot; you can write very useful assembly routines with just a few of the many assembler instructions. Some of the most daunting difficulties to beginning assembly language programmers—finding a way to data and procedures in remote modules—aren't a problem in the relatively short, self-contained, one-procedure assembly routines that concern us here. But there are new difficulties in getting at parameters on and off of the stack; this chapter tells you all you need to know about how it is done.

When you are in the midst of composing your Turbo masterpiece, with Pascal syntax coursing through your veins, it can be hard to shift gears into the very different realm of assembly language programming. With the tools provided here, you will find that with a bit of practice you can quickly write a finished assembly routine without much distraction. What makes it so easy is the program INLINE.COM, which is found on one of the accompanying diskettes. INLINE.COM automatically converts your assembler code into the **Inline** format used by Turbo Pascal. What's more, INLINE.COM allows you to include Pascal statements in the assembly code, including procedure or function declarations, so that INLINE.COM can generate a file containing a complete Turbo Pascal routine. Every routine in this collection was generated by INLINE.COM. It has been tested with versions 1.0 and 2.0 of the IBM assembler and version 4.0 of the Microsoft assembler.

INLINE.COM makes use of the .LST file that is optionally created by the assembler when it assembles your code and generates an object file (the .OBJ file is not used—there is no linking). An assembler works with INLINE only if it uses the IBM .LST file format. Without a conversion program like INLINE, writing and editing Inline code is a painstaking experience; you must manually transfer the code from the .LST file to the Turbo routine, and you may also need to make some quite elaborate adjustments in the code. INLINE uses the symbol table in a .LST file to take care of variable names and to calculate jump addresses. Since the machine code is written as hexadecimal pairs, without a program like INLINE, everything quickly turns to gobbledygook, errors creep in, and rebooting becomes a way of life.

Turbo Pascal does, in fact, offer another way of incorporating assembly language code. This is done with the reserved word **external**, which draws the code into the Turbo program from a .COM file. The chief problem with this approach is that the routine cannot make direct references to the data segment, while the Inline format lets you name a Pascal variable right in the assembly-language code. Another drawback is that the *external* method doesn't let you include lines of Pascal code in the same file, so that a routine's declaration and other code must be kept separately. Since Inline code is entirely in text form, it can mix Pascal and assembler instructions. Using Inline, every bit of a routine can reside in one file, and, if desired, the entire file can be permanently incorporated into the main Pascal source file. Because of its versatility, we are concerned only with the Inline format here. If you want to try the *external* method, you will find it well-documented in the Turbo Pascal manual and in Borland's *Turbo Tutor*.

Here is an example of Inline code:

```
Procedure BitCopy16(var Target: integer; Source,TStart,SStart,Number: integer);
Begin
  Inline
    ($C4/$BE/TARGET/$26/$8B/$15/$8B/$46/$0A/$BB/$01/$00/$8B/$F3/$8A/$6E/$04/
     $8A/$4E/$06/$D3/$E6/$8A/$4E/$08/$D3/$E3/$85/$C6/$75/$08/$F7/$D3/$23/$D3/
     $F7/$D3/$EB/$02/$0B/$D3/$D1/$E6/$D1/$E3/$FE/$CD/$75/$EA/$26/$89/$15);
End;
```

BitCopy16 copies a bit field of specified length from any position in one integer to any position in another. It is used for bit-packing. **Number** bits are copied from **Target** to **Source**, starting from the respective bit positions **TStart** and **SStart**. The Inline code consists of a series of hexadecimal values, each corresponding to a byte of machine code. The values are divided by slash symbols, enclosed in parentheses, and terminated with a semicolon. The entire assemblage is really nothing more than a single Pascal statement. A Pascal procedure or function may consist entirely of one Inline sequence, or there may be many such sequences interspersed among Pascal statements.

A single assembler instruction consists of from one to six bytes of code, and notes may be inserted to show the corresponding assembler mnemonics and their accompanying notes:

```
Procedure BitCopy16(var Target: integer; Source,TStart,SStart,Number: integer);
Begin
  Inline
    ($C4/$BE/TARGET/      {       LES   DI,TARGET[BP]  ;point to Target        }
     $26/$8B/$15/         {       MOV   DX,ES:[DI]     ;move to DX             }
     $8B/$46/$0A/         {       MOV   AX,[BP+10]     ;source to AX           }
     $BB/$01/$00/         {       MOV   BX,1           ;bit mask for target    }
     $8B/$F3/             {       MOV   SI,BX          ;bit mask for source    }
     $8A/$6E/$04/         {       MOV   CH,[BP+4]      ;number bits            }
     $8A/$4E/$06/         {       MOV   CL,[BP+6]      ;source start bit        }
     $D3/$E6/             {       SHL   SI,CL          ;mask bit to start pt    }
     $8A/$4E/$08/         {       MOV   CL,[BP+8]      ;target start bit        }
     $D3/$E3/             {       SHL   BX,CL          ;mask bit to start pt    }
     $85/$C6/             { L1:   TEST  AX,SI          ;test source bit         }
     $75/$08/             {       JNZ   L2             ;jump if '1'             }
     $F7/$D3/             {       NOT   BX             ;reverse mask            }
     $23/$D3/             {       AND   DX,BX          ;zero out bit            }
     $F7/$D3/             {       NOT   BX             ;re-reverse mask         }
     $EB/$02/             {       JMP   SHORT L3       ;jump ahead              }
     $0B/$D3/             { L2: OR DX,BX               ;set bit                 }
     $D1/$E6/             { L3: SHL SI,1               ;shift mask up by one    }
```

```
        $D1/$E3/            {    SHL  BX,1       ;ditto                      }
        $FE/$CD/            {    DEC  CH         ;dec bit field counter      }
        $75/$EA/            {    JNZ  L1         ;loop till finished         }
        $26/$89/$15);       {    MOV  ES:[DI],DX ;set value for return       }
End;
```

As you can see, the notes are nested within braces, just like any other Pascal note. You may ask the ROUTINES program that generates the individual routines from eight compressed files to strip away the Inline code and braces to make an assembly-language source file. The assembler file can be modified and then reconverted to Inline form with the INLINE program.

The first thing to note about the code sample is that there is no **RET** instruction at the end of the sequence; Turbo automatically inserts it for you. Next, notice that the word **TARGET** is in the code. In a few special instances Turbo Pascal adds code to the Inline series. Variable names may be placed in the code when the **LES, LDS, LEA**, or **MOV** instructions are used. When Turbo Pascal processes the code, it replaces the names with the proper addresses. We will turn to the methods of getting at variables in a moment. But first you must understand how Turbo Pascal moves parameters to and from a function or procedure.

Reading parameters

When the procedure or function containing the Inline code is called, all parameters (or addresses of parameters) declared by the procedure are pushed onto the stack. The assembly routine fetches the parameters directly from the stack. Or, if a parameter is preceded by **var**, the routine takes from the stack the double-word *address* of the parameter, and it uses that address to find the parameter in memory. For a function, extra room is left for the return value, and the routine writes this value into the stack before returning; the compiler sees to it that the value is then conveyed to whatever statement called the function.

The Inline statement makes it easy to move byte or integer values from the stack into registers. Simply place the name of the parameter in the code. For example, **$80/$8E/LNGTH/** moves the parameter LNGTH into the CX register. The code is generated by the assembler statement, **MOV CX,LNGTH[BP]**, where **[BP]** relates the variable to the stack. For the assembler to do its job, **LNGTH** is set up as a dummy variable.

The ability to name parameters in the Inline code helps with program clarity, but it has certain limitations. Most important, strings pushed onto the stack are accessed byte by byte, and a routine needs a register pointing at the string. Inline provides no help in this case. Another problem is that the size of the string (its type declaration) may determine the location of other parameters on the stack; a routine cannot, for example, set up a pointer to a second string on the stack without it. But Inline does not give this information. Finally, when you want to access local or global variables without passing them as parameters, Inline does not provide a double-word address. This means that your routine cannot access pointer variables directly. And routines that access *any* variable directly risk becoming obsolete if future versions of Turbo Pascal allow a larger memory model.

For these reasons, an unusual approach was taken in devising this library, one that does not use the usual Inline facilities for naming parameters and variables within the Inline code. A line or two of Pascal code is added to some routines to force crucial information onto the stack. And the parameters are taken from the stack by calculating offsets from the BP register.

The BP register acts as a fixed pointer to the stack. On entry to a procedure or function, BP points to the memory location that is 4 bytes lower in memory than the lowest of the parameters. The SP register points lower in memory still. Because the stack grows downward in memory, SP is said to point to the "top" of the stack; its value changes as your routine pushes and pops registers.

If a procedure has but one parameter and it is an integer, BP+4 points to the low byte of that integer, and **MOV AX,[BP+4]** moves the integer into AX. A second integer parameter would be found at **BP+6**, a third at **BP+8**, and so on. In the declaration of the parameters, the *rightmost* parameter is the closest to BP. As a result, in **Procedure SetCursor(Row,Column: integer);** *(Column)* is at **BP+4** and *Row* is at **BP+6**. Figure 10-1 shows these relationships.

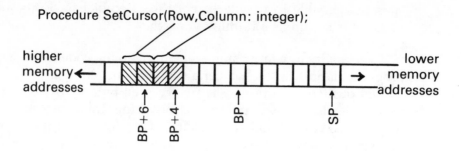

Figure 10-1.   Integer parameters on the stack

Recall that when the BP register is used for addressing, it automatically points to the stack without the use of a segment override. There is no need to write **MOV AX,SS:[BP+4]; MOV AX,[BP+4]** does the job. Your routines can change BP, but they must always restore the original value when they terminate, or the program will crash. Note that the same applies to the DS, SS, and SP registers. No other register ever needs to be saved with initial PUSHes and terminating POPs. Offsets relative to BP can be made with SI and DI, as in **MOV AX,[BP][SI]** and **MOV AX,[BP],[SI+1]**. Or, use the segment override to allow registers to address the stack without BP, as in **MOV AX,SS:[BX]**. In this case, if BX were to point to the rightmost parameter, you would need to first move the current value of BP into it, and then add four. A missing **SS:** prefix, an easy bug to introduce, can be a surprisingly difficult one to spot.

Of course, there are five other types of variables in Turbo Pascal besides the integers shown above. *Real* values take up six bytes on the stack. *Boolean, Byte,* and *Char* values nominally take up only one byte. But because the 8088 and 80286 chips push only sixteen-bit values onto the stack, all of these variable types take up a full word, just like an integer. The value is placed in the low part of the word. Thus in the declaration, **Procedure WhatFor(X: Boolean; Y: real, Z: byte)**, **BP+4** points to the *byte* value *Z*, **BP+6** points to the *real* value *Y*, and **BP+12** points to the Boolean valued *X*, as Figure 10-2 illustrates. (Note that Booleans hold **0** for FALSE and **1** for TRUE.)

The remaining variable type, *string*, isn't quite so straight-forward. A string takes up as much room on the stack as is assigned to it by its type declaration, plus one more byte for the string's descriptor byte. Thus, if the variable **Title** is declared as being of **stype**, and **stype** is **string[20]**, **Title** is given twenty-one bytes of stack space. These twenty-one bytes are allocated no matter what length string **Title** actually contains. The byte lowest in memory (closest to BP) is the descriptor giving the length of the actual string. The descriptor holds a value from 0 to 20, in which 0 indicates a null string. The byte following the descriptor (the next highest in memory) is the first in the string.

Now, it is important to know that this string would take up exactly twenty-one bytes of stack space, and not twenty-two bytes so that it would end on a word-boundary, the way byte, char, and Boolean values do. Consider the declaration **Procedure FindString(Num: integer; Strg: stype)**. If **stype** is **string[10]**, the string descriptor will be found at **BP+4**, and the last byte of the string will be at **BP+14**. The integer **Num** will begin at **BP+15**, that is, at 4 + 11. This may be a bit disconcerting, since you will quickly become accustomed to parameters falling at even-numbered stack positions, and strings can throw this pattern out of kilter. Figure 10-3 shows the stack contents for this case.

This is all well and good, but what if you want to write a general-use function that can accept a string parameter of any length? The number of bytes on the stack allotted to the string will vary depending on the string type specification. One time it

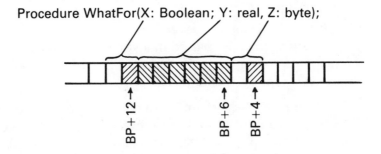

Procedure WhatFor(X: Boolean; Y: real, Z: byte);

BP+12   BP+6   BP+4

Figure 10-2.   Different type parameters on the stack

Procedure FindString(Num: integer; Strg: stype);

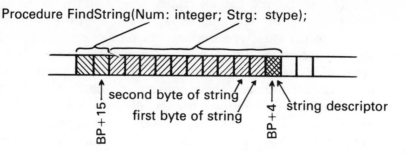

Figure 10-3.   A string on the stack

might be **stype = string[20]** and another time it could be **stype = string[200]**. Say that the procedure declaration is **Procedure Scramble(X: integer; Strg: stype; Y: real);**. How can you fish the integer X from the stack when you have no idea how far it is from BP because of the varying value of *stype*?

One solution is always to make the string parameter the leftmost in the declaration, placing it at the highest memory position. But what if there are two strings? Or what if you are writing a function? A function's return value goes to a still higher memory position.

A second solution is to use **var** in the string's declaration, so that it becomes: **Procedure Scramble(X: integer; var Strg: stype; Y: real);**. We'll learn about the nature of **var** in a moment; for now, suffice it to say that **var** causes the address of a variable (string or otherwise) to be pushed onto the stack instead of the variable itself. The address always takes up four bytes, and as a result, a routine can navigate the stack no matter the size of the string type. Using **var**, however, limits the flexibility of a routine, since the string must be placed in a variable before it can be used as a parameter. You can write **Scramble(3,StrgVar,3.45)**, but not **Scramble(3,'WhoopDeDoo',3.45)**.

A third possibility is simply to make *stype* equal to the largest possible string used by the program and then turn off type-checking so that Turbo Pascal will allow the routine to receive string parameters of a different type declaration. You could design all of your routines so that they expect *stype* to be

string[255]. Yet for a routine to be the most useful, it should be able to work with Pascal's type-checking in full operation. While it is easy enough to write a routine to expect a string of a particular size, what happens when you want to reuse the routine in another program where that particular size is different? Keeping the stack accesses correct might call for much recoding. What is needed is a way for the routine to find out how large *stype* is.

The solution to the problem is roundabout, but it works well. Turbo Pascal provides the *SizeOf* function to return the size of a variable. When applied to a string, it returns the size set by the string's type declaration, *plus* one more for the string descriptor. If **Strg = string[20]**, then **SizeOf(Strg)** equals twenty-one. While you could simply have the string size sent as an additional parameter, that would be clumsy and wasteful. Instead, the information can be sneaked onto the stack, enabling the routine to pick it up and use it to calculate the locations of values on the stack higher in memory than the string.

The procedure or function should begin with the declaration or an integer variable, say, **X**. Then immediately before the Inline code begins write the statement **X = SizeOf(stype)** (or whatever name is used for the string type). The value given to **X** is promptly pushed onto the stack at **BP-4** and the routine can retrieve it from that position. If there is more than one string, declare more variables and precede the Inline Code with more *SizeOf* assignments. The second value will be found at BP-6 and so on. Note that the order of the values as they are found below BP depends on the order in which the variables are declared, not the order in which the assignments are made. Here is an example:

```
Procedure Scramble(Num: integer; Strg: stype);
  Var
    X: integer;
  Begin
    X := SizeOf(stype);
    Inline
    .
    .
```

To find the integer **Number** in this procedure, get the size of **Strg** and add 4 for the offset to the start of the string. For example:

```
MOV   SI,[BP-4]        ;get the SizeOf Strg
ADD   SI,4             ;add BP offset to start of string
MOV   AX,[BP][SI]      ;place Num in AX
```

Now you have a routine that is self-adjusting—it can work with any string size. If only one string size is used, type-checking may be left in force. When several string sizes are served, *stype* would be set to the largest and type-checking would be switched off. Incidentally, note what would happen if you were to set *stype* to, say, 60, and then were to send a 70-byte string to the routine with type-checking switched off. The last ten bytes would spill over into the space allotted for the integer above, the routine would read two bytes of the overflow as an integer value, and all kinds of fun and games would begin.

Now let's consider the last of the topics on stack access: using *var*. As noted, *var* causes the address of the parameter to be pushed onto the stack. When a procedure is to make a permanent change in a variable, it must use *var* to reach the place where the variable is stored. Otherwise, the routine receives only a copy of the variable (the one placed on the stack), and the copy disappears when the routine returns and the stack space is reclaimed.

The two words that *var* causes to be placed on the stack constitute a standard segment:offset address. The offset is at the lower position in memory, closer to BP. Your routine needs to load the segment value into DS or ES, and the offset into SI, DI, or BX. Of the two ways to do this, one is to simply grab the values directly from the stack in two separate operations. For example, for the declaration **Procedure Scramble(var Garbage: stype)**:

```
MOV   AX,[BP+6]        ;get the segment
MOV   ES,AX            ;place it in ES
MOV   DI,[BP+4]        ;now ES:DI pts to Garbage
```

The second method uses the LDS or LES instructions. Recall that these require a double-word address for the variable they refer to. In your assembly language source code the data segment would require this construction to get at the variable **Garbage**:

```
GUCK      DB   21 dup(?)
GARBAGE   DD   GUCK
```

Then the code would include the statement:

```
LES  DI,GARBAGE[BP]
```

and DS:DI would be left pointing to *Garbage*. The **[BP]** appended to the statement is required to reference the stack. When you use LDS or LES in an assembly-language subroutine, you must set up the data segment as shown, although the number of bytes given to *Guck* will be irrelevant (it is the location of the first byte that matters). When the INLINE program converts the assembler .LST file to Inline form, it finds only an offset for the variable in the code. INLINE looks up the variable name corresponding to the offset and replaces the numbers with the variable name, leaving the name in the midst of the hexadecimal code. When Turbo Pascal reads the Inline code, it looks up the address of the variable name in its own symbol table and inserts the correct address.

Should you write some Inline code without the help of the INLINE conversion program, you need to know that LDS and LES generate a segment-override prefix when used with the **[BP]** suffix. The prefix appears in the .LST file as **3E:**. This code confuses the compiler and must be removed. The INLINE program makes this deletion selectively; it leaves ordinary **SS:** overrides intact.

Returning values from functions

The value returned by a function is placed on the stack starting at the first byte following the last occupied by the parameters. Enough space is allocated to hold whatever data type is returned; if it is a string, there are as many bytes as were allotted to the string type, and one more for the string descriptor. The return value can begin at an *odd* numbered position on the stack. This occurs when a string in the function's parameter list has a size that is odd-numbered. Values of *byte*, *char*, or *Boolean* type, however, continue to take up two bytes of stack space even when they are the highest on the parameter list. Hence, for the declaration **Function Gimme(This: char; That: integer): integer;**, the integer value to be returned would be placed at **BP + 8**. But if the parameters were **Gimme(Strg: stype;That: integer): integer;**, and *stype = 2*, giving a string size of 3, then the return value would be placed at **BP+9**. Figure 10-4 diagrams the two cases.

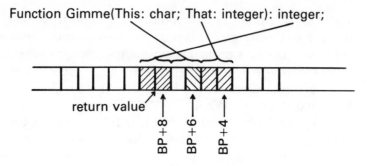

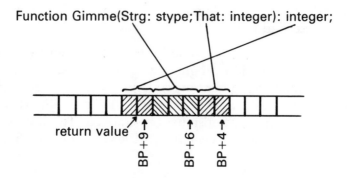

Figure 10-4. A function's return value on the stack

Getting at variables

Next, let's consider how to access a variable without sending it to the routine as a parameter. There are a number of occasions when this is necessary, as when a variable holds a constant always required by the routine. For example, the memory-mapping video routines in this collection require the address of the video buffer, which varies between monochrome and color systems. It would be senseless to require the programmer to pass this value as a parameter each time a video output routine is called.

Version 3.0 of Turbo Pascal is restricted to a 64K data segment, which means that any variable in the data segment can be accessed using a 16-bit offset, supplied by the mnemonic **LEA**. To find the integer variable XYZ, set up a (fake) variable named XYZ in the data segment of your assembly code:

```
XYZ    DW  ?
```

Then write the statement:

```
LEA   SI,XYZ
```

DS:SI would then point to XYZ, which could be read, or written to, by these two statements:

```
MOV   AX,[SI]
MOV   [SI],AX
```

Much as for the LDS and LES instructions, the INLINE program searches the symbol table of an assembler .LST file for the name of a variable referenced by LEA, and it places that name in the Inline code it creates. Turbo Pascal inserts the proper address when it processes the code.

Could you use LES and LDS to reach variables directly? No. But since LEA does the job just fine, what would be the point? One reason would be to get at pointer variables in Turbo's heap. Another reason is that future versions of Turbo Pascal may have a larger data model, in which double-word addresses are used throughout. If routines are to survive changes in the compiler, they need to anticipate this change. For this reason, all direct variable accesses made by the routines in this library use double-word addresses.

But how do you get a double-word address for a variable when LDS and LES won't do the job? The solution is similar to that for finding out string size. Start the routine with Pascal code that declares two integer variables, say, X and Y. Then use the Turbo Pascal *Seg* and *Ofs* functions to assign to X and Y the segment and offset of the variable in question. The first value will be pushed onto the stack at **BP-4**, and the second at **BP-6**. The routine can fish the values from the stack and set up segment and offset pointers. This example points DS:SI to the variable *Gotcha*:

```
Procedure WhatsIt(Strg: stype);
Var
  X,Y : integer;
Begin
  X := Seg(Gotcha);
  Y := Ofs(Gotcha);
  Inline
  .
  .
```

The Inline code would point DS:SI to *Gotcha* in this way:

```
PUSH DS                        ;save Turbo's DS
MOV  AX,[BP-4]                 ;segment of Gotcha
MOV  DS,AX                     ;set DS
MOV  SI,[BP-6]                 ;offset of Gotcha
  .
  .
MOV  [SI],DX                   ;set value into Gotcha
  .
  .
POP  DS                        ;restore original DS
```

Note how DS is saved and later restored. With version 3.0 of Turbo Pascal, the contents of DS in fact do not change. But in future versions, data could be spread over many memory segments. Perhaps Turbo Pascal will continue to be limited to a 64K data segment, making this precaution unnecessary; but much work will be saved if a larger memory model appears. The extra Pascal and assembly code required by this measure add roughly twenty bytes to a routine.

Also note two minor points. First, it is easier to point to variables with ES, since you're saved the trouble of saving and restoring DS. Second, any number of values can be pushed onto the stack from **BP-4** downward. You can reach more than one variable this way, or you can combine this ploy with the one that uses *SizeOf* to find out a string's size.

One other point must not be overlooked. Pascal usually protects the programmer from all but the most suicidal of wrong moves. When Turbo Pascal writes a string into the data segment, it won't make a mistake. But a half-cooked assembly language routine can work absolute marvels in the realm of error production. When your code works its way into an infinite loop, you won't have much trouble knowing it—you will have to turn the machine off to restart. The virtue of this sort of error is that it announces its presence. But when errors occur during direct accesses to the data segment, the damage may appear only much later. If your routine overwrites a string variable and destroys adjacent data, that data could be read minutes later, returning nonsense values without any explanation. You could spend hours looking for the problem in the related Pascal code! The two solutions are to be always very, very careful and very, very suspicious.

Limitations in writing assembly language subroutines

There are several constraints in writing assembly language subroutines. For starters, consider the problem of intermediate results. In ordinary assembly-language programming, when the registers are fully occupied, you can create all the variables you need to hold intermediate values. But not here. The assembler lists variables in *relocatable* form; their relative addresses are not fixed. Since the routine isn't sent through a linker, it cannot find variables it creates for its own use.

This problem has several remedies. Least acceptable is to declare some variables through Turbo Pascal, setting aside a bit of the data segment for use by assembly subroutines. Forgetting the inconvenience (and confusion) to the programmer using the routine, so many registers would be kept busy pointing to the variables that the whole point of their existence would be defeated.

A second remedy is to rely heavily on the stack to hold intermediate results. This gets messy, since the value you need may not be the next in line for a POP. To avoid the sequencing problem, read values from the stack without POPing them. **SP** points to the last value pushed, **SP+2** points to the previous value, and so on. Since **SP** can't be used directly for addressing, its value must be moved to another register. For example, if three integers have been pushed and you need to get the second into AX, write:

```
MOV   BX,SP
MOV   AX,SS:[BX+2]
```

By far the best way of dealing with intermediate results is to place them on the stack in the same positions used to pass parameters. Of course, you will need to have taken the parameters from these positions beforehand. If you look at the code for the *DrawBox* routine in Chapter 8, for example, you will see that immediately after the parameters that describe the box to be drawn are removed from the stack, the various block graphic characters are moved to **BP+4**, **BP+6**, and so on.

Another limitation is that one cannot very easily set up procedures within the routine. As with local variables, this problem occurs because procedure addresses are relocatable, and Turbo does not perform linking. The INLINE program supports the creation of one procedure within a routine, although only along very rigid lines. You can see it in many of the memory-mapping versions of the screen-oriented routines, in which the code checking the graphics-card retrace timing is called repeatedly. The procedure is called indirectly by placing its address in, say, BX and writing **CALL BX**.

To insert a procedure into a routine, do the following: Make **MOV BX,$** the first line of the assembly code. This particular combination causes the INLINE program to generate the instruction-pointer address in the format Inline understands **$BB/*+5**. Make the second instruction **JMP ZZ**, where ZZ may be any label. Then write the procedure, saving changed registers, and ending it with **RET**. Immediately follow the procedure's RET instruction with the ZZ label (or whatever) and the first line of the routine proper. When the routine is entered, the procedure address is deposited in BX. Write **CALL BX** whenever you want to call the procedure, or move the address to some other register (say, DI) and instead call the procedure from there **CALL DI**. That is all there is to it. Here is an example:

```
MOV  BX,$          ;instruction pointer to BX
JMP  ZZ            ;skip over the routine
PUSH AX            ;---the procedure begins
PUSH SI            ;save registers your routine needs
     .
     .
```

```
        POP  SI              ;restore registers
        POP  AX              ;ditto
        RET                  ;---internal procedure ends
  ZZ: MOV  DI,BX             ;shift proc address to other
                             ;register
        MOV  DL,[BP+4]       ;the routine proper begins
          .
          .
          .
        CALL DI              ;call the procedure
          .
          .
          .
        CALL DI              ;call the procedure
          .
          .
          .
    etc.
```

The **JMP** instruction presents another problem. The machine code that describes *short* jumps includes a one-byte offset. A *long* jump has a two-byte offset, but it is treated as a relocatable by the assembler. This means that if you are going to write Inline code without the help of the INLINE program, you will have to count the number of bytes of machine code between the instruction and the label (the counting differs by the direction, incidentally). INLINE figures all this out and inserts the proper values. One demon lurks here, however. Never insert LEA, LDS, or LES instructions between a jump instruction and its label, since Turbo will generate some extra code when it encounters the name of the variable referenced by these three instructions, and that will throw the jump off.

Using the INLINE conversion program

The INLINE program is very easy to use, but it places certain rigid rules on the format of your program. The reason is that it looks for particular information at precise locations in the assembler .LST files, and that information is present only if it is properly positioned in the original assembler source file.

First, you must mark off the beginning and end of the code to be converted by placing the lines **;BEGIN** before the first line of the code and **;END** after the last line of code. These markers must be at the very beginning of the line (that is, flush with the left margin of the screen). They may be written in any combination of upper- and lowercase letters. The markers are to occur only once in a particular assembler file, always in the code segment. You may still need to set up a data segment to allow the code to assemble, but the assembler's data segment or stack is irrelevant to the finished Inline code. INLINE handles 480 132-character lines of code—as much as Turbo Pascal's data segment can hold. If you need more, resize the array for shorter lines and recompile the source code.

Second, the **NOP** instruction is used to include Pascal code in the assembler file. For example, Inline converts **NOP;X :=SizeOf(MyVar)** to the Pascal statement, **X := SizeOf(MyVar)**. The NOP mnemonic is required to carry the code over to the .LST file (lines holding only notes are not carried over). Insertions of Pascal code must come at the beginning or end of the assembly language sequence; Pascal code cannot be inserted *within* the Inline machine code, breaking it into two or more parts.

The NOP instructions aren't included in the finished Inline code. Rather, when the INLINE program spots a NOP instruction, it strips away the machine-language codes and formats the text that follows as Pascal code. Since the NOP instructions lead or follow the assembler code, deleting them doesn't interfere with jump instructions. Always immediately follow the NOP mnemonic with a semicolon and then the desired Pascal text. Here is a simple example of a function that adds two integers and returns the result:

```
;BEGIN
    NOP;Function AddInts(X,Y: integer): integer;
    MOV  AX,[BP+4]        ;get one value
    ADD  AX,[BP+6]        ;add the second
    MOV  [BP+8],AX        ;set the return value
;END
```

The programming strategies using *SizeOf*, *Seg*, and *Ofs* require an initial declaration of integer variables. The INLINE program is specially tailored to format these code lines. For example, the following code accesses a variable named *SoWhat*:

```
         ;BEGIN
             NOP;Function AddInts(X,Y: integer): integer;
             NOP;Var
             NOP;X,Y : integer;
             NOP;Begin
             NOP;X := Seg(SoWhat);
             NOP;Y := Ofs(SoWhat);
             MOV   AX,[BP-4]          ;get segment of SoWhat
             MOV   ES,AX              ;ES:DI will point to
SoWhat
             MOV   DI,[BP-b]          ;get offset of SoWhat
               .
               .
               .
             etc.
               .
               .
               .
         ;END
```

When INLINE finds no NOP instructions, it generates the assembler code in Inline format, places it in parentheses, and adds the word "Inline" at the start and a semicolon at the end. When INLINE finds one initial instance of NOP, it assumes that it is the declaration for a procedure or function. In this case, IN-LINE automatically adds lines of Pascal code reading **Begin** and **End;** on the two sides of the Inline code. Everything is indented prettily to make a complete Pascal routine. When more than two initial NOP instructions are encountered, you must write in the word **Begin**, as in the example above. INLINE looks for it, and the word *Var* too, and sees to it that everything is properly indented. The letters in "Begin" and "Var" may be any combination of uppercase and lowercase. INLINE becomes confused when it encounters initial NOP instructions not immediately followed by Pascal statements.

NOP instructions may be written at the end of the Inline code for two reasons. The first is to include Pascal statements. You will see this at the end of the *InputInteger* and *InputReal* routines in Chapter 5, in which a final Pascal statement uses the Pascal library to convert numbers from string to numeric form, avoiding duplication of code. Again, one simply follows the NOP mnemonic with a semicolon and the desired Pascal text. Any number of lines are allowed. The other use of a trailing **NOP**—and it must be the very last line before **;END**—is to show the position of a final label that points to the position following the last assembler instruction; that is, it points to the RET instruction that Turbo Pascal fills in for you. When a final label is on a line with a NOP instruction that is *not* followed by a semicolon and text, the INLINE program gives the label its own line in the notes that INLINE generates to the left of the hexadecimal codes. Without this feature the position of a final label would be unclear. Here is an example:

```
        .
        .
        OR    DX,DX          ;zero result?
        JZ    L5             ;then return default
        SUB   DX,AX          ;else adjust result
        MOV   [BP+8],DX       ;set it for return
    L5: NOP
```

As you can see from the files that make up this library, IN-LINE nicely formats the Inline code and accompanying notes. The layout takes up exactly eighty columns. It allots enough space for all possible Inline-code sequences, and the rest is given over to the assembler mnemonics and notes. The assembler source files must follow a precise format if they are to be formatted in the same way as the routines in this library. If you use another format, the program will continue to work properly but may create lines longer than eighty columns.

To follow the proper assembler file format, write the code close to the left edge of the display. Use two-character labels; labels take up columns 1 through 3 (for example, **L1:**). Column 4 is left blank to leave space between the labels and the mnemonics. The mnemonics begin at column 5. The semicolons marking the beginning of a note fall at column 25; the notes must not extend beyond column 52. Those are the rules. With some editors, it is actually quite easy to keep track of columns 25 and 52. Set up two keyboard macros with Borland's *SuperKey* or a similar program. Start the macros with a command that returns the cursor to the left margin, then follow with 25 or 52 single cursor moves to the right.

INLINE always converts the assembler mnemonics to notes in the file it creates. It automatically capitalizes all mnemonics and variable names, but it makes no changes in the assembler notes.

Now that you know how to set up an assembler file for IN-
LINE, you need to know how to use the program. It operates
entirely from the command line. Simple type **INLINE** and the
name of the .LST file to be converted. Say that your assembly
language source file is called **FROGS.ASM**. When you assemble,
the assembler offers the choice:

```
Source Listing [NUL.LST]:
```

By typing in the word FROGS before striking ‹enter›, the assembler creates the file FROGS.LST. Once the assembler's work is
done, type:

```
INLINE FROGS.LST
```

or simply:

```
INLINE FROGS
```

INLINE creates a file named FROGS.PAS containing the Inline
code. When only this much information is given, INLINE expects
to find the .LST routine in the current directory, and it also writes
the output file in that directory. To find the input file in another
directory, write a DOS path along with the file name:

```
INLINE C:\ASM\ROUTINES\FROGS.LST
```

   . . . or . . .

```
INLINE C:\ASM\ROUTINES\FROGS
```

To write the output in a directory other than the current one, add
a second command-line parameter, as in:

```
INLINE C:\ASM\FROGS   C:\ROUTINES
```

   . . . or . . .

```
INLINE C:\ASM\FROGS   A:
```

When the .LST file is in the current directory and you want the
output file directed to a different one, you must still write the
first parameter, giving the full path to the current directory.

INLINE displays a message when it is finished. A 100-line routine takes about five seconds to process on a 6 MHz IBM PC AT.

Error-Checking

Most routines require some amount of error-checking on the input parameters. Turbo Pascal may ensure that the parameters are the proper type, but other things can go wrong. A routine must be prepared to receive a null string when a string parameter is passed, and it must deal with numeric values outside the acceptable range. For example, a procedure that draws a line on the screen could be told to make it zero pixels long. There is no rational reason for making this request (not to mention a line -20 pixels long), but mistakes happen, particularly when the parameter is generated elsewhere in the program.

Often you will find yourself deciding just how much error-checking to add to a routine. Besides the extra work, extensive error-checking can increase the size of a routine considerably, and sometimes it may even limit the usefulness of the routine for applications other than the one at hand. It is convenient to think of three levels of error checking:

1. **Errors that hang the machine.** For example, when the zero-length of a null string acts as a counter variable, the CX register immediately steps down to 65535, causing a loop to be executed that many times. Of course, code should always be included to avoid such an error, and all routines in this collection are minimally checked to this level. When the crash occurs, there will be no error messages from Turbo and no pointer to the spot in the code where control was lost. Although you can be pretty sure that the culprit is an assembly language routine, it may be hard to know which one went awry when the program has many. In particular, if the offending parameter is generated by another routine, it can be extremely difficult to isolate the bug.

2. **Errors resulting from parameters out of range.** Range-checking is easy to perform, and often necessary to keep the machine from crashing. A cursor column position on the screen,

for example, should fall within 0–79 (or 1–80 for consistency with the Turbo *GotoXY* statement). But what should the routine do if it doesn't? It could substitute the maximum value, which may be no help at all. Or the routine can simply return without doing anything, although this could leave the programmer wondering what happened. It is easy to set up an error code reporting system, but a great deal of extra Pascal code is required to check the code, and the program is still stuck with the problem of what to do. Often the best solution is not to bother with range checking if the machine won't crash and the location of the error will be clear. Keep in mind that a sort of crash occurs when a numeric parameter is accidentally made so large that it takes minutes for the routine to return. When the maximum size of the parameter is below 256, an easy way to avoid this problem is by using only the low byte of integer parameters.

3. **Errors resulting from improper application.** This kind of error is the most difficult to check for. Consider the case of a routine that draws a box on the screen with block characters. Parameters specify a width and depth of ten characters, which is perfectly acceptable. But if the position coordinates for the top left corner of the box place it at column 75, a kind of error has occured—there is not enough room for the box at the right edge of the screen. Here the parameters are "correct," but the logic isn't. Since it can take a good deal of extra code to avoid all such cases, you must ask if it is worth the trouble or the code space.

Debugging

Your wonderful assembly language debugging tools may not be very useful when writing subroutines for high level languages. If the routine is very long and complex, you may want initially to set it up as an assembly program, artificially pumping the parameters through to it. But once it is set up to take its parameters from Turbo's stack, all the Pascal code and the Turbo runtime module come between your debugger and your assembly routine. Although you can run the whole assemblage within a debugger, finding your way around can be a tremendous headache, particularly if your routine is in the mood to crash. Recently, *memory-resident* versions of commercial debuggers have been released, and they may allow better access.

Most assembly-language routines are short and don't require much debugging. But hard-to-find bugs nonetheless can occur, and you'll need a way to watch what is going on. One of the diskettes holds a short program called TURBOBUG.COM. The assembly-language source code for the program is also on the disk as TURBOBUG.ASM.

TURBOBUG is *not* a debugger. There is no single-stepping, no breakpoints or passpoints, none of the usual goodies. Rather, TURBOBUG is a very simple *debugging tool*. Though it does little, it is quite useful and takes only a couple of minutes to learn to use. Its three functions are to:

— Display the stack, marking the position pointed to by BP and offsets from that pointer.

— Display the content of any Turbo Pascal variable (presumably the one your routine is altering).

— Display the contents of the CPU registers and indicate where changes have occurred.

TURBOBUG is a memory-resident program. If you want to use it, you must load it before starting up Turbo Pascal or a compiled Turbo Pascal program. Simply enter **TURBOBUG** at the DOS prompt; the message "TURBOBUG loaded" appears and the DOS prompt returns. The program is accessed through unused interrupt vectors. Since there is no keyboard access to TURBOBUG, you don't need to worry about the order in which it is loaded with other memory-resident programs. You may want to load the program from the AUTOEXEC.BAT file, because it is easy to forget to reload it after rebooting from a crash; of course, the machine will hang if TURBOBUG is called without having been loaded.

In its present form, TURBOBUG uses interrupt vectors 80H–82H. To begin the series elsewhere in the vector table, simply change the equate at the start of the source code and reassemble. The vectors correspond to the following functions:

80H   Writes the stack on the top five lines of the screen.

81H   Writes the contents of a memory position (a variable) on the sixth line of the screen.

82H   Writes the contents of the CPU registers at the bottom of the screen, scrolling prior values upward to as far as the seventh row.

TURBOBUG could well win the crowded-screen-of-the-year award. With all features in use, hardly one spot on the display goes unused. It displays data through direct memory-mapping to the video buffer. The version on the diskette is set for a monochrome video system, in which the video buffer begins at B000:0000. To run the program on a color display, change the equate at the start of the source code to **0B800H**, then reassemble.

Since the program takes up the whole screen, it is easy for the main Pascal program to overwrite its output. You will use TURBOBUG mostly to watch the CPU registers, leaving the top six lines of the screen free for Pascal output. Or, Turbo Pascal can write a single line at row six when the stack is displayed, but not a memory variable. In graphics programming, however, the only solution is to run a second video system at the same time, using both color and monochrome monitors and adaptors. Set the video buffer equate for the monochrome system that displays the TURBOBUG output.

Use Turbo's *Clrscr* command to clear the screen before accessing TURBOBUG. With a second video system, you'll need to insert extra code in your routine to clear the noncurrent display. You won't want to repeatedly clear the screen from within the assembly routine since it erases the accumulating record of CPU register changes, as described below.

Displaying the stack

INT 80h displays the stack on the top five rows of the screen; it preserves all registers. The two leftmost columns hold labels, and then each of the seventy-eight positions to the right show a byte from the stack. The sequence moves left to right from higher to lower stack positions (that is, from lower to higher memory addresses). For procedures, the top end of the highest parameter lies at the left edge; for functions, the top of the return value is on the left. BP lies somewhere to the right, or possibly off the scale when a parameter or return value is a large string.

The third row of the display holds the ASCII character representing the byte at the corresponding position. The two rows below hold a vertically written hexadecimal value that gives the numeric value held in the byte, from **00** to **FF**. The top two rows of the screen form a scale by which to orient yourself. BP is clearly labeled, providing it is on the screen. A numeric scale runs in both directions outward from BP, letting you count your way to any particular stack offset. You can get lost when the BP position is off-screen; temporarily resizing string variables lets you bring it back to view.

Consider this function:

```
Function TryAgain(Strg: stype; Num: integer): integer;
```

Say that **stype** is **15** and that the function is sent **'123456789012345'** for **Strg**, 65 for **Num**, and that **97** is returned by the function. Furthermore, assume that the expression **X :=** **SizeOf(Strg)** is placed at the start of the routine to find out the size of **stype**. After the return value has been reset, the stack appears as follows:

```
                                       BP + 4
                              2           1     ↓       B           1           2
stack position  {   321098765432109876543 21 P 1234567890123456789012
ASCII character {   a5432109876543210⋆A·······►·················
                   0633333333333333330 04XXXXX01XXXXXXXXXXXXXXXXX
hex equivalent  {   0154321098765432 1F 01XXXXX00XXXXXXXXXXXXXXXXX
```

This diagram shows only 46 bytes of the 78 displayed. Note BP at the top center. **BP + 4** is four positions to the left, under the numeral **4**. This position marks the low byte of the integer, **Num**. It holds **65**, which is represented by the ASCII character **A**, and by hexadecimal **41**, which is written below in the same column. The column at **[BP + 5]**—the high byte of **Num**—holds zero, and its associated ASCII symbol is a blank.

The next column to the left, the position at **BP+6**, holds the string descriptor for **Strg**. Next comes the first character of the string and so on. The two columns at the far left hold the return value, **97**. This is represented by the ASCII character **a** in the low byte, and by null in the high byte.

Finally, see how the value of **SizeOf(Strg)** appears to the right of BP, at **BP–4**. The low byte of the integer is there and holds **16**, and the high byte at **BP+3** holds zero. Note that this value is one greater than the value of the string descriptor on the left. Everything else in this illustration is filled in by periods and Xs. In reality, random symbols will occupy these positions.

Displaying a variable

When **var** is used with a parameter's declaration, the double-word address pushed onto the stack allows the routine to permanently change the variable at its location in the data segment. INT 81H displays such a variable on the sixth line of the screen. By calling INT 81H repeatedly from inside a loop in your routine, you can watch the variable change (providing you simultaneously use INT 82H, which halts the loop after each turn, as explained below).

Before calling INT 81H, place in BX the offset from BP to the lowest byte of the double-word address on the stack. If the parameter is the farthest right in the declaration, its address would extend from **BP+4** to **BP+7**, so **4** would be placed in BX. The routine preserves all registers, but if your program is using BX, then the current value must be pushed beforehand.

A label reading **VAR:** is written at the left edge of the sixth row of the screen. Then an expanse of 76 bytes of memory is displayed, reaching to the right edge of the screen. The byte farthest left is the lowest byte of the variable pointed to by the address on the stack. If the variable is a character, only that first byte will be significant. If it is an integer, the second byte will be the high byte of the value. If it is a string, the entire length of the line may be of interest.

Displaying the registers

Whenever INT 82H is called, the CPU registers are displayed on the twenty-fourth row of the screen. The bottom row labels the registers. Before the registers are written, the eighth through twenty-fourth rows are scrolled upward by one line. As a result, a series of up to eighteen readings of the registers may be displayed at one time. The register readings form parallel columns stretching upward from the bottom of the screen and scrolling out of view. Note that the interrupt exits with all registers unchanged.

The register contents are shown in both ASCII and hexadecimal form. The two ASCII characters representing the register contents are shown side-by-side in reverse video. To both the right and left of these two characters are pairs of equivalent hexadecimal digits. If the AX register contains 4142H, it will be displayed as 41**AB**42, with AH on the left and AL on the right.

When INT 82H is called again, the prior register readings are scrolled up a line, as are all readings from prior scrolls. So you can easily compare the registers from one reading to the next. The strategy is to place the INT 81H instruction in one or more critical places in the code or perhaps within a loop. Although this is much less convenient than stepping through the code instruction after instruction, it usually can get you out of trouble in small routines.

Each time the register contents are rewritten, TURBOBUG compares the current values with those written the previous time. If there has been no change, the ASCII characters are written, but the hexadecimal equivalents aren't. Hence, with one glance, you can look over 18 register changes and see where values have altered.

When INT 82H is placed in a loop, register readings can scroll offscreen far more quickly than you can read them, let along figure them out. For this reason, the interrupt comes to a stop once it has drawn the registers; then it waits for permission to exit, returning control to the calling assembly language subroutine. Permission is given through the keyboard's *shift keys,* which avoid the limitations imposed by the keyboard typematic rate. There are three choices:

1. When the *left* shift key is depressed, it steps forward at about 100 register readings per minute (providing there is no other code in the loop to slow it down). The stepping stops when the key is released. The timing is done with the BIOS clock, so the stepping rate is the same on any machine.

2. When the *right* shift key is depressed, it steps forward as fast as it can, again stopping when the key is released. Because the scroll-and-compare operations take time, a brief touch of the key results in just ten readings.

3. When the Alt key is depressed, the interrupt is disabled, and the assembly routine speeds along without making any more writes on the screen. This feature was added for cases in which the loop variable accidentally becomes such a large number that it would take ages to step through to the end.

That is all there is to TURBOBUG. If you make it a habit to load the program before starting an assembler subroutine, you'll come to appreciate the ease with which you can peer into the registers anytime merely by adding a few keystrokes to the assembler code. Since the source code for TURBOBUG is on one of the diskettes—TURBOBUG.ASM—you may customize it if you like.

This is just about all there is to say about writing assembly-language subroutines. The rest depends on your programming skill. You would do well to set up a little system to ease writing subroutines. Devote a subdirectory on your hard disk to the necessary tools. Create an empty, preformatted template file for assembler programs to get all of the busy work of setting up segments out of the way. Have TURBOBUG loaded at boot-up. And make up keyboard macros to call up your editor, the assembler, and INLINE. With your system set up just right, and with a little experience, you may find that taking time out to write assembly-language subroutines can be, well, *fun*.

General Index

A

Absolute disk sectors   291
Alt key   182
Assembly language   1–3
Attributes
  files   297, 301
  screen   xviii, 18–20, 72, 78, 86, 205, 206–218
AQA *see* Expanded memory

B

Background color   205, 208
Backspace key   148, 153, 157
Bank switching   37
BIOS data area   28, 311
Bit fields   67
  copy bits   77, 88
  set bits   77, 80, 82, 86
Blink attribute   20, 185, 191, 206
BP register   339, 348
Buffer
  keyboard   147, 149, 150, 155, 161
  video   17–20

C

CapsLock   180, 182, 184
Carriage-return/line-feed   317
CGA *see* Color graphics adaptor
Clear screen   18, 257, 260, 262, 264
Code bytes   8

Color   xviii, 18–21, 205, 208, 211, 219

Color graphics adaptor   30
  presence   28
Compression
  data   77
  text   126
Conversions
  binary to byte   71
  binary to integer   71
  bit field to binary   74
  bit field to numeric   72
  byte to binary   69
  byte to hexadecimal   70
  integer to binary   69
  integer to hexadecimal   70
  integer to string   114
  real to string   114
Critical error message   34, 35, 313
Ctrl-break   150, 151
Ctrl key   182
Current adaptor   28, 30
Cursor
  on/off   196, 200
  position   198, 202, 219
  shape   196, 197, 200

D

Data
  compression   77, 90, 92, 126
  exchange   38
  move   38

Subroutine Index

File Name Index